W9-BQZ-614

Scaffolding Reading Experiences

Scaffolding Reading Experiences

Michael F. Graves

and

Bonnie B. Graves

Christopher-Gordon Publishers, Inc.
Norwood, Massachusetts

Credit Lines

Chapter 2: Figure 2–1 copyright © 1976 by the National Council of Teachers of English. Reprinted by permission.

Chapter 3: Figure 3–1 copyright © 1977 by Lawrence Erlbaum Associates, Inc. Reprinted by permission. Figure 3–2 copyright © 1983 by P. David Pearson and Academic Press. Reprinted by permission.

Chapter 4: Preview for "The Signalman" copyright © 1983 by the International Reading Association. Reprinted by permission.

Chapter 5: "Buffalo Dusk" from *Smoke and Steel* by Carl Sandburg, copyright © 1920 by Harcourt Brace & Company and renewed 1948 by Carl Sandburg. Reprinted by permission. "I'm Thankful" from *The New Kid on the Block* by Jack Prelutsky, copyright © 1984 by Jack Prelutsky. Reprinted by permission of Greenwillow Books, a division of William Morrow & Company, Inc. "Weather is Full of the Nicest Sounds" from *I Like Weather* by Aileen Fisher, copyright © 1963 by HarperCollins Children's Books. Reprinted by permission.

Appendix A: Original text material for "Text Difficulty and Accessibility" copyright © 1989 by Randall J. Ryder and the International Reading Association. Reprinted by permission.

Christopher-Gordon Publishers, Inc.
480 Washington Street
Norwood, MA 02062

Printed in the United States of America

10 9 8 7 6 5 4 3 2   99 98 97 96 95

ISBN: 0–926842–35–8

To our daughters, Julie and Erin, and to their teachers in the Minneapolis, Minnesota, Ouray, Colorado, and Bloomington, Minnesota public schools, who nurtured their growing literacy

Table of Contents

Chapter Four
Prereading Activities   45

Appendix A
Text Difficulty and Accessibility   203

Appendix B
Sources of Information on Children's Books   217

Preface

Nearly 20 years ago, one of us coauthored a book for the National Council of Teachers of English titled *Structuring Reading Activities for English Classes* (Graves, Palmer, & Furniss, 1976). Since that time, the booklet, updated versions of the booklet, and ideas derived from the booklet have been used in scores of reading courses offered at the University of Minnesota and in a variety of workshops, conferences, and inservice sessions from New Hampshire to California. We have learned a lot from the thousands of teachers who have taken the classes and attended the workshops. We have learned, for example, that the ideas are not just relevant to English teachers; they are relevant to any teachers whose courses include a reasonable amount of reading. They are particularly relevant to intermediate and middle-grade teachers, whose students are increasingly reading both narrative and expository texts that offer some challenges.

The notions that prompted the booklet have held up well, something that gives us some satisfaction in light of the tremendous advances that have been made in the field of reading over the past 20 years. At the same time, we have learned a great deal from these advances, and our understanding of reading and the teaching of reading has grown. Consequently, the original notions have been modified and supplemented to make the plan we present in this book, *Scaffolding Reading Experiences*, more effective and more easily handled and to make the teaching activities we describe more engaging for students. We believe that the plan we present here can make reading more enjoyable, more successful, and more understandable for students. We further believe that it can make teaching reading more manageable, more exciting, more effective, and more rewarding for teachers. We hope that you find this to be true. We hope that reading our book proves to be a rewarding and successful experience, an experience that provides you with some new insights and a number of practical tools for teaching.

Reference

Graves, M.F., Palmer, R.J., & Furniss, D.W. (1976). *Structuring reading activities for English classes*. Urbana, IL: National Council of Teachers of English. The roots of the thinking underlying *Scaffolding Reading Experiences* first appeared here.

Acknowledgements

The thinking behind *Scaffolding Reading Experiences* goes back nearly 20 years. As a consequence, many people have contributed to the book's development. We wish first to thank the thousands of students and teachers who have considered our ideas about scaffolding, responded to them, added ideas of their own, and created Scaffolded Reading Experiences for their students. We also thank Rebecca Palmer and David Furniss, who coauthored a booklet in which we introduced some of the ideas elaborated here. More recently, we were aided by informal reviews from our friends and colleagues, Barbara Brunetti, a teacher at MacGregor Primary School in Albany, California, Gerald Brunetti, a teacher at St. Mary's College in Moraga, California, Susan Watts, a teacher at the University of Minnesota in Minneapolis, and the members of the Augsburg Park Library writers' group. We were further aided by the formal reviews of Becky Ardren, a reading specialist in the Duluth Minnesota Public Schools, Lorraine Gerhart, a reading specialist in the Elmbrook Schools in Brookfield, Wisconsin, Mary Joffre, a reading resource instructor in the Dade County Florida Public Schools, Margaret McKeown, a research scientist at the University of Pittsburgh's Learning Research and Development Center, Denise Muth, professor and head of elementary education at the University of Georgia, and Pam Ryder, reading/language arts coordinator for the Whitefish Bay Wisconsin Public Schools. Our thanks to these reviewers is much more than perfunctory. Each of their reviews was thorough, insightful, and very helpful in strengthening the book. We also appreciate the very thoughtful feedback of Daniel Casper and Clinton Franklin, two graduate students at the University of Minnesota. Finally, we wish to thank Suzanne Canavan of Christopher-Gordon for her encouragement and assistance throughout the project and Susan Folan of Christopher-Gordon for her help with the myriad of details associated with publishing the book.

1

Introduction
and Overview

Imagine a classroom somewhere in America a few years ago, 30 students and one teacher. One small, curly-haired boy named Charlie gazes at the chalkboard and reads the assignment: *Read pages 65–74 in your science book and, on a separate sheet of paper, answer the questions on page 76.* He opens his book reluctantly. After muddling through the ten pages, he tries to answer the questions, with predictably little success. He hands his paper to the teacher and never sees or thinks about the chapter or the questions again. Reading his answers, his teacher might conclude that he has learned nothing. But that's not at all true. He has, in fact, learned two things: Neither school nor reading is much fun.

As you know from your own experience, either as a reader or a teacher, to enjoy reading and get the most out of what you read, you need to be actively involved with the text. You need to feel some sense of ownership for both the task and the material. Essential to effective reading are having the prerequisite skills and background knowledge to deal with a particular selection, being motivated and prepared to read, and having some purpose for reading. Say you are glancing through the newspaper and this headline catches your attention: "New Technique Successful in Teaching All Students to Read." Right away you're motivated to read, although you may well be skeptical of the claim. You're a teacher with 28 third graders, six of whom are struggling readers. In a split second your brain pulls out of memory the faces of those six students, an image of your busy classroom, and the methods and materials you've used. You're more than prepared to see what this article has to tell you about teaching reading; in fact, you can't wait to get started. You want to know just what this technique is and whether or not the technique really can work with all students. Once you begin reading, you combine what you know about students, teaching reading, and classrooms with what is presented in the text, building meaning as you go. What the author says either refutes or confirms what you know. You might become intrigued, amused, discouraged, angered, or enlightened, but two things are certain—you are neither lost nor uninterested. After you read, you will be able to recall what has been presented in the text—to ponder it, to consider the author's arguments, and to apply or reject what you have learned.

How can we foster and encourage this kind of involvement in our students' reading? One way is by providing appropriate kinds of experiences before students read, while they are reading, and after they read—experiences that will ensure they get the most out of what they read, whether it be novels or short stories, folk tales or poems, chapters in textbooks, magazine articles, or cookbooks.

The central ideas we present for implementing these kinds of experiences revolve around the concept of **scaffolding.** We believe that the term *scaffolding* was first used in its educational sense by Harvard psychologist Jerome Bruner, who used it to characterize mothers' verbal interaction when reading to their young children. Thus, for example, in sharing a picture book with a child and attempting to assist the child in reading the words that label the pictures, a mother might at first simply page through the book familiarizing the child with the pictures and the general content of the book. She might then focus on a single picture and ask the child what it is. After this, she might point to the word below the picture, tell the child that the word names the picture, ask the child what the word is, and provide him or her with feedback on the correctness of the answer. The important point to focus on is that the mother has neither simply told the child the word nor simply asked him or her to say it. Instead, she has built an instructional structure, a scaffold, that assists the student in learning. Scaffolding, as Wood, Bruner, and Ross (1976) have aptly put it, is "a process that enables a child or novice to solve a problem, carry out a task, or achieve a goal which would be beyond his [or her] unassisted efforts" (p. 90).

In this book, we use the term *scaffolding* to refer to a set of prereading, during-reading, and postreading opportunities and experiences designed to assist a particular group of students in successfully reading, understanding, learning from, and enjoying a particular selection. The process of reading a selection is somewhat like taking a journey. As with any successful journey, there are certain essentials, things that should be done before, during, and after the trip to make it a worthwhile and meaningful experience. A Scaffolded Reading Experience (SRE) is designed to provide students with the essentials that will make their reading experience worthwhile and meaningful. As we will explain and illustrate throughout this book, the more unfamiliar the territory, the greater the need for substantial amounts of preparation, guidance, and follow-up.

The remainder of this book is divided into seven chapters. Chapter 2, What Is a Scaffolded Reading Experience?, defines Scaffolded Reading Experiences, gives a list and brief explanations of their components, describes the two phases of Scaffolded Reading Experiences, models the thinking involved in constructing a Scaffolded Reading Experience for a science chapter, and explains what Scaffolded Reading Experiences are not.

Chapter 3, The Thinking Behind Scaffolded Reading, describes a variety of considerations that influenced us as we developed and refined the notion of Scaffolded Reading Experiences. These influences have, as we suggested before, come over a 20-year period, and they are many and varied. They include theoretical constructs such as schema theory, concerns about students such as the importance of their experiencing success in reading, and pedagogical notions such as the benefits of reflective teaching.

Chapters 4, 5, and 6 parallel each other. Chapter 4, Prereading Activities, describes ten types of prereading activities and gives specific examples of each of them. Chapter 5, During Reading Activities, describes five types of during-reading activities and gives examples of each. Chapter 6, Postreading Activities, describes and provides examples of seven types of postreading activities. Because we believe that models are extremely useful in precisely conveying our meaning, we have included a lot of detailed examples. Along with each example, we have included a discussion of the types of reading selections with which the activity would be useful and our reflections on the activity—our assessment of it, some of its unique features, and some general pedagogical considerations it suggests.

Chapter 7, Comprehensive Scaffolded Reading Experiences, begins by describing the thinking that goes into selecting an appropriate set of prereading, reading, and postreading activities for a particular group of students reading a particular text. The chapter then presents three examples of complete Scaffolded Reading Experiences. We have deliberately made these three SREs very different from each other to show the range of possibilities the Scaffolded Reading approach invites.

Chapter 8, Incorporating Scaffolded Reading Experiences in Your Classroom, addresses several considerations to keep in mind as you begin using SREs. First, it describes some of the decisions you face. After that, it considers ways of adjusting postreading tasks when you see that students are not likely to be successful unless postreading activities are somehow modified, ways of preparing students for cooperative learning, and ways of involving students in constructing SREs. Finally, the chapter places the Scaffolded Reading approach in the context of a comprehensive reading program by describing nine other components that are vital to a comprehensive program.

This book concludes with two appendices and several indexes. Appendix A, Text Difficulty and Accessibility, presents a reflective approach to choosing appropriate reading selections for your students. Appendix B, Sources of Information on Children's Books, describes a variety of sources of information about fiction and nonfiction books for young readers. Finally, the sample activities are indexed by author, title, grade level, and subject; and the book itself is indexed by academic author and academic subject.

As we have mentioned, besides a general description of the Scaffolded Reading approach and the ideas that inform it, this book contains a number of detailed samples of Scaffolded Reading activities. These activities are designed to illustrate the general ideas we discuss, to serve as models you can use in developing similar activities for your classroom, and to act as springboards for critical and creative thinking as you reflect upon how these ideas might be implemented in your particular teaching situation. They are not meant to be scripts or blueprints. As you are well aware, each reading situation is slightly different from every other one. Moreover, given the dynamics of actual classrooms, even the most carefully crafted lessons have a way of taking on a new life of their own. At the same time, even though your plans will often change as they unfold in the classroom, having carefully considered plans for facilitating students' reading puts you in the best possible position to assist and encourage students to become competent, avid, and lifelong readers.

Reference

Wood, D.J., Bruner, J.S., & Ross, G. (1976). The role of tutoring in problem-solving. *Journal of Child Psychology and Psychiatry, 17* (2), 89–100. Our introduction to the concept of *scaffolding* and an insightful examination of parent-child interactions.

2

What Is a Scaffolded Reading Experience?

In this chapter, we explain what a Scaffolded Reading Experience is and what it is not.

What a Scaffolded Reading Experience Is

A Scaffolded Reading Experience is a set of prereading, during-reading, and postreading activities specifically designed to assist a particular group of students in successfully reading, understanding, learning from, and enjoying a particular selection. As such, a Scaffolded Reading Experience is somewhat similar to traditional instructional plans such as Emmett Betts' Directed Reading Activity (1946) and Russell Stauffer's Directed Reading-Thinking Activity (Stauffer, 1969). However, a Scaffolded Reading Experience differs markedly from these other instructional plans in that a Scaffolded Reading Experience is not a preset plan for dealing with whatever reading selections students encounter. Instead, it is a flexible framework that provides a set of options from which you select those that are best suited for a particular group of students reading a particular text for a particular purpose.

On the following page, we list here those options and describe the framework in which we have placed them. Although some of these categories of activities are self evident, others are not. Thus, it may be helpful to say a few words about each of them here. We deal with each of them in more depth and provide detailed examples of each in later chapters.

Prereading Activities

Prereading activities prepare students to read the upcoming selection. They can serve a number of functions, including getting students interested in reading the selection, reminding students of things they already know that will help them understand and enjoy the selection, and preteaching aspects of the selection that may be difficult.

Table 2-1 Possible Components of a Scaffolded Reading Experience

---

Prereading Activities
- Motivating
- Relating the Reading to Students' Lives
- Activating Background Knowledge
- Building Text-Specific Knowledge
- Preteaching Vocabulary
- Preteaching Concepts
- Prequestioning
- Predicting
- Direction Setting
- Suggesting Strategies

During–reading Activities
- Silent Reading
- Reading to Students
- Guided Reading
- Oral Reading by Students
- Modifying the Text

Postreading Activities
- Questioning
- Discussion
- Writing
- Drama
- Artistic, Graphic, and Nonverbal Activities
- Application and Outreach Activities
- Reteaching

Prereading activities are particularly important because with adequate preparation the experience of reading will be enjoyable, rewarding, and successful.

By **Motivating Activities** we refer to any activity designed to interest students in the upcoming selection and entice them to read it. Although a variety of prereading activities can be motivational as well as accomplish some other purpose, we list motivating activities as a separate category because we believe that it is perfectly appropriate to do something solely for the purpose of motivating students. Moreover, we believe that motivating activities should frequently be a part of reading activities.

Relating the Reading to Students' Lives is so self-evident a category its leaves little to say. We will, however, point out that, because showing students how a selection relates to them is such a powerful motivator, it is something we like to do often.

Activating Background Knowledge and **Building Text Specific Knowledge** can conveniently be considered together because they are contrasting, yet complementary, activities. Activities that activate background knowledge prompt students to bring to consciousness already known information that will be helpful in understanding the upcoming text. For example, before reading a science article on tributaries of the Nile, students can discuss what they have learned about tributaries of other rivers. In addition to activating background knowledge, it is sometimes necessary to build background knowledge, knowledge that the author has presupposed—probably tacitly—readers already possess. The author of a story set in a movie theater is likely to presuppose that students are quite familiar with American movies and movie theaters. However, we might have to explain quite a bit about these and related concepts to a Hmong student who has just arrived in the United States.

In contrast to activities that activate or build background knowledge, activities that build text-specific knowledge give students information that is contained in the reading selection. Providing students with advance information on the content of a selection—giving students the seven topics discussed in an article on whales, for example—may be justified if the selection is difficult or densely packed with information.

Preteaching Vocabulary and **Preteaching Concepts** are other activities that are closely related and can conveniently be considered together. We list these as two different activities rather than a single activity to contrast teaching words that are merely new labels for concepts that students already know to teaching new and potentially difficult concepts. For example, you would be teaching vocabulary—a new label—if you taught fourth graders the word *crimson,* meaning "red." On the other hand, if you wanted to teach these same fourth graders anything like the full meaning of *velocity,* you would be dealing with a new concept. It often makes sense to take five minutes and preteach half a dozen new vocabulary words before an upcoming selection, but it seldom makes sense to attempt to preteach half a dozen new and difficult concepts in anything like the same amount of time. Teaching new and difficult concepts takes significant amounts of time.

We have listed **Prequestioning, Predicting,** and **Direction Setting** together because we believe that they are similar activities. With any of them, we are focusing students' attention and telling them what is important to look for as they read. Such focusing is often necessary because without it students may not know what to attend to.

In the final prereading activity we have listed, **Suggesting Strategies**, the key word is *Suggesting.* As we will explain at the end of this chapter, Scaffolded Reading Experiences are not designed to *teach* strategies. Teaching strategies—actually instructing students in how to do something they could not do previously—almost always requires more time than we allot to Scaffolded Reading Experiences. However, it is often appropriate to suggest as part of a Scaffolded Reading Experience that students use strategies they already know. Occasionally, these strategies may be ones that students have learned on their own, but in most cases the strategies will have been deliberately taught in the past.

During-reading Activities

During-reading activities include both things that students themselves do as they are reading and things that you do to assist them as they are reading. In this category, we include **Silent Reading, Reading to Students, Guided Reading, Oral Reading by Students,** and **Modifying the Text**.

We have deliberately listed **Silent Reading** first because we believe strongly that it should be the most frequently used during-reading activity. The central long-term goal of reading instruction is to prepare students to become accomplished lifelong readers, and most of the reading students do in life—in secondary school, in college, and in the world outside of school—will be silent reading. It is both a basic rule of learning and everyday common sense that one needs to practice repeatedly the skill he or she is attempting to master. If we choose appropriate selections for students to read and adequately prepare them to read the selections, students will often be able to read the selections silently on their own.

Reading To Students can serve a number of functions. Hearing a story or piece of exposition read aloud is a very pleasurable experience for many youngsters and also serves as a model of good oral reading. Reading the first chapter or the first few pages of a piece can help ease students into the material and also serve as an enticement to read the rest of the selection on their own. Reading to students can make difficult material accessible to those who find certain texts difficult, either because of their complex structure or difficult vocabulary. In these instances, reading aloud—or playing an audio tape for the same purpose—is sometimes necessary. However, in most instances, students should read silently on their own. One gets good at reading through reading.

Guided Reading refers to any activity that you use to focus students' attention on particular aspects of a text as they read. Guided reading can be used to assist students in understanding a text or to assisting them in enjoying and appreciating it. Guided reading often begins as a prereading activity—perhaps with your setting directions for reading—and is then carried out as students are actually reading. For example, to help students appreciate an author's craft and to give them examples of the sort of language they might like to include sometimes in their own writing, you might have them jot down examples of colorful or figurative language while they read a humorous short story. As another example, if you find that an expository piece on seashells is actually divided into half a dozen sections but contains no headings or subheadings, you might give students a semantic map that includes titles for the sections and ask them to complete the map as they are reading. Often, with guided reading activities, students' goal is to learn something from their reading rather than just read for enjoyment. Thus, guided reading activities are frequently used with expository material. However, it is also possible to guide students in responding to narratives, for example, to recognize the plot structure of a novel or learn about the main characters and their motives in a short story.

Of course, one long-term goal is to enable and motivate students to engage in active and responsive activities as they are independently reading. Thus, with less challenging selections and as students become increasingly competent over time, your support can be less specific and less directive, perhaps consisting only of a prereading suggestion: "After reading this chapter, I have a suggestion for you. Try reading it with a partner and stopping after each section to take notes. This should help you understand and remember the material better." Or, "You'll find that Toby is quite a character and that he changes a lot during the story. Using a journal to record the changes he undergoes and writing down how you feel about the changes may help you better appreciate what he's going through."

In most classrooms, **Oral Reading by Students** is a relatively infrequent activity. As we previously mentioned, most of the reading students do once they leave elementary school is silent reading. Nonetheless, oral reading has its place. Certainly, poetry is often best and most effective when read orally. Also, poignant or particularly well-written passages of prose are often appropriate for oral reading. Reading orally can also be helpful when the class or a group of students is studying a passage and trying to decide on alternative interpretations or on just what is and is not explicitly stated in the passage. Additionally, students often like to read their own writing orally. Thus, while oral reading may not be a frequent activity, it is a very useful one and something to include among the many options you offer students.

Modifying the Text is sometimes necessary to make the reading material more accessible to students. This may involve presenting the material on audio or video tapes, changing the format of a selection, or simplifying or shortening a text. Modifying the text is called for in situations in which reading selections present too much of a challenge because of their length or difficulty. Assuming students can and will read the original selection, will they get as much out of reading a modified version of it or from listening to it on tape? Probably not. But assuming they cannot or will not read all of the original selection, hearing it or successfully reading part of it is certainly preferable to failing to read all of it.

Postreading Activities

Postreading activities serve a variety of purposes. They provide opportunities for students to synthesize and organize information gleaned from the text so that they can understand and recall important points. They provide opportunities for students to evaluate an author's message, his or her stance in presenting the message, and the quality of the text itself. They provide opportunities for you and your students to evaluate their understanding of the text. They also provide opportunities for students to respond to a text in a variety of ways—to reflect on the meaning of the text, to compare differing texts and ideas, to imagine themselves as one of the characters in the text, to synthesize information from different sources, to engage in a variety of creative activities, and to apply what they have learned within the classroom walls to the world beyond the classroom.

Questioning, either orally or in writing, is a frequently used and frequently warranted activity. Questioning activities give you an opportunity to encourage and promote higher order thinking—to nudge students to interpret, analyze, and evaluate what they read. Questions can also elicit creative and personal responses—"How did you feel when . . . ?" "What do you think the main character would have done if . . . ?" Sometimes, of course, it is appropriate for students to read something and not be faced with some sort of accountability afterward. However, in many cases, neither you nor your students will be sure that they gained what they needed to gain from the reading without their answering some sort of questions. Of course, teachers are not the only ones who should be asking questions after reading. Students can ask questions of each other, they can ask you questions, and they can ask questions they plan to answer through further reading.

Some sort of **Discussion**—whether it is discussion in pairs or small groups or discussion involving the entire class—is another frequent activity and often very appropriate. Certainly, if there is a chance that some students did not understand as much of a selection as they need to—and there is often this chance—discussion is warranted. Equally important, discussion gives students a chance to offer their personal interpretations and responses to a text and hear those of others. Discussion is also a vehicle for assessing whether or not reading goals have been achieved and to evaluate what went right about the reading experience, what went wrong, and what might be done differently in the future.

Writing is a postreading task that ought to be used more frequently than it is. In recent years, there has been a good deal of well-warranted emphasis on the fact that reading and writing are complementary activities and often should be dealt with together. We certainly agree. However, we want to stress that writing is often a challenging activity, and it is thus important to be sure that students are adequately prepared for writing. Among other things, this means that if students are expected to write about a selection, you usually need to be sure they have comprehended the selection well. We say *usually* because sometimes students can write to discover what they have comprehended in a selection.

Drama offers a range of opportunities for students to get actively involved in responding to what they have read. By drama, we refer to any sort of production involving action and movement. Given this definition, short plays, skits, pantomimes, and Readers Theatre are possibilities.

Artistic, Graphic, and **Nonverbal Activities** constitute additional possibilities for postreading endeavors. In this broad category, we include visual art, graphics, music, dance, and media productions such as videos, slide shows, and audio tapes, as well as constructive activities that you might not typically think of as artistic. Probably the most frequent members of this last category are graphics of some sort— maps, charts, trees, diagrams, schematics, and the like. Other possibilities include constructing models or bringing in artifacts that are somehow responses to the selection read. Artistic and nonverbal activities can be particularly useful because they are fun, may be a little different from typical school tasks, and provide opportunities for students to express themselves in a variety of ways, thus creating situations in which students of varying talents and abilities can excel. This is not to say that such activities are frills, something to be done just to provide variety. In many situations and for many students, artistic and nonverbal activities offer the greatest potential for learning information and for responding to what has been read.

Application and **Outreach Activities**. Here, we include both concrete and direct applications—cooking something after reading a recipe—and less direct ones—attempting to change some aspect of student government after reading something about state government that suggests the possibility. Here, we also include activities that extend beyond the campus—planning a drive to collect used coats and sweaters after reading a news article on people in need of winter clothing or taking a field trip to a local art museum after reading about one of the artists represented there. Obviously, there is a great range of application and outreach options.

The final postreading activity we consider is **Reteaching**. When it becomes apparent that students have not achieved their reading goals or the level of under-standing you deem necessary, reteaching is often in order, and the best time for reteaching is usually as soon as possible after students first encounter the material. In some cases, reteaching may consist simply of asking students to reread parts of a selection. In other cases, you may want to present a mini-lesson on some part of the text that has caused students problems. In still other cases, students who have understood a particular aspect of the text may assist other students in achieving similar understanding.

Planning Scaffolded Reading Experiences

We have described a fairly lengthy list of possible activities, far too many to be used with a single selection. Again, however, this is a list of options. From this set of possibilities, you choose only those that are appropriate for your particular students' reading a particular text for a particular purpose. Suppose, for example, you are working with a class of fourth graders on social studies. The class is reading an article on the Declaration of Independence, and their goal is to learn the most important information in the article. In this situation, you might provide prereading instruction that includes a motivational activity, the preteaching of some difficult vocabulary, and a questioning activity—an activity in which students pose *who, when, where, what, how,* and *why* questions they expect to be answered in the article. Next, for the during-reading portion of the lesson, you might read part of the article orally and then have students read the rest silently, looking for answers to their questions. Finally, after students have finished the selection, they might break into discussion groups of three or four and answer the questions they posed during prereading. After this, the groups might come together as a class and share their answers. Here is a list of the activities.

Prereading:	Motivating
	Preteaching Vocabulary
	Questioning
During Reading:	Reading to Students
	Silent Reading
Postreading:	Small Group Discussion
	Answering Questions
	Large Group Discussion

There are probably two main characteristics of this example particularly worth recognizing at this point. For one thing, this combination of prereading, during-reading, and postreading activities is only one of a number of combinations you could have selected. For another, you selected the activities you did based on your assessment of the students, the selection they were reading, and their purpose in reading the selection.

We can highlight both of these characteristics of a Scaffolded Reading Experi-ence (SRE) by giving another example. Suppose the same fourth-graders were reading a simple and straightforward narrative, something like the opening chapters of Beverly Cleary's *Ramona and Her Father.* Suppose further that their primary purpose for reading the story was simply to enjoy it. In this case, prereading instruction might consist of only a brief motivational activity, the during-reading portion might consist entirely of students' reading the story silently, and the postreading portion might consist of their voluntarily discussing the parts of the story they found most interesting. In this SRE, there is little instruction because neither your students, the story itself, nor their purpose for reading the story require it.

We can make the general plan for an SRE more tangible and perhaps more memorable with the aid of the diagram below. As shown in Figure 2-1, a Scaffolded Reading Experience has two phases. The first phase is the **Planning Phase**, during which you create the entire experience. The second phase is the **Implementation Phase**, the activities you and your students engage in as a result of your planning.

Planning takes into account the students, the reading selection, and the reading purpose. These factors are interrelated, and decisions made about any one factor influence and constrain the decisions that can be made about the other two. If, for instance, you are teaching sixth-grade students, there are only certain texts and certain topics that are likely to be appropriate. If you want students to learn something about the migration of whales, you will have a limited number of texts to choose from—probably one or two. Moreover, although sixth graders can certainly

Figure 2-1   Two Phases of a Scaffolded Reading Experience

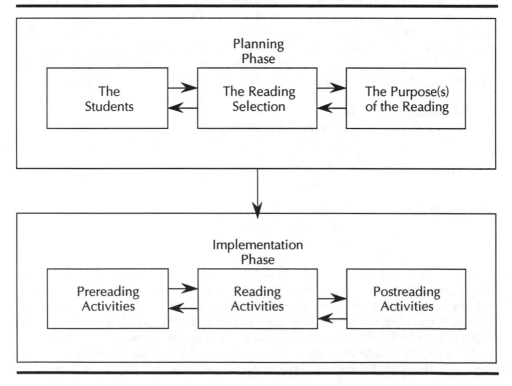

learn some things about whale migration, they will still be years of study away from becoming experts on the topic when they finish reading. Still, if all students are reading the same selection, you have the option of arranging a healthy set of activities to assist them with the reading. If, on the other hand, you are teaching third graders and your purpose is to have students read a humorous story for the pure enjoyment of it, you will have a lot of selections to choose from. In fact, you may want to offer students individual choices from the classroom or school library. And because students have selected their own books, they are likely to be interested in what they read and quite successful in reaching your goal of reading just to enjoy a humorous story. On the other hand, your decision to allow students to self-select materials means that they will be reading from a variety of materials and you will not have much opportunity to arrange activities to help them with their reading.

The result of your planning—taking into account the interdependent factors of students, texts, and purposes—is the creation of the total SRE with its various activities. As shown in Figure 2-1, the possible components of the implementation phase are prereading, during-reading, and postreading activities. As is the case with the three factors considered in planning, the three components of the implementation phase are interdependent. If, for example, you decide to have all your sixth graders read a relatively difficult article on whale migration for homework, at least some students in a heterogeneous class are likely to need a good deal of prereading instruction. If, on the other hand, your choice is to have students read a relatively simple selection solely for enjoyment and there is to be no postreading task, prereading activities are likely to be minimal.

A Sample Planning Experience

Consider, for example, the planning you might do and the SRE you might construct for a chapter on waves in a fifth-grade science text (Hackett & Moyer, 1991). Your students are fifth graders of average to high ability, and the class includes two ESL students for whom reading English is a challenge. After reading the chapter, you decide the important reading purposes are for students to understand the concept of **waves**, note some of the properties of waves, describe several different types of waves, and come away with the understanding that waves are important physical phenomena, a scientific topic they will meet again and learn more about in later grades.

Thinking again about your class, you decide that your students can handle the chapter, with your help. Again considering the chapter, you identify the concepts you want to stress and note that the chapter contains some material they do not need to deal with at the present time. You also note that the chapter is 10 pages and about 3,000 words long and estimate it will take your students 20 to 30 minutes to read through it once.

All of this thinking—these considerations about your students, the chapter, and reading purposes—are in your mind as you plan the SRE. (As a matter of fact, in actually planning an SRE you would probably consider more factors than we have listed in this brief example.) With those considerations firmly in mind, you come up with pre-, during-, and postreading activities. Here is an outline of what your plan might look like.

Scaffolded Reading Experience

Planning

Students	Selection	Purpose
Fifth graders of average-to-high ability; the class includes two ESL students.	Chapter titled "Waves" in fifth-grade science text	To understand and recall the concept of waves, some wave properties, and types of waves

Implementation

Prereading Activities	During Reading Activities	Post Reading Activities
Motivating: Act out the motion of a wave.	**Reading Aloud:** Read first section aloud to students.	**Discussion:** Small groups discuss chapter and add information to outline.
Preteaching a Concept: Teach the concepts amplitude and frequency.	**Modifying the Text:** Tape chapter and make tape available to ESL students.	**Reteaching:** Reteach and extend central concepts as necessary.
Building Text-Specific Knowledge: Use the headings in the chapter to preview and predict its contents.	**Silent Reading:** Students read chapter on their own.	**Writing:** Have students write an imaginative tale in which a wave goes berserk.

For prereading, you decide to include a motivational activity that will relate the topic of **waves** to students' lives and preteach the concept. You include motivation because you believe that some sort of motivation is almost always a good idea and because students will not automatically be interested in waves. You have students demonstrate a wave by arranging themselves in a line across the front of the room and then successively standing up and sitting down—much as fans do at a football game. Following this demonstration (students will probably have to practice the wave several times before it becomes rhythmic and looks like a wave), you point out various attributes of their wave and of waves generally. For example, their wave and all waves are rhythmic and have amplitude and frequency. You might go on to explain these related concepts and then have students again demonstrate several different wave forms, changing the amplitude of their wave by raising both hands rather than standing up and changing its duration by standing up and sitting down or raising and lowering their hands at different rates. Finally, you might draw several wave forms on the board to illustrate the rhythmic patterns and the different amplitudes and durations waves can have.

Motivating students might also include stressing that **waves** is an important science topic, reminding them that they are already familiar with some sorts of waves—those in oceans or lakes—and asking them what other sorts play parts in their daily lives; microwaves and TV waves are likely responses.

Next, because the chapter contains several difficult concepts, more really than you would like, you decide to preteach two of the most important ones. These are the concepts of **amplitude** and **frequency** as they apply to waves. You begin by defining each of the concepts. The amplitude of a wave is the height of the wave from its origin to its crest. The frequency of a wave is the number of cycles of a wave to pass through a point in a certain amount of time. Next, you remind students that their own wave had amplitude and frequency; its amplitude was perhaps a foot or two, and its frequency might have been 10 cycles a minute. After this, you might show a video that illustrates the two concepts. Finally, you could ask students if they know of other words or phrases that express concepts similar to those expressed by amplitude and frequency; *height, size,* and *how often something happens* are possible responses. Of course, these brief activities have not fully taught the concepts, but students will be better prepared to understand them when they come up in the chapter.

As the next activity, to prepare students to deal with both the content and the organization of the chapter, you write the headings and subheadings from the chapter on the board, being sure to preserve the features the text used to show subordination. For example, the superordinate topics might be in all caps and left justified, while the subordinate topics might be in a mixture of upper and lower case letters and indented. You then ask students to identify the superordinate and subordinate topics by noting their placement and the type of letters used. Finally, you ask students to brainstorm on what they can learn just from the headings. For example, the first heading might be HOW DO WAVES TRANSFER ENERGY?, indicating that one thing waves do is transfer energy. You write this on the board and continue through the rest of the outline with the class jotting down similar information gleaned from the outline.

For during-reading activities, you decide to make an audio tape of the chapter for your ESL students. Your plan also includes reading the first section of the chapter aloud to all students to ease them into it and to point out new information that can be added to the outline on the board. After the first section, the ESL students will listen to the tape and the rest of the class will finish the chapter by reading silently to themselves. Before students begin their listening or reading, however, you remind them that they shouldn't try to learn everything in the chapter but should focus their attention on the topics included in the outline—the properties of waves and the different sorts of waves described.

In deciding on postreading activities, you would probably take into account the fact that the chapter is challenging and that you do want students to remember the major concepts dealt with in it. You might, therefore, hand out a discussion guide that parallels the chapter outline you wrote on the board and offer students 20 minutes to discuss these concepts in small groups. After that, the class could come back together, and each group could report one piece of information it discovered about waves. Also, it is likely that some of your students will probably need extra work with concepts such as **amplitude** and **frequency**, and you might offer to join a group of students if there are any that would like to consider these ideas further. Finally, because many of your students have a creative bent and because you believe that **waves** and related concepts might prompt interesting fantasy tales, you suggest that students work alone or in small groups to create stories, sketches, or poems in which waves play central roles. Then, once students have completed their creations, they could either present them orally or post them around the room.

All in all, your students might spend three or four days with this SRE. Your purpose in designing these activities—and the purpose in planning and carrying out any SRE—is a straightforward one: You want to do everything possible to ensure that students have a successful reading experience. As we suggested before, we believe that a successful reading experience is one in which students understand the selection, learn from it, and enjoy it. Moreover, our goal includes students' realizing that they have been successful, recognizing that they have dealt competently with the selection because that is exactly what they have done. If students are to become successful lifelong readers—persons who voluntarily choose to read to understand themselves and their world better, gain information, and experience the joy of reading—the vast majority of their reading experiences must be successful ones.

What a Scaffolded Reading Experience Is Not

To conclude our explanation of what a Scaffolded Reading Experience is, we want to explain what an SRE is not and what goals SREs are not designed to achieve.

We will begin with the obvious. A Scaffolded Reading Experience is not a complete plan for a reading program. It does not deal at all with word identification skills—phonics, syllabication, blending, words parts, use of context, and the like. It does not provide a systematic program of vocabulary instruction. It does not take the place of literature circles or of a recreational reading, independent reading, or free reading program. Moreover, SREs do not provide instruction in reading strategies.

SREs assist students in understanding, enjoying, and learning from the selections they read. These successful experiences will produce more avid readers and better readers: Success breeds success. Again, however, SREs do not include direct attempts to teach students strategies that they can use in their reading. They do not, for example, directly teach students how to determine important information, make inferences, outline material, or summarize it.

Is teaching such strategies important? In our judgment, absolutely yes! Students need instruction in these sorts of strategies, but describing such instruction is simply not our purpose here. Are assisting students in understanding individual selections they read, enhancing students' enjoyment of individual selections they read, and helping them learn from selections they read also important? Again, absolutely yes! A complete reading program will include instruction that accomplishes both of these objectives.

Although this book is not intended to prepare you to construct a comprehensive reading program, because we believe that the most effective reading programs are comprehensive ones, at the end of Chapter 8 we discuss the components of comprehensive programs and suggest key readings on these components.

Concluding Comments

In this chapter, we have attempted to give a fairly thorough overview of what a Scaffolded Reading Experience is and what it is not. In doing so, we have defined an SRE, listed its components, briefly described each of them, given examples of activities and how we would go about planning them, and directly explained what Scaffolded Reading Experiences are not designed to do. The next chapter examines the thinking that prompted us to develop the notion of the Scaffolded Reading Experience as we have.

References

Betts, E. (1946). *Foundations of reading*. New York: American Book. This general methods text contains the original presentation of the Directed Reading Activity, the framework that for decades served as the lesson framework for basal readers.

Moore, D.W., Readence, J.E., & Rickelman, R.J. (1989). *Prereading activities for content area reading and learning* (2nd ed.). Newark, DE: International Reading Association. Presents a variety of activities for preparing students to read as well as strategies students can use independently as they approach content area reading selections.

Neal, J.C., & Langer, M.A. (1992). A framework of teaching options for content area instruction: Mediated instruction of text. *Journal of Reading, 38,* 227–230. Briefly describes a before-, during-, and after-reading framework for dealing with content area reading selections.

Olson, M.W., & Homan, S.P. (Eds.). (1993). *Teacher to teacher: Strategies for the elementary classroom*. Newark. DE: International Reading Association. A collection of more than 100 teacher-constructed reading activities from the "In the Classroom" section of *The Reading Teacher*.

Stauffer, R.G. (1969). *Directing reading maturity as a cognitive process*. New York: Harper & Row. Contains the original presentation of the Directed Reading–Thinking Activity. Still a valuable resource.

Tierney, R.J., Readence, J.E., & Dishner, E.K. (1990). *Reading strategies and practices: A Compendium* (3rd ed.). Boston: Allyn and Bacon. This very valuable and extensive compendium — nearly 500 pages in length — describes and evaluates more than 75 reading strategies and practices. These activities are grouped into 14 units, including Comprehension Development, Response to Literature and Drama, and Content Area and Text-based Comprehension.

Wood, K.D., Lapp, D., & Flood, J. (1992). *Guiding readers through text: A review of study guides*. A detailed, lucid, and useful description of 17 types of study guides that teachers can use to focus students' attention and guide them toward understanding as they are reading.

Yopp, R.H., & Yopp, H.K. (1992). *Literature-based reading activities*. Boston: Allyn and Bacon. Describes pre-, during-, and postreading activities for literary selections.

Children's Books Cited

Cleary, B. (1975). *Ramona and her father*. New York: William Morrow.

Hackett, J.K., & Moyer, R.H. (1991). "Waves," *Science in Your World*, Level 6. New York: Macmillan/McGraw-Hill.

3

The Thinking Behind Scaffolded Reading

The past 25 years has been an enormously exciting and productive time in the field of reading, and we believe that the wealth of information available today makes it possible to improve the reading performance of all youngsters markedly and, equally important, to instill in students a lifelong love of reading. We agree, therefore, with the view expressed in the 1985 report of the Commission on Reading: "The knowledge is now available to make worthwhile improvements in reading throughout the United States. If the practices seen in the classrooms of the best teachers in the best schools could be introduced everywhere, improvements in reading would be dramatic" (Anderson, Hiebert, Scott, & Wilkinson, 1985, p. x). We are confident that these best practices can indeed be introduced in all schools. Moreover, a great deal has been learned since 1985, and teachers are in an even better position today to improve children's reading than they were several years ago.

In this chapter, we discuss the ideas that most influenced us as we developed the Scaffolded Reading approach. Some of these ideas, as the above paragraph suggests, are new; others have existed for some time. Some of the ideas are rather formal and properly deserve the term *theories;* others are much less formal and are better termed *notions.* Some are complex, obscure, and not easily grasped; others are simple, obvious, and common sense. Some are supported by a good deal of research; others have very little research support. All in all, it is a diverse set of ideas, linked by a single unifying theme: Each of these ideas makes a direct and practical statement about what can and should be done to assist students in reading and enjoying specific selections.

We have, of course, already introduced one of these ideas, that of scaffolding; the concept of **scaffolding** is at the center of the plan we are presenting. As we noted in Chapter 1, a scaffold is a temporary supportive structure that enables a person to successfully complete a task he or she could not complete without the aid of the scaffold. Training wheels for young children's bicycles are an excellent example of a scaffold used to assist youngsters in mastering a challenging physical task. Training wheels are temporary, they are supportive, they can be adjusted up or down to provide more or less support, and they enable a child to ride a bicycle when he or she might otherwise not be able to do so. This is precisely the function that a Scaffolded Reading Experience serves in supporting students' reading.

We have grouped the other ideas underlying the Scaffolded Reading approach under four headings—**Student Engagement, Cognitive Learning Concepts, Instructional Concepts**, and **Pedagogical Orientations**. We stress, however, that the topics included in one of these areas could in some cases have been placed in another, and that the collection of topics within a single area is sometimes quite diverse. Our central concern in choosing the ideas to discuss here is that they matter in terms of what you do in your classroom rather than that they fit into some neat category system.

Student Engagement

The theme of this section is that students' reading abilities will grow in direct proportion to the extent to which they see reading as an activity that they succeed at, an activity that is under their control and something they can improve at, and an activity that is a worthwhile and enjoyable. In keeping with this theme, here we consider three topics—the critical importance of **Success, Attribution Theory and Learned Helplessness**, and the significance of creating **a Literate Environment** that will nurture children's reading and writing development.

Success

The dominant thought motivating not just this section of the chapter but the whole of this book is the overwhelming importance of success. As Harold Herber (1970) pointed out some years ago and as the research on teaching effectiveness has repeatedly verified (see, for example, Brophy, 1986), if students are going to learn to read effectively, they need to succeed at the vast majority of reading tasks they undertake. Moreover, if students are going to become not only proficient readers but also avid readers—children and later adults who voluntarily seek out reading as a road to information, enjoyment, and personal fulfillment—then successful reading experiences are even more important.

There are, of course, a variety of ways in which reading experiences can be successful. Several of them are particularly important. First, and most important, a successful reading experience is one in which the reader understands what he or she has read. Of course, understanding may take more than one reading, it may require your assistance or that of other students, and it will often require the reader to manipulate the ideas in the text actively—summarize them, discuss them with classmates, or compare them to other ideas. Second, a successful reading experience is one that the reader finds enjoyable, entertaining, informative, or thought provoking. Of course, not every reading experience will yield all of these benefits, but every experience should yield at least one of them. Finally, a successful reading experience is one that prepares the student to complete whatever task follows the reading.

To a great extent, children's success in reading is directly under your control. You can select and allow them to select materials that they can read. To the extent that the material they read presents challenges, you can provide support before, during, and after they read that will enable them to meet those challenges. You can also select and help them select postreading activities that they can succeed at.

Doing this—choosing selections, arranging activities, and selecting doable postreading tasks so that students are successful in their reading—is the essence of the Scaffolded Reading approach, of the whole of this book. Here, we give three brief examples of ways in which you can help ensure students' success. Suppose you have a group of students who read at about 100 words a minute and a 15-minute period in which they will be reading. Giving students a selection slightly shorter than 1,500 words will ensure that they at least have time to complete it, whereas giving them a selection much longer than 1,500 words will leave them frustrated and ensure failure.

As another example, suppose you have a group of students who will be reading a science chapter on the ecology of fresh water lakes but who have virtually no concept of ecology, who have never even thought about the relationships among organisms and their environments. Preteaching the concept of ecology—quite possibly in a fairly extensive lesson—will greatly increase the possibilities that students will understand the chapter and not simply flounder in a sea of new ideas. As a third example, suppose that you have a group of students for whom the questions at the end of a social studies chapter on Reconstruction are likely to present more of a challenge than they can handle. In such a case, you might cue students to the places where the questions are answered in the text. Or you might work through the first few questions as a group to get students off to a good start. The point, once again, is to do everything possible to ensure success.

In concluding this section, we want to point out a qualification advanced by Frank Smith (1976). Saying students should succeed at the reading tasks you ask them to complete and that you should do everything possible to ensure success does not mean spoon-feeding them. Unless readers undertake some challenging tasks, unless they are willing to take some risks and make some attempts they are not certain of and get feedback on their efforts, there is little room for learning to take place. To develop as readers, children need to be given some challenges. However, it is vitally important for teachers to arrange and scaffold reading activities so that students can meet these challenges.

Attribution Theory and Learned Helplessness

Attribution theory deals with students' perceptions of the causes of their successes and failures in learning. As Merlin Wittrock (1986) explains, in deciding why they succeed or fail in reading tasks, students can attribute their performance to ability, effort, luck, the difficulty of the reading task, or a variety of other causes. All too often, children who have failed repeatedly in reading attribute their failure to factors that are beyond their control—to an unchangeable factor such as their innate ability or to a factor that they can do nothing about such as luck. Once this happens, children are likely to lose their motivation to learn to read generally, and they are likely to doubt their capacity to successfully read and comprehend specific selections. From their perspective, there is no reason to try because there is nothing they can do about it. Moreover, as long as they do not try, they can't fail; you can't lose a race if you don't enter it.

As Peter Johnston and Peter Winograd (1985) have pointed out, one long-term outcome of children's repeatedly attributing failure in reading to forces that are beyond their control is their falling into a passive failure syndrome. Children who exhibit passive failure in reading are apt to be nervous, irritable, withdrawn, and discouraged when they are faced with reading tasks. They are unlikely to be actively engaged in reading, to have goals and plans when they read, to monitor themselves when they are reading to see if the reading makes sense, or to check themselves after reading and see if they have accomplished their reading goal. Finally, even when they are successful—and this is not likely to be often—children who are passive failures are likely to attribute their success to luck, or their teacher's skill, or some other factor over which they have no control.

Obviously, we need to break this cycle of negative attributions and learned helplessness. Here, we suggest three approaches. The first, and almost certainly the most powerful, is something we just stressed: Make reading a successful experience; make it so frequently successful for students that they will be compelled to realize that they, and not some outside force, are responsible for the success. Second, tell students that their efforts make a difference, and when they are successful in a reading task, talk to them about the activities they engaged in to make them successful. If, for example, after reading an informational piece about dinosaurs students successfully answer several questions about dinosaurs that they generated before reading the selection, discuss how generating those questions beforehand helped them focus their attention so that they could find the answers to the questions as they read. Third, try to avoid competitive situations in which students compare how well they read a selection to how well others read it; instead, focus students' attention on what they personally gained from the selection. Finally, provide a number of reading activities in which the goal is to enjoy reading, have fun, and experience something interesting and exciting rather than only offering reading activities that are followed by answering questions or some other sort of external accountability.

A Literate Environment

Recently, the phrase *literate environment* has been used to describe a classroom, school, and home environment in which literacy will be fostered and nurtured (see, for example, Goodman, 1986; Huck, 1992). Probably the most important component of a literate environment is the modeling done by people children respect and love. In the best possible literate environment, children's teachers, principals, parents, brothers and sisters, and friends read a lot and openly display the pleasure reading gives them, the fact that reading opens up a world of information to them, the value they place in reading, and the satisfaction they gain from reading. To be most effective, of course, this modeling should occur not just once but repeatedly—all the time, really. Also, this modeling should include both repeated demonstrations—your reading along with students during a sustained silent reading period, your looking up an answer to a question children have about a book, and your sharing a favorite poem with your class—and direct testimonials—"Wow! What a story." "I never knew what fun river rafting could be till I read this article; I sure wish I'd read it sooner." "Sometimes I think the library is just about my favorite place."

Another important component of a literate environment is the physical setting in which children read; for teachers, this generally means the classroom. In the best possible literate environment, the classroom is filled with books, books that are readily accessible for students to read in school or take home. The walls are covered with colorful posters that advertise books and the treasures they offer. And there are several comfortable and inviting places to read—a carpeted corner of the room where children can sit on the floor and read without interruption, bean bags or other comfortable chairs that entice young readers to immerse themselves in a book, places where students can gather in groups to read to each other or discuss their reading, and some tables for students to use when reading prompts them to write.

Still another component of a literate environment is the content of the books, magazines, and other reading materials that are available to students. The reading materials you have available for your students need to reflect the diversity of your classroom—the range of abilities, interests, and cultural, linguistic, and social backgrounds of your students—as well as the diversity of the larger society outside your classroom. What students read must connect with their individual experiences if reading is to have meaning for them; what students read must connect them to the larger society if both students and the larger society are to prosper.

A final and equally important component of a literate environment is the atmosphere in which children read; for teachers, this again means the classroom. In the best possible literate environment, everything that happens in the classroom sends the message that reading—learning from what you read, having personal responses to what you read, talking about what you read, and writing about what you read—is fantastic! In such a classroom, children are given plenty of time to read, they are given ample opportunities to share the information they learn and their responses to what they have read with each other, they are taught to listen to and respect the ideas of others, and they learn that others will listen to and respect their ideas. A literate atmosphere is a thoughtful atmosphere in which values and ideas are respected—values and ideas in books, one's own values and ideas, and other people's values and ideas.

In concluding this section on student engagement, we emphasize that the concepts described here—*success, attribution theory and learned helplessness,* and *literate environment*—are interrelated. Frequent success is crucial. One reason it is crucial is that it precludes learned helplessness; successful students are simply not faced with the repeated failures that lead them to attribute failure to factors beyond their control. Finally, a literate environment nurtures success and provides students with a secure place that enables them to deal positively with the small failures they will inevitably encounter from time to time.

Cognitive Learning Concepts

From about 1930 to about 1970, the dominant psychological orientation in the United States was behaviorism. Behaviorist psychologists viewed people as rather passive respondents to their environment and gave little attention to the mind and its role in learning. Beginning in the 1960s, behaviorism began to be replaced by the cognitive orientation, and for the past two decades cognitive psychology has been the dominant psychological orientation in this country. Cognitive psychologists view the mind as central to learning and the study of learners' thought processes as a central focus of their work. They also view learners as active participants who act on rather than simply respond to their external environment as they learn. Four concepts that have emerged from cognitive psychology—**Schema Theory**, the **Interactive Model of Reading**, **Automaticity**, and **Constructivism**—are particularly important to understanding reading and reading instruction.

Schema Theory

Schema theory is concerned with knowledge, particularly with the way knowledge is represented in our minds and its importance to learning. According to the theory, knowledge is packaged in organized structures termed schemata. As described by David Rumelhart (1980), schemata constitute our knowledge about "objects, situations, events, sequences of events, actions, and sequences of actions" (p. 34). We have schemata for objects such as a house, for situations such as being in a class, for events such as going to a football game, and for sequences of events such as getting up, eating, showering, and going to work. We interpret our experiences—whether they are direct encounters with the world or vicarious experiences gained through reading—by comparing, and in most cases matching, those experiences to an existing schema. In other words, we make sense of what we read and of our experiences more generally by a tacit process that in essence tells us "Ah ha. This is an instance of such and such."

Obviously, both what we learn and the ease or difficulty of the learning are heavily influenced by our schemata. The more we know about something, the easier it will be to deal with that topic and learn more about it. Three sorts of schemata that children possess to varying degrees are particularly important to consider as we plan reading instruction. One of these is knowledge of the world and its conventions— knowledge about the makeup of families, about daily events such as children going to and returning from school and adults going to and returning from work, about institutions such as churches and the government, about holidays such as Memorial Day and Martin Luther King's Birthday, about places such as zoos and the beach, and about a myriad of other events, places, institutions, objects, and patterns of behavior. Children acquire a good deal of this knowledge simply by growing up in and experiencing the world. This knowledge will generally serve students well in understanding narratives—stories, plays, and novels—because this is the principle sort of knowledge that narratives require. However, if children grew up in a culture different from that depicted in the narrative, the world and conventions they understand may be different from those depicted in the narrative, and they will need some help developing appropriate schemata for the narrative. Additionally, of course, if your classroom includes students representing several cultural backgrounds, you will want to take into account students' cultural backgrounds when you choose reading selections and deliberately choose some selections particularly appropriate for each of the cultural groups represented in the class.

Another sort of schema that children possess to varying degrees is schemata about the ways in which different types of texts are organized. Most children have relatively well developed schemata for the organization of narratives because most narratives mirror the temporal order of the world they live in and most narratives have a similar structure. Most narratives have a beginning, a middle, and an ending; most have characters that are involved in a plot that includes some sort of complication; and most end with some type of resolution to the complication. Moreover, most children have had numerous experiences with narratives both in school and at home. Unfortunately, most children do not have well developed schemata for the structure of expository material, the informational material they encounter in social studies, math, science, health, and the like. This is true because children often have not had much experience with expository material, because expository material can have a number of different structures, and, unfortunately, because a good deal of the expository material children read is not very well structured. Many times students will benefit from additional help in dealing with expository material.

The third sort of schemata that children possess to varying degrees are schemata for the content of various subjects—knowledge about science, about history, and about geography. Most of this knowledge does not come from simply living in the world; it comes from formal schooling. Each year, schools build students' knowledge in such areas as history, health, math, and science. Until students build up their schemata for various content areas, they will often need assistance in successfully reading in these areas.

As a final comment on the importance of schemata in reading, we quote a particularly eloquent statement by Marilyn Adams and Bertrand Bruce (1982): "Without prior knowledge, a complex object such as a text is not just difficult to interpret; strictly speaking, it is meaningless" (p. 23).

The Interactive Model of Reading

Schema theory emphasizes the importance of the reader's knowledge in understanding a text. The interactive model of reading, on the other hand, serves to remind us that both the reader and the text play important roles in reading. In arriving at the meaning of a text, as Rumelhart (1977) has explained, readers use both their schemata and the letters, words, phrases, sentences, and longer units in a text. Moreover, they use these various sources simultaneously and in an interactive fashion. They do not, for example, look at a sentence with no idea what it will be about, zero in on the first word, first recognize the letter *t* and then the letter *h* and then the letter *e*, decide that the word is *the*, and then move on to do the same thing with the next word. Instead, readers begin a passage with some idea of what it will be about, encounter the letter string *t-h-e* and decide that it is the word *the* partly because it's followed by the noun *cat* and partly because *the* is often the first word in a sentence, and determine that the third word in the sentence is *meowed* partly because that's what cats do, partly because of its spelling, and partly because it makes sense in the sentence.

Good readers need to rely appropriately on the texts they are reading and their background knowledge to arrive at meaning, and teachers need to provide students with the sorts of texts and tasks that promote their doing so. For example, giving students a selection that deals with a largely unfamiliar topic and that includes a lot of difficult vocabulary may force them to give undue attention to the individual words they encounter, to neglect summoning up their prior knowledge to bear on their understanding of the text. More seriously, having students do a lot of oral reading, emphasizing their being 100 percent correct in their oral reading, and putting students in a position where they face a penalty for being incorrect will almost certainly force them to give undue attention to the text and focus on words and letters rather than sentences, paragraphs, and ideas. For example, having less able students read orally in front of their peers without adequate preparation for doing so is likely to lead them to focus almost all their attention on correctly pronouncing individual words and thus give little attention to meaning.

Conversely, having children only read silently and providing no follow-up to what they read, or having them repeatedly engage in postreading discussions that are only vaguely related to what they read, may encourage students to give too little attention to the text itself. In such situations, some students may largely ignore the words and sentences on the page, frequently guess at the meaning of what they are reading, and make little use of the text in confirming their guesses. For example, giving students a steady diet of individualized reading may not provide them with sufficient opportunities to check their understanding of what they have read with you or with other students, and without such checks they may fall into the habit of guessing a great deal. Again, an appropriate balance of attention to the text itself and to prior knowledge is the goal.

Automaticity

An automatic activity is one that we can perform instantly and with very little attention. As David LaBerge and S. Jay Samuels (1974) pointed out in their pioneering work on automaticity in reading, the mind's attentional capacity is severely limited; in fact, we can only attend to about one thing at a time. If we are faced with a task in which we are forced to attend to too many things at once, we will fail. For example, a number of people have reached a level of automaticity in driving a stick shift car. They can automatically push in the clutch, let up on the accelerator, shift gears, let out the clutch, and press on the accelerator; and they can do all this while driving in rush hour traffic. Beginning drivers cannot do all of this at once; they have not yet automated the various subprocesses, and it would be foolish and dangerous for them to attempt to drive a stick shift car in rush hour traffic.

Reading includes a number of subprocesses that need to take place at the same time—processes such as recognizing words, assigning meanings to them, constructing the meanings of sentences and larger units, and relating the information gleaned from the text to information we already have. Unless some of these processes are automated, readers simply cannot do all of this at once. Specifically, readers need to perform two processes automatically; they need to recognize words automatically and to assign meanings to words automatically. For example, if a student is reading and comes across the word *imperative*, he or she needs to automatically recognize the word and automatically—immediately and without conscious attention—know that it means "absolutely necessary." If the student needs to pause often and go through some sort of mental process to recognize and assign meanings to words, reading will be difficult and laborious and the student will not understand much of what he or she is reading.

Fortunately, the road to automaticity is a very straight one. To become automatic at an activity, we need to practice the activity a lot in non-taxing situations. To become automatic in reading, students need to do a lot of reading in materials they find relatively easy, understandable, interesting, and enjoyable and to do that reading in situations in which they can read for enjoyment and not be faced with difficult questions or requirements based on the reading. In brief, you need to encourage students and give them a lot of opportunities for independent reading in material they find interesting and enjoyable.

Constructivist Theory

Constructivism is a philosophical and psychological position that holds that much of the meaning an individual gleans from a text is constructed by the individual. As Arthur Applebee (1992) notes, constructivism is a diverse construct with a number of roots. Exactly how much texts shape and constrain meaning is a matter of debate (Jonassen, 1991); however, most constructivists place a good deal of emphasis on the reader's contribution. Many constructivists also hold that the social world in which we live heavily influences our interpretations (Gergen, 1985). These two views—the belief that much of the meaning a reader arrives at when reading a text is actually constructed by the reader and the belief that social interactions heavily influence readers' constructions—have important implications for reading instruction. Here we discuss three of them.

Most obviously, constructivism serves as a direct reminder that comprehending a text is an active, constructive process. Constructivists often use the phrase "making meaning" to emphasize the reader's active role in comprehending texts. Students cannot just passively absorb meaning from texts. A truly passive reading would leave the reader simply having turned the pages. Instead, readers must actively engage with the text, consider what they are reading, and link the information they are gleaning from the text with ideas, topics, and events they already know. Moreover, the more difficult a text becomes for students—the more new and challenging information it presents—the more actively engaged readers must be.

Constructivism also supports reader response theory, a theory with important implications for literature instruction. Reader response theory, first proposed by Louise Rosenblatt in 1938 and now a prominent influence on literature instruction (see Beach, 1993; Langer, 1992), stresses that readers will have a range of responses to literary works and encourages teachers to promote and accept a range of responses. Particularly when reading complex literary texts, students will come up with a variety of interpretations. Many literary texts simply do not have a single correct interpretation, and readers should be allowed a variety of interpretations if they can support them. Moreover, responses to literary works can and should involve many things besides answering questions. Students may sometimes respond to what they read through drawing or painting; they may respond to a short story by writing one of their own; or they may be prompted by reading a particular poem to relate some personal incident that the poem reminds them of. Encouraging students to respond to texts in a variety of ways and giving them the freedom to respond to texts that invite diverse interpretations with their own interpretations makes good sense.

Finally, the constructivist tenet that gleaning meaning from texts is a social process supports the use of group projects and group discussion. Students need to be given opportunities to work together in preparing to read texts, in considering alternate interpretations of texts, in writing about what they read, in preparing and delivering oral presentations on their reading, and in completing projects prompted by the reading. Group work gives students chances to talk through and gradually build up their interpretations of a text in a non-threatening setting. Group work also gives students opportunities to teach each other, to learn from each other, to get actively involved in learning, and to learn that others often have alternate interpretations of texts. More generally, as many educators note (e.g., Johnson, Johnson, & Holubec, 1990; Slavin, 1987), group work gives students the opportunity to learn to work together, a skill that is becoming increasingly important in today's interdependent world.

In concluding this section on cognitive learning concepts, we briefly review the major educational implications of each concept. *Schema theory* emphasizes the importance of making sure that students have the background knowledge to read the texts you assign. The *interactive model* is a reminder that the reader needs to use both the text and his or her background knowledge in understanding selections. The notion of *automaticity* stresses the importance of students' doing a lot of relatively easy reading—the kind of reading we as adults do when we read the newspaper, a magazine, or a novel—so that reading becomes automatic. Finally, *constructivist theory* highlights the fact that reading is an active constructive process, explains that responses to literature can and should vary, and underscores the value of group work.

Instructional Concepts

In addition to producing some rather general learning principles such as those described in the previous section, the past 20 years of educational theory and research have produced a number of more specific concepts that have direct implications for instruction. In this section of the chapter, we consider five of them—the **Tetrahedral Model**, the **Zone of Proximal Development**, the **Gradual Release of Responsibility Model**, the distinction between **Informational and Aesthetic Reading**, and the concept of **Generative Learning**. Each of these ideas is closely linked, and together they suggest some very powerful approaches to instruction.

The Tetrahedral Model of Learning

The tetrahedral model of learning was originally developed by James Jenkins (1976) to explain the diversity of results that appear in psychological research on learning and memory. Jenkins noted that psychological experiments that appear to be dealing with the same phenomena often produce a variety of results. For example, one experiment showed that in some cases children who were asked to "learn" written material behaved very differently than those simply told to "look at" written material, while in other cases these different directions had no effect on children's behavior. The explanation of these contrasting results was that something else besides the instructions differed in the two experiments. In this case, it was the age of the children; the children who did not behave differently to the instructions to "learn" or to "look at" material were younger than those who did. Or consider another example, this one concerning chess experts. Experiments have shown that, compared to novices, chess experts have hugely superior memories for the arrangement of chess pieces on a board. However, experiments have also shown that this superiority does not always hold. If chess pieces are arranged randomly on the board, then both experts and novices have similar difficulty recalling their placement. The explanation here is that it is the orderly arrangement of pieces in a way that makes sense in the game of chess that gives the chess expert the advantage.

Jenkins employed the tetrahedral model, a version of which is shown in Figure 3-1, to remind researchers that the outcome of an experiment will be influenced by at least four different factors—characteristics of the learner, the nature of the materials, the learning activities, and the criterial tasks. If you compare Jenkins' model to the diagram of a Scaffolded Reading Experience shown in Chapter 2, you will see that the Planning Phase of a Scaffolded Reading Experience deals with three of these factors—the learner, materials, and task—while the implementation phase deals with the other factor—the learning activities. Thus, the Scaffolded Reading approach is heavily based on Jenkins' model.

Figure 3-1   The Tetrahedral Model of Learning

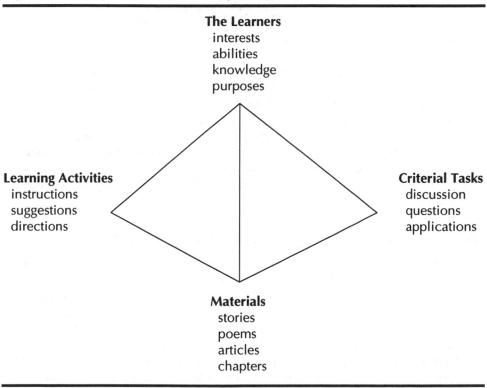

The Learners
interests
abilities
knowledge
purposes

Learning Activities
instructions
suggestions
directions

Criterial Tasks
discussion
questions
applications

Materials
stories
poems
articles
chapters

The Zone of Proximal Development

The concept of the zone of proximal development is primarily attributed to the Russian psychologist Lev Vygotsky (1978). The notion places major emphasis on the social nature of learning and emphasizes that learning is very much a social phenomenon. We learn much of what we learn in our social interchanges with others. The notion is therefore consistent with constructivist theory; in fact, it is one of the ideas that stimulated social constructivist thinking. According to Vygotsky, at any particular point in time, children have a circumscribed zone of development, a range within which they can learn. At one end of this range are learning tasks that they can complete independently; at the other end are learning tasks that they cannot complete, even with assistance. In between these two extremes is the zone most productive for learning, the range of tasks at which children can achieve *if* they are assisted by some more knowledgeable or more competent other.

If left on their own, for example, many third graders might learn very little from a *National Geographic World* article on the formation of thunderstorms. Conversely, with your help—with your spending some time getting them interested in the topic, focusing their attention, preteaching some of the critical concepts such as the effects of rising heat, and arranging small groups to discuss and answer questions on certain parts of the article—these same students may be able to learn a good deal from the article. However, with other topics and other texts—for example, with a chapter on motion from a high school text—no amount of outside help, at least no reasonable amount of outside help, will foster much learning for these third graders. The topic of motion and its presentation in the high school text is simply outside the third graders' zone of proximal development.

Outside of school, many people can and do serve as more knowledgeable or more competent others—parents and foster parents, brothers and sisters, aunts and uncles, friends, and clergy. As a teacher creating Scaffolded Reading activities, you may occasionally be able to bring in outside resources to assist students. More often, however, you will arrange reading situations so that you serve as the more knowledgeable other who assists students in successfully reading selections they could not read on their own. Additionally, in many cases students will be able to pool their resources and assist each other in dealing with reading selections they could not successfully deal with alone.

The Gradual Release of Responsibility Model

The gradual release of responsibility model depicts a progression in which students gradually assume increased responsibility for their learning. The model was first suggested by Joseph Campione in 1981, and since that time it has been used as the basis for designing a good deal of reading instruction. David Pearson and Margaret Gallagher (1983) have presented a particularly informative visual representation of the model, and we have included a slightly modified version of that representation in Figure 3-2.

What the model depicts is a temporal sequence in which students gradually progress from situations in which the teacher takes the majority of the responsibility for their successfully completing a reading task (in other words, does most of the work for them) to situations in which students assume increasing responsibility for reading tasks and finally to situations in which students take total or nearly total responsibility for reading tasks. In considering the model as it applies to SREs, we emphasize three notions—the meaning and importance of gradual release, the part that the text and students' development play in deciding on how much responsibility is appropriate for teachers and how much is appropriate for students, and the view that the model depicts a recursive process, one that students will cycle through many times throughout their schooling.

Here, we give several concrete examples to illustrate these notions. Consider a kindergarten or first grade teacher in early October seated in a circle with a group of children and displaying a big book. The book has a colorful cover with a picture providing some good clues as to what the book is about and a similarly revealing title. The teacher reads the title aloud and talks a little bit about what it and the picture on the cover bring to mind. Then, he asks the children what the title and picture make them think of and what the book might be about. After listening to their responses and trying to emphasize and highlight those that are likely to help students understand the story, the teacher begins reading. Even though there is only a handful of words on each page and the story is a simple one, the teacher stops every two or three pages, asks students what has happened, summarizes the story up to that point if their responses suggest a summary is necessary, and perhaps asks students what they think will happen next. After completing the story, the teacher may ask students a few questions to see if they understood it. Or he may get some other kinds of responses from them—how they felt about one of the characters, if they have had any experiences similar to those in the story, or what emotions the story aroused in them. The teacher might also share his understanding of the story and some of his personal responses to it. But whatever he does afterward, he will try to ensure that each student has gotten something from the story and leaves the experience feeling good about it.

At home, many of the children will tell their parents what they did in school, and

Figure 3-2   The Gradual Release of Responsibility Model

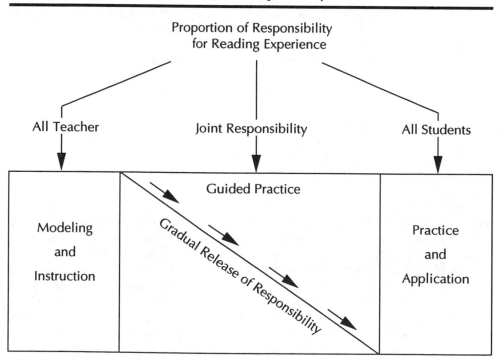

many will say that they read a story. They really didn't read a story, of course; the teacher selected the book, gathered the children together, previewed the story and built their interest for it, read it to them, checked on their understanding and summarized events when necessary, and engaged them in postreading tasks they could accomplish. Appropriately, the teacher took a huge proportion of the responsibility for their reading the story.

Now consider this same teacher and class in January. Over the past four months, the teacher has continued to take much of the responsibility for students' reading. He has done a lot of building interest, reading to students, checking on understanding, and the like. Additionally, over this same period, he has gradually introduced children to longer and more challenging books. At this point, when students go to read something like the simple picture book they read in October, he will let them handle it largely on their own, perhaps having children self-select books and then pair off to read and share them. With the more challenging books, however, the teacher will continue to scaffold activities.

This same process of gradually releasing responsibility holds for older students— for fourth graders, for eighth graders, for high school students, and even for college students. As students progress through school, they assume increased responsibility for their learning. The gradual release of responsibility model emphasizes that over time the goal is to dismantle the scaffolds we have built to ensure students' success. However, students do not repeatedly deal with the same sorts of text over time; rather, students deal with increasingly challenging texts and with a broader range of texts as they progress through school. At any particular point in time, they are likely to be—and should be—dealing with some texts that are more challenging and some that are less challenging. Many fourth graders will be able to take full responsibility for reading an easy novel such as *Skinnybones* by Barbara Park. These same students may need you to assume some of the responsibility for their successfully dealing with a somewhat challenging historical novel such as *Pedro's Journey* by Pam Conrad, and they may require you to assume a great deal of the responsibility for their successfully dealing with an expository article on acid rain. Eighth graders may be able to take full responsibility for reading an article on acid rain much like the one fourth graders needed your help with; they may need you to assume some of the responsibility for their successfully reading a thought-provoking novel such as John Steinbeck's *The Red Pony*, and they may require you to assume a great deal of the responsibility for their successfully dealing with a challenging short story such as Ray Bradbury's "The Foghorn."

As a concluding comment emphasizing that the recursive process of gradually releasing responsibility continues at all levels, we point out that even college teachers need to assume much of the responsibility for students' success with some texts. One of our daughters, for example, is a college junior majoring in molecular biology. Last year, her instructor for a cell biology class told the class *not* to read the text until after he had given the lecture on the appropriate chapter. Additionally, in this and other classes, there are discussion groups and individual help sessions available in which graduate students assume some of the responsibility for undergraduates' learning. Later, if she goes to graduate school, our daughter may have the opportunity to lead discussion groups and help sessions and herself assume some of the responsibility for undergraduates' learning. However, even in graduate school, she will find herself dealing with challenging texts in seminars in which other students and a professor assume parts of the responsibility for successfully processing difficult material.

Informational and Aesthetic Reading

As we mentioned in the section on constructivism, reader response theory, which explains why students are likely to respond to literary works in a variety of ways and encourages teachers to promote and accept such a diversity of responses, is currently a major influence on literature instruction. What we did not discuss is that reader response theory applies primarily to certain types of texts and certain purposes for reading. As part of explaining when and where reader response theory applies, Rosenblatt (1978) points out that there are two primary types of reading—informational reading and aesthetic reading. In informational reading, the reader's attention is focused primarily on what he or she will take from the reading—what information will be learned. Much of the reading that both students and adults do is done for the sake of learning new information, answering questions, discovering how to complete a procedure, or gleaning knowledge that can be used in solving a particular problem. Much of the reading done in such subjects as health, science, math, and geography is informational reading.

The other sort of reading Rosenblatt considers, aesthetic reading, is quite different. In aesthetic reading, the primary concern is not with what you remember about a text after you have read it but with what happens to you as you are reading. The primary purpose when reading aesthetically is not to gain information but to experience the text. Although the aesthetic reader, like the reader whose goal is gaining information, must understand the text, he or she must "also pay attention to associations, feelings, attitudes, and ideas" (Rosenblatt, p. 25) that the text arouses. For the most part, literature is written to provide an aesthetic experience. Most adults read literature for enjoyment; they do not read literature to learn it. Students need to be given opportunities to do the same.

In considering how this distinction between aesthetic and informational reading affects what you do in the classroom, several points should be kept in mind. First, reader response theory does not imply that one sort of reading is superior to the other. Students need to and deserve to become adept at reading as an aesthetic experience; students also need to and deserve to become adept at reading to gain information. Second, although much of the reading students do in textbooks and in other material used in content areas is informational reading and much of the reading they do in the novels and short stories they encounter is aesthetic reading, literary texts often contain useful information, and informational texts can often yield aesthetic enjoyment and pleasure. Finally, as noted above, to have an appropriate aesthetic response, some understanding of a text is necessary; if youngsters read *The Red Pony* and do not understand that Jody feels partly responsible for the pony's death, it would be difficult for them to have a full response to the piece. Moreover, if students are to learn about literary texts, to learn how literary texts are constructed and how to understand them better and more fully enjoy them, students sometimes need to treat literary texts as information to be studied.

Generative Learning

The concept of generative learning is one that applies primarily, although not exclusively, to informational reading. The concept was developed by Merlin Wittrock, who first proposed the term in 1974 and has further investigated and amplified on the concept since that time (Wittrock, 1986, 1990). According to generative learning theory, meaningful learning—the sorts of learning that result in real understanding, in remembering what is learned, and in being able to apply what has been learned in new situations—occurs when learners themselves generate meaningful relationships involving the ideas in a text. These meaningful relationships include both relationships among the ideas in a text and relationships between the ideas in a text and ideas that the reader already knows, believes, and has experienced. For example, in reading about characteristics of alpine forests, a sixth grader might generate relations between ideas in the text by linking the fact that such forests occur at high elevations with the fact that alpine trees are often dwarfed. The student might then generate a relationship between the text and his or her experiences by recalling seeing diminutive forests on a trip to Rocky Mountain National Park. In keeping with generative learning theory, much of the teacher's role is to arrange situations in which such generation takes place.

Considered further, the generative model suggests three processes that teachers need to be concerned with—motivating students, directing students' attention, and taking students' schemata into account. Generating relationships requires a good deal of mental effort, and students need to be motivated to expend this effort. Typically, such motivation will consist of explaining to students that considering relationships among ideas will greatly aid them in understanding and remembering what they read and will help them learn the material in less time than if they just relied on rote memory.

It is not sufficient for students to generate relationships among any ideas in a text; they need to generate relationships among just those ideas in the text that are important to correctly understanding the concepts presented. For example, in reading the selection on alpine forests, students might learn that spruce trees can be found in alpine forests and falsely assume that it is something unique to spruce trees that creates alpine forests. In this case, the teacher would need to prompt students to consider the relationship among elevation, temperatures, precipitation, and other factors crucial to developing alpine forests.

Finally, students' prior knowledge about the topic being studied will influence their ability to identify crucial elements in the text and, of course, their ability to relate ideas in the text to their existing knowledge. Thus, for example, a student who has never seen an alpine forest, who has never seen or even thought about miniature plants such as bonsai, and who lives in the Midwest where flat land and fields extend for hundreds of miles in all directions will have a difficult time understanding and appreciating alpine environments.

Wittrock (1990) has listed a number of activities that can be used to generate relationships among ideas. On the following page, we present some of the activities he has listed and some of our own. If you are engaged in generating relationships among the ideas in this text, you will recognize that this list includes a number of specific examples of the activities we have suggested for SREs.

Generative Learning Activities

Activities Involving Ideas in the Text	Activities Relating Ideas in the Text to Prior Knowledge
Composing Titles	Giving Personal Examples
Composing Headings	Creating New Examples
Writing Questions	Drawing Pictures and Other Artwork
Paraphrasing	Giving Demonstrations
Writing Summaries	Making Comparisons
Making Charts and Graphs	Drawing Inferences
Articulating Main Ideas	Reflecting on Ideas
	Solving Problems
	Creating Stories, Plays, Essays, and Other Sorts of Writing

In concluding this section on instructional concepts, we briefly summarize each of the constructs presented. The *tetrahedral model* suggests that any learning situation is influenced by the learner, the learning activities, the materials used, and the criterial tasks that the learner is expected to complete. The concept of *the zone of proximal development* indicates that there is a circumscribed range within which children can learn, that the assistance of a more knowledgeable or competent other person extends this range, and that instruction should be targeted to present learning tasks that are within this range. *The gradual release of responsibility model* indicates that we can think of instruction on new and difficult material as beginning with the teacher doing all or most of the work and ending with students doing all or most of the work. The distinction between *informational and aesthetic reading* points out that there are two quite different purposes for reading, two quite different kinds of text, and different activities and expectations appropriate for these differing situations. Finally, the *generative learning* model stresses the importance of generating relationships among ideas in order to learn and suggests a number of approaches to generating relationships.

Pedagogical Orientations

In this last section of the chapter, we discuss four pedagogical orientations, four contemporary stances toward teaching and learning. These include **Teacher Decision Making, Reflective Teaching, Whole Language and Literature-based Instruction,** and **the Relationship between Reading and Writing**.

Teacher Decision Making

As we noted earlier in the chapter, cognitive psychologists view the study of human thought processes as a central focus of their work. Not surprisingly, then, the investigation of teachers' thought processes as they make instructional decisions has become an important area of study. Several outcomes of this work are particularly important to the concept of Scaffolded Reading.

One outcome, or perhaps realization, of the research on teacher decision making is that the classroom is an enormously complex place. Every day, most teachers face at least 30 and perhaps as many as 150 students—each with his or her particular store of background knowledge, each with a unique personality, each with a variety of out-of-school concerns and interests, and each with different motivation to partici- pate and learn from the day's activities. Every day, teachers are faced with an equally complex set of goals for students' learning—general goals such as learning to read, learning to write, and learning to compute; subject specific goals such as learning about what makes up a desert or learning how Lewis and Clark explored the North- west Territory; and social goals such as learning how to work effectively with other students. And every day, teachers are faced with a multitude of teaching and learning activities from which they must choose—reading aloud, reading silently, discussion, small group work, writing, and many others. Given this complexity, teachers need organizational structures that assist them in imposing order on what might otherwise be overwhelming. The Scaffolded Reading approach is one such structure.

A second outcome of the research on teacher decision making is that teachers sometimes make decisions after considering only some parts of the learning situation. For example, Gerald Duffy and his colleagues (Duffy, Roehler, & Putman, 1987) suggest that "once reading groups are formed and organizational patterns are estab- lished, most instructional decisions focus on maintaining student attention rather than on issues of content and student understanding" (p. 359). In such situations, the purposes of the reading students are doing seem to have been lost, and the emphasis is simply on getting through the material. The Scaffolded Reading framework serves as a reminder that there are at least four aspects of any learning situation that teachers need to attend to as they make instructional decisions—the students, the materials, the purposes, and the activities that will be used to help students use the materials to achieve the purposes.

A third outcome of the work on teacher decision making is the realization that it is unwise, inappropriate, and probably impossible to try to take away or radically constrain teachers' decision-making powers. Management systems, teacher-proof materials, and rigid scope and sequences of skills that suggest mechanical ap- proaches to classroom instruction just do not work. Such systems ignore the com- plexities of the classroom and fail to acknowledge the decision-making role that only a teacher working with a particular group of students in a particular setting can fill. As Richard Shavelson (1983) has pointed out, "Teachers are rational professionals who, like other professionals such as physicians, make judgments and carry out decisions in an uncertain, complex environment" (p. 392). Teachers are able to operate in this sort of complexity by constructing simplified models of reality and then using those models as they form their thoughts, make judgments, and arrive at decisions. As suggested in the above paragraph, one requirement of such models is that they be relatively easy to use without ignoring important aspects of the learning environ- ment. The Scaffolded Reading approach is designed to meet this requirement.

Reflective Teaching

As described here, the concept of reflective teaching is closely related to that of teacher decision making. In fact, reflective teaching is one aspect of teacher decision making, an aspect of teachers' thought processes that we want to endorse and promote. The concept was first introduced by John Dewey (1909/1933), who saw the reflective teacher as a person who deliberately and consciously reflects on his or her instruction and its effects on students. More recently, the concept of reflection was revived and elaborated on by Donald Schön (1983), who examined the place of reflection for professionals such as engineers, architects, and managers.

As applied to teaching, reflection is a cyclic process in which teachers repeatedly view their ongoing instruction and the results of that instruction as a series of problems to be examined and temporarily solved. We say temporarily solved because a central tenet of reflective teaching is that there is no single or ultimate solution to instructional questions; the context in which instruction takes place will heavily influence what is appropriate in any particular case. In reaching these temporary solutions, reflective teachers use knowledge they have acquired formally in their own education, their experience and intuitions, and the ongoing events of the classroom. A reflective teacher consciously reflects on all aspects of the learning situation—the students, the materials, the learning activities, and what is learned—the aspects of learning considered in the tetrahedral model and the Scaffolded Reading approach. Additionally, the literature on reflective teaching (e.g., Calderhead, 1992) indicates that one very important object of reflection ought to be the values inherent in the materials being taught and in the teaching itself.

Considering all aspects of the learning situation in planning a particular reading experience, in observing the experience as it unfolds in the classroom, and in evaluating that experience is essential to optimizing your ability to create the best possible reading experiences for students. Moreover, to the extent that you share your reflections with students, you will not only be honing your own teaching but also assisting them in becoming more conscious about what does and does not work for them as they are reading.

Suppose, for example, that your class is reading a selection about world hunger, a selection that you judge to be fairly easy for students and something that would gain their attention and for which you consequently did little prereading preparation. A few minutes after students begin reading, however, you notice that quite a few of them are not engaged in the reading. A few students are talking, a few heads are nodding, and quite a few pairs of eyes look a bit glazed. A reflective teacher would first notice the situation and then decide what to do about it. The decision, of course, could only be made in the context of a specific class reading a specific selection. One alternative, however, would be interrupting the class at that point and attempting to kindle or rekindle interest and commitment in the topic. Another would be deciding that an interruption at this point would be counterproductive and instead making alternative plans for students' next encounter with a similar topic. If the latter were your choice, further reflection might focus on whether you could find texts that were intrinsically more interesting or whether with such topics you need to include more motivational and interest-building activities as part of prereading instruction. Finally, the fact that the topic of world hunger and the materials and approach used in presenting the topic did not result in much engagement on the part of students would itself be a matter for reflection.

As another example, suppose you plan a set of activities for a health lesson on communicable diseases and decide that since many of the concepts are difficult ones you are going to need to do a lot of preteaching concepts and building background knowledge. As a result, you prepare a substantial set of prereading activities. However, when you begin working with the prereading activities, you quickly learn that your initial assessment of students' knowledge on communicable diseases was incorrect; your students, in fact, know a lot about the topic. One appropriate step here would be to truncate the planned prereading instruction and let students get on with the reading itself. Beyond that, however, as a reflective teacher you would want to consider what led you to underestimate students' knowledge in the first place and make a conscious effort to avoid doing so in the future.

A central tenet of reflective teaching is that such reflection should be a continuing process, that it is not something that only new teachers do or that you do only until you get it "right." The complexities of the classroom—the ever changing combination of students, texts, learning activities, and goals—require that reflection be an ongoing part of teaching.

Whole Language and Literature-based Instruction

The whole language orientation to reading instruction and the development of literacy skills more generally originated in the 1970s and has now become a central theme behind much instruction. The term *"literature-based instruction,"* on the other hand, is relatively recent and represents a special emphasis supported by many whole language teachers. Here, we deal primarily with whole language and then add a note about literature-based instruction.

As Kenneth Goodman (1986) and other whole language theorists (e.g., Harp, 1993) have repeatedly pointed out, whole language is a general viewpoint about literacy and how children learn to be literate rather than a specific approach to instruction. As Goodman and others also note, there is no single set of instructional practices that constitute a whole language approach to teaching; instead, individual teachers create quite different whole language programs depending on the situations in which they find themselves and their students' needs. This makes whole language difficult to describe, and rather than attempting to describe all of the viewpoint, here we concentrate on just those aspects of whole language that inform the Scaffolded Reading approach.

Perhaps the most prominent whole language principle is that students should read whole texts and not excerpts or snippets of texts. One argument against excerpts is that because they are not complete and self-contained they may be confusing and unsatisfying. Another is that, outside of school, we typically read complete texts or decide for ourselves when to read parts of them. Both arguments seem valid, and as a consequence all of the texts used as examples in this book are complete texts.

Another very prominent principle of whole language is that the primary purpose of reading is and must always be to attain meaning rather than to learn or practice skills. All of the activities students engage in as part of a Scaffolded Reading Experience serve to assist them in attaining meaning—to help them understanding what they read, learn from what they read, enjoy reading, relate ideas and experiences read about to situations beyond the reading, and extend the ideas and experiences they read about.

Another whole language principle is that the situation in which children learn and use their literacy skills is crucial to their success. The supportive and encouraging literate environment described earlier in this chapter is the sort of situation in which literacy flourishes.

Still another whole language principle is that risk taking is a necessary part of learning to read. We have already noted the importance of risk taking in qualifying our emphasis on the importance of success with the caution that students do need to face some challenges if their reading and other literacy skills are to grow. Also, the approach of considering students' zone of proximal development and providing the support they need to achieve at the outer limits of their competence is one method of encouraging and supporting risk taking.

The final whole language principle we highlight, and one we will return to, is that reading and writing are supportive skills that should often be integrated with each other. We discuss the close relationship between reading and writing in the next section.

The general tenets of literature-based instruction are consistent with those of whole language. In fact, the two terms are sometimes used interchangeably. However, advocates of literature-based instruction such as Bernice Cullinan (1992) put special emphasis on the value and importance of quality children's literature in the reading program. Good literature is seen as particularly valuable and supportive of children's growing competency in reading because it deals with important and widely applicable themes. Good literature often has great emotional appeal and thus has the potential to foster students' love of reading—to create readers who are both competent and motivated to read. Good literature also presents sentence structures and vocabulary that can stretch children's growing competence with language and serve as models for their own writing.

Finally, a lot of good literature consists of narratives—stories. Narratives offer a particular advantage to beginning readers because, as we have noted, they follow an organizational structure that children are already familiar with. They involve a setting, a cast of characters, a plot with some sort of complications, and a resolution to those complications. Such familiar structures nourish children's understanding and memory for what is read and thus make the task of learning to read easier. However, children also need to learn to read and learn from expository material—informational materials, including textbooks. Scaffolded Reading activities are designed to support both reading narrative literature and reading expository material—textbooks, informational trade books, magazine articles, and the like.

The Relationship Between Reading and Writing

As we noted in discussing whole language, the fact that reading and writing are supportive skills that should often be integrated with each other is a central principle of whole language. Whole language, however, is certainly not the only source of support for integrating reading and writing. In fact, as Timothy Shanahan's (1992) collection of essays on reading and writing indicates, there appears to be universal support for integrating these two facets of language, and there are certainly many good reasons for doing so.

One reason for linking reading and writing is that doing so is economical for both you and your students. There simply is no reason for routinely presenting reading during one segment of the day and writing during another, and doing so is bound to take more time than integrating the two.

Another is that reading is an excellent prompt for writing. Frequently, one of the biggest problems facing students as they begin to write is having something to write about. But reading often solves that problem. The student who has just finished Avi's *The True Confessions of Charlotte Doyle* is likely to have an easy time writing about how he would feel if he suddenly found himself in Charlotte's shoes, alone on a ship with a cruel and murderous captain and a crew bent on reaping their revenge before the voyage ends. And fiction is not the only sort of reading that can stimulate writing. The student who has studied a chapter dealing with black widow spiders has gained a lot of information that could be used in writing a descriptive piece about some creepy and crawling creature she has encountered.

Of course, it is not just that reading provides a good stimulus for writing; writing also complements and aids students with their reading. The student who writes about how he would feel if he were in Charlotte's predicament is learning to relate to fictional characters, empathize with them, and consider how their experiences are similar to and different from his own. The student who writes the descriptive piece prompted by what she has read about black widows is engaged in generative learning, establishing a relationship between information in a text and her existing knowledge and experiences. The writing should improve both her understanding of what she has read and her memory for the information. More generally, it is worth noting that a lot of activities suggested by the generative learning model—composing headings, writing questions, paraphrasing, writing summaries, and others—involve writing. Writing is an excellent study technique, one that is typically active and constructive.

Still another advantage of linking reading and writing is that students can learn a lot about reading from writing. As Robert Tierney and David Pearson (1983) have explained, it is useful to view reading as a composing process, as a situation in which a reader must actively construct meaning. Particularly for students who are not active readers, the process of composing may serve as a cue to the importance of their getting actively involved in their reading. Additionally, students can learn a lot about reading from writing because both processes employ the same organizational structures. A student who has just written a narrative and has found that organizing the piece was almost automatic is in an excellent position to discuss just what constitutes the narrative form and to realize that most narratives follow a prototypic form. Conversely, a student who has just written an informational piece and found that he or she had to struggle with a number of different ways of organizing the piece is in a good position to recognize the fact that expository writing can have many structures and that dealing with the organization of expository materials when reading them may be a demanding task.

Finally, reading, writing about what they read, and sharing that writing with other students allow students to appreciate a host of different features of reading and writing. Writers usually write for some purpose; they have information they want to communicate, a position they want to support, or an idea or feeling they wish to convey. Readers usually read for some purpose; they may want to learn something, they may wish to be entertained, or they may seek an aesthetic experience from reading. Writers often have to strive to convey their messages, and despite the attempt not all messages are successful. Authors must write in different ways for different readers; what will inform or please one reader will not necessarily satisfy another. Different readers will come away from the same text with quite different messages and quite different responses. The list is nearly endless, and such facts are not learned simply because reading and writing are taught and practiced together; however, combining experiences in reading and writing can certainly help to promote such learning.

As with the previous sections, we conclude this one with some brief comments on each of the topics considered. This time the topics fall into two pairs. Both the first two and the last two are closely linked. *Teacher decision making* and *reflective teaching* are related because making situationally appropriate instructional decisions requires that teachers be reflective about their teaching. The *whole language* orientation and the motivation to *integrate reading and writing* instruction are linked in that both stem from many similar considerations. Both see the various language arts as interrelated, both view reading and writing as meaning-making activities, and both see children as active learners, who will learn best when they work with language in real communicative situations.

Concluding Comments

In this chapter, we have described much of the thinking that prompted us to develop the Scaffolded Reading approach and that has shaped the approach. The ideas that motivated us have, as noted earlier, been diverse. They include affective concerns such as the importance of success, traditional cognitive concerns such as the importance of prior knowledge, general instructional concepts such as the existence of a zone of proximal development within which children can best learn, and current ideas about teaching such as the value of integrating reading and writing instruction. While somewhat less diversity might at first seem desirable, we have decided that this is not the case for two reasons. One is that the Scaffolded Reading approach is itself diverse and multifaceted because it is designed so that you can tailor activities to different students, different texts, and different purposes for reading. The other is that we believe that a variety of perspectives offer useful ideas about teaching and that no single perspective or small set of perspectives can offer all the ideas teachers need to meet the challenging goal of making each reading experience a successful one for all students.

References

Adams, M., & Bruce, B. (1982). Background knowledge and reading comprehension. In J. A. Langer & T. M. Smith-Burke (Eds.), *Reader meets author: Bridging the gap* (pp. 2–25). Newark, DE: International Reading Association. A brief and very readable discussion of the importance of background knowledge to reading comprehension.

Anderson, R. C., Hiebert, E. H., Scott, J. A., & Wilkinson, I. A. G. (1985). *Becoming a nation of readers*. Washington, D. C.: National Institute of Education. Although written some years ago, this continues to be an excellent and balanced summary of current thinking about reading instruction.

Applebee, A.N. (1992). The background of reform. In J.A. Langer (Ed.), *Literature instruction: A focus on student response* (pp. 1–18). Urbana, IL: National Council of Teachers of English. A brief description of several aspects of current literature instruction along with consideration of some major issues in improving the teaching of literature.

Beach, R.W. (1993). *A teacher's introduction to literary-response theories*. Urbana, IL: National

Council of Teachers of English. An extended and sophisticated treatment of a variety of theories of literary response.

Brophy, J. (1986). Teacher influences on student achievement. *American Psychologist, 41,* 1069–1077. Concise summary of the findings of the teacher effectiveness research.

Calderhead, J. (1992). The role of reflection in learning to teach. In L. Vali (Ed.), *Reflective teacher education: Cases and critiques* (pp. 139–146). New York: SUNY Press. A lucid treatment of the importance of reflection in becoming an effective teacher.

Campione, J. (1981, April). *Learning, academic achievement, and instruction.* Paper presented at the second annual Conference on Reading Research of the Center for the Study of Reading, New Orleans, LA. The original source of Campione's widely endorsed and very useful gradual release of responsibility model.

Cullinan, B.E. (1992). Learning with literature. In B.E. Cullinan (Ed.), *Invitation to read: More children's literature in the reading program* (pp. viii–xxii). Newark, DE: International Reading Association. Useful overview of the content and spirit of literature-based instruction.

Dewey, J. (1909/1933). *How we think.* Lexington, MA: D.C. Heath. Dewey's classic text on the relationship of reflective thinking to effective teaching.

Duffy, G.G., Roehler, L.R., & Putnam, J. (1987). Putting the teacher in control: Basal reading textbooks and instructional decision making. *The Elementary School Journal, 87,* 357–366. A forceful argument for the importance of teachers' being active decision makers.

Gergen, K.J. (1985). The social constructionist movement in modern psychology. *American Psychologist, 40,* 266–275. One of the most readable introductions to social constructionist thinking.

Goodman, K. (1986). *What's whole in whole language?* Toronto, Canada: Scholastic TAB. A concise overview of the whole language approach by one of the founders of the movement.

Harp, B. (1993). The whole language movement. In B. Harp (Ed.), *Assessment and evaluation in whole language programs* (pp. 1–18). Norwood, MA: Christopher-Gordon. Cogent summary of the whole language approach.

Herber, H.L. (1970). *Teaching reading in content areas.* Englewood Cliffs, NJ: Prentice-Hall. The classic text on reading in content areas.

Huck, C.S. (1992). Books for emergent readers. In B.E. Cullinan (Ed.), *Invitation to read: More children's literature in the reading program.* Newark, DE: International Reading Association. An excellent source of books for those just beginning to read.

Jenkins, J.J. (1976). Four points to remember: A tetrahedral model of memory experiments. In L.S. Cermak & F.I.M. Craik (Eds.), *Levels of processing in human memory.* Hillsdale, NJ: Erlbaum. The original source of Jenkins' widely cited and very useful tetrahedral model, the model underlying much of the Scaffolded Reading approach.

Johnson, D.W., Johnson, R.T., & Holubec, E.J. (1990). *Circles of learning: Cooperation in the classroom* (3rd ed.). Edina, MN: Interaction Book Company. A concise yet very complete description of what cooperative learning is and how to prepare students to succeed in cooperative learning groups.

Jonassen, D.H. (1991). Objectivism versus constructivism: Do we need a new philosophical paradigm? *ETR&D, 39,* 5–14. An introductory comparison to these two very different views of the world.

Johnston, P.H., & Winograd, P.N. (1985). Passive failure in reading. *Journal of Reading Behavior, 17,* 279–301. A powerful and important explanation of this destructive phenomenon.

LaBerge D., & Samuels, S. J. (1974). Toward a theory of automatic information processing in reading. *Cognitive Psychology, 6,* 293–323. The original description of this simple yet powerful concept.

Langer, J.A. (Ed.). (1992). *Literature instruction: A focus on student response* (pp. 1–18). Urbana, IL: National Council of Teachers of English. An excellent selection of interesting perspectives on the response approach to literature instruction.

Pearson, P.D., & Gallagher, M.C. (1983). The instruction of reading comprehension. *Contemporary Educational Psychology, 8,* 317–344. Still a useful summary of the research on teaching reading comprehension.

Rosenblatt, L. (1938). *Literature as exploration.* New York: Appleton-Century. Rosenblatt's original presentation of her response theory.

Rosenblatt, L. (1978). *The reader, the text, the poem: The transactional theory of the literary work.* Carbondale, IL: Southern Illinois Press. Another presentation of Rosenblatt's response theory; both this and her 1938 book have had enormous influence on the teaching of literature.

Rumelhart, D. E. (1977). Toward an interactive model of reading. In S. Dornic (Ed.), *Attention and performance* (Vol. 6, pp. 573–603). Hillsdale, NJ: Erlbaum. The original description of the interactive model, done by one of the major researchers in the area.

Rumelhart, D. E. (1980). Schemata: The building blocks of cognition. In R. J. Spiro, B. C. Bruce, & W. F. Brewer (Eds.), *Theoretical issues in reading comprehension* (pp. 33–58). Hillsdale, NJ: Erlbaum. One of the original descriptions of schema theory, done by a pioneer researcher on the topic.

Schön, D. (1983). *The reflective practitioner.* New York: Basic Books. The book that first prompted current interest in the importance of teacher reflection.

Shanahan, T. (Ed.). (1990). *Reading and writing together: New perspectives for the classroom.* Norwood, MA: Christopher-Gordon. A rich and diverse set of views on the relationships between reading and writing.

Shavelson, R.J. (1983). Review of research on teachers' pedagogical judgments, plans and decisions. *Elementary School Journal, 83,* 392–413. A concise review of the research on teacher decision making by a prominent researcher in the area.

Slavin, R.E. (1987). *Cooperative learning: Student teams* (2nd ed.). Washington, D.C.: National Education Association. A brief overview of several of Slavin's approaches to cooperative learning.

Smith, F. (1976). Some limitations on spoken and written language learning and use. In H.H. Spectner, N.S. Anastasiow, & W.L. Hodges (Eds.), *Children with special needs: Early development and education.* Minneapolis, MN: University of Minnesota. An early paper advancing some of the central tenets of what is now the whole language view.

Tierney, R.J., & Pearson, P.D. (1983). Toward a composing model of reading. *Language Arts, 60,* 568–580. A cogent perspective on reading as an active, constructive process.

Vygotsky, L.S. (1978). *Mind in society.* Cambridge, MA: Harvard University Press. One of Vygotsky's classic texts, probably best known for its description of the zone of proximal development.

Wittrock, M.C. (1974). Learning as a generative process. *Educational Psychologist, 11,* 87–95. Wittrock's original description of his generative learning theory.

Wittrock, M.C. (1986). Students' thought processes. In M.C. Wittrock (Ed.), *Handbook of research on teaching* (3rd. ed., pp. 297–314). New York: Macmillan. An authoritative review of the research on the effects of teachers and instruction on various aspects of students' perceptions, motivation, understanding, and the like.

Wittrock, M.C. (1990). Generative processes of comprehension. *Educational Psychologist, 24,* 345–376. Another view of generative comprehension processes.

Children's Books Cited

Avi. (1990). *The true confessions of Charlotte Doyle.* New York: Orchard.

Bradbury, R. (1990). The foghorn. In *The stories of Ray Bradbury.* New York: Alfred A. Knopf.

Conrad, P. (1991). *Pedro's journal.* Honesdale, PA: Boyds Mills.

Park, B. (1982). *Skinnybones.* New York: Alfred A. Knopf.

Steinbeck, J. (1955). *The red pony.* New York: Bantam.

4

Prereading Activities

Prereading activities motivate and prepare students to read a selection. Taking time to prepare students before they read can pay big dividends in terms of their understanding what they read and finding reading an enjoyable experience. The kind of preparation you do, of course, will depend on your students, their overall purpose for reading, and the reading material itself. Thus, the way in which you prepare a class of low-achieving sixth graders to read a chapter on weather in a science text is vastly different from how you prepare a group of precocious first graders to read a trade book such as Arnold Lobel's *Days With Frog and Toad.* The students, the purpose for reading, and the selection dramatically influence your planning and implementing reading experiences.

Thinking of prereading activities as activities that motivate and prepare students for the text they will read brings to mind various prereading activities. As noted in Chapter Two, we have described ten categories of prereading activities.

Prereading

1. Motivating
2. Relating the Reading to Students' Lives
3. Activating Background Knowledge
4. Building Text-Specific Knowledge
5. Preteaching Vocabulary
6. Preteaching Concepts
7. Prequestioning
8. Predicting
9. Direction Setting
10. Suggesting Strategies

The list, while in no way inclusive, can serve as a guide in planning prereading activities. In this chapter, we discuss each of the categories of activities and give one or two detailed examples of each. As you consider the categories, you will find that a number of them overlap. An activity that builds background knowledge can also motivate, for example. We realize this; we list and discuss ten categories to empha-size that many kinds of activities can be useful as you prepare students to read, not to suggest an elaborate system of mutually exclusive categories.

As mentioned earlier, initially planning a Scaffolded Reading Experience requires you to consider three things—the students, the selection, and the purpose or purposes for which students are reading. After either you or your students have selected the text to read and after you have read through it and identified topics, themes, potentially difficult vocabulary, and other salient features of the material, you begin to map out the entire SRE. What is your students' overall goal for reading—is it primarily for an aesthetic experience, or is it to gain information or insights? The kinds of activities students will be involved in before, during, and after reading will reflect these goals.

As you plan prereading activities, ask yourself such questions as, "How can I get these students really interested in this selection? What sort of background knowledge do they have on this topic? What might they need to know to profit most from their reading? Is there anything in the material I can relate to their lives? Are there any concepts or vocabulary in the selection that students might benefit from working with? Could they use any of their repertoire of reading strategies to help them better understand the material?" After answering these questions or similar ones, you begin planning.

Guide to Activities for Chapter 4

Motivating:	*Nate the Great*
	Share and Tell
Relating the Reading to Students' Lives:	*Common Threads*
Activating Background Knowledge:	*1-2-3*
Building Text-Specific Knowledge:	*In a Nutshell*
	The Coming Attraction
Preteaching Vocabulary:	*Paired Questions*
	Word Clues
Preteaching Concepts:	*Multimedia*
	Is It? Or Isn't It?
Prequestioning:	*What Do YOU Think?*
Predicting:	*I Predict*
Direction Setting:	*Looking for Old, Looking for New*
	Looking for Answers
Suggesting Strategies:	*Sum It Up*

Because ten is a large number of categories to treat as discrete items and because these ten categories serve four major functions, we have grouped them in four sections. The first section deals with **Motivational Activities**; it contains only the Motivating category. The second section deals with **Building or Evoking Background Knowledge**; it contains the Relating Reading to Students' Lives, Activating Background Knowledge, Building Text-Specific Knowledge, Preteaching Vocabulary, and Preteaching Concepts categories. The third section deals with **Focusing Attention**; it contains the Prequestioning, Predicting, and Direction Setting categories. The fourth section deals with **Suggesting Strategies**; it contains only the Suggesting Strategies category.

Motivational Activities

A big part of preparing students to read is motivating them. Whatever the task, it is always more interesting, exciting, and meaningful if we have a good reason for wanting to do it. Think about yourself and your own reading. What motivates you to pick up the evening newspaper, to read an article in *The Instructor* or a mystery novel? Is there a particular purpose you have in mind? Do you read to be informed, enlightened, inspired, entertained? We all read for a combination of reasons but usually because we expect the text is going to give us something we need or want—information, inspiration, entertainment, whatever. To ensure a successful reading experience for students, we need to be certain that they have this sort of motivation to read.

Motivational activities are just that—activities that incite enthusiasm, an eagerness to delve into the material. Sometimes, you will undoubtedly use activities that serve primarily to motivate students. However, motivational activities frequently overlap with other kinds of prereading activities—activating background knowledge, relating reading to students' lives, and preteaching concepts. In general, motivational activities will draw upon the interests and concerns of the particular group doing the reading. Puppets and puppies might be part of a motivating activity for first and second graders, a rap song or challenging puzzle for fourth, fifth, and sixth graders. You know what kinds of things interest and excite your students. Use these to help motivate their reading.

Motivational activities will often involve hands-on experiences, active student participation, drama, and intrigue:

"Feel this fabric and tell me what it makes you think of and how it makes you feel."

"Think of your favorite color. Walk around the room and touch three things that have that color in them."

"Guess what's in this box?"

"Look at this picture. Imagine you are there. What are you doing? How are you feeling?"

Now, once students' interest is piqued, comes the next step—transferring that interest to the reading material.

"Robbie, the little boy in the story you will read today, has a special blanket made of the fabrics you were feeling—flannel and satin."

"*Hailstones and Halibut Bones* is a poem all about colors . . . ."

"I guess my clues were good ones, and you're pretty good detectives. The material I put in the box is pumice, and we'll be reading about it and other kinds of igneous rocks in our science chapter today."

"The picture you were looking at shows the village of San Paulo in Argentina. Pedro, the main character in the story you will be reading, lives in a village very much like it . . . ."

In the next few paragraphs, we give a detailed example of a motivational activity. It is one a teacher we'll call Ms. Monihan used with a group of low-to-average second graders in a midwestern suburb. The selection the students were going to read was *Nate The Great* by Marjorie Sharmat. In this trade book for beginning readers, young Nate the detective solves the mystery of his friend Annie's missing picture. Ms. Monihan's purpose for this prereading activity was to pique her students' interest and to build upon their concept of a detective.

After Ms. Monihan had her students' attention, she began placing items on a table in front of them—a chalkboard eraser, a book, a red marker, her watch, a bell, an orange, and a painter's cap. Without saying anything, she wrote the word *detective* on the board. From a grocery sack she pulled out a Sherlock Holmes style hat and put it on. Then she pointed to the word *detective* and asked the students, "What is a detective?" After she had gotten a number of varied responses from the children, she asked, "What must a detective *be?*" Quickly, she whipped a magnifying glass from the grocery sack and began using it to study the items on the table. Next, she wrote the word *observant* on the board. "Good detectives must be observant," she explained. "They must look carefully at things, people, places, and search for clues. Clues that will help them solve the cases that people hire them to solve."

While the second graders' attention was focused on her, Ms. Monihan began placing the items on the table back in the grocery bag. "Now," she told the children, "let's see how observant you were!" She then asked the children to name the items in the bag. As they named them, she asked them to tell as many things as they could about each item. After they had done so, she removed each item from the bag, one at a time, and set it back on the table. When all the items had been identified and placed back on the table, Ms. Monihan explained to the students that the reason they were talking about detectives and being observant was that they were going to read a story about a detective, a detective named Nate the Great.

At this point, she pulled the book, *Nate the Great*, out of the bag and showed the students the cover illustration, which shows Nate dressed in Sherlock Holmes-type attire. Then she continued her introductory remarks. "When you read this story, I would like you to think about all the things that Nate does to show he's observant, or a good observer. Good detectives are observant, you know," she said, picking up the magnifying class and observing a few items in the classroom. "They notice details about who, what, when, where, how, and why."

This or a similar activity might also be used to motivate these same students to read something like Marjorie Sharmat's *Nate the Great Goes Down in the Dumps* or to motivate advanced second graders or third or fourth graders before reading *Meg Mackintosh and the Mystery at the Medieval Castle* by Lucinda Landon.

As Ms. Monihan's technique aptly illustrates, motivating activities should be fun.

They get students interested and involved. They also direct their thinking toward the themes, topics, and concepts of the material you are preparing them to read.

In the next section, we present another sample motivational activity, this time using the format we will use in the remainder of the sample activities. As you will notice, the activity also serves additional prereading functions. You may want to consider what those functions are as you read through the sample.

At the end of this and of each sample activity in this book, we have included a section called "Reflections." This section serves a function somewhat similar to that of dialog journals. Dialog journals, as you know, are used to share a common interest or to work out a common problem with someone else. Unfortunately, a book format doesn't allow us to hear your responses, but these sections do allow us to expand on ideas and issues that emerge from the activities in a conversational style. In these informal remarks, we have tended to do two different things. Most of the time, we comment on the activity itself—what it did, what it did not do, how it might be changed, and the like. Less frequently, we comment on a general principle the activity reminds us of. We hope you find these informal reflections helpful and that they encourage your reflection.

Motivating Sample Activity: *Share and Tell*

Share and Tell uses cooperative learning groups as a forum for students' sharing knowledge about a topic to stimulate interest and activate prior knowledge.

Selection: "Exploring the Ocean" in *Science in Your World* (Hackett & Moyer, 1991). This chapter in a science text discusses the features of the ocean floor, including the continental shelf, rift zones, trenches, and the various forms of life in the ocean. It concludes with the issue of protecting the ocean.

Students: Fourth graders of average to high ability.

Reading Purpose: To add to old knowledge and gain new information about the ocean's features, ocean life, and protecting the ocean.

Goal of the Activity: To pique students' interest in learning more about the ocean, to activate their prior knowledge, and to give specific information about the topics and organization of the text.

Rationale: Sharing what they know about a topic can serve to stimulate interest, activate prior knowledge, and focus students' attention on the material that will be covered in the reading selection.

Procedure: Write the chapter title and subtopics on the chalkboard.

EXPLORING THE OCEAN

Ocean Features	Ocean Life	Protecting the Ocean

Tell students that the chapter they are going to read in their science books is "Exploring the Ocean" and that the chapter talks about the features of the ocean, ocean life, and protecting the ocean. Point out that they know something about the ocean from things they've read or from trips to the ocean and that you'd like them to share that knowledge with each other.

Divide the class into groups of about six students each and appoint a facilitator and recorder for each group. Before the groups meet, talk about what they are to discuss—what they *know* about each of the three topics.

Explain that the facilitator will call on people to tell what they know about each of the topics and the recorder will write down the information that students share. Briefly review the topics with students and discuss some of the things they will want to think about for each. For example, you might write these prompts on the board:

> **Ocean Features:** Think about what you would see if you could drain all the water from the ocean.
>
> **Ocean Life:** Think about all the different kinds of living things that make their home in the ocean.
>
> **Protecting the Ocean:** Think about the things that can be harmful to the ocean.

After discussing the prompts, give students about ten minutes to discuss the three topics. At the end of the discussion time, let the recorder for each group read the responses for each topic. Also, spend a little time evaluating the activity, what worked, what didn't, and how students can improve on the activity.

Adapting the Activity: *Share and Tell* can be used to build interest in any selection with a topic or theme that is somewhat familiar to students; for example, you could use *Share and Tell* before your ethnically diverse fifth graders read Russell Freedman's *Immigrant Kids,* before your California fourth graders read *Earthquakes* by Seymour Simon, or before curious and scientifically inclined third graders read *Insect Metamorphosis: From Egg to Adult* by Ron and Nancy Goor.

Reflection: After reading through the sample, you may wonder why we included it under Motivational Activities *rather than* Activating Prior Knowledge *or* Building Text Specific Knowledge. *Obviously, the activity serves each of these functions. In fact, it certainly serves as much to evoke and build knowledge as it does to motivate. However, we put it in the motivating category because we have found social interaction highly motivating for most students, particularly gregarious ten year olds. Having students' thinking stimulated and challenged by their peers is an excellent way to pique their curiosity and get them interested and actively involved with a topic.*

It is worth emphasizing that what students need to get interested and actively involved with is the ideas that will help them as they read. As two of our reviewers pointed out, it is extremely important that motivating activities do direct students' attention to the important themes, topics, and concepts in the upcoming reading. With motivating activities we are not just trying to get students interested and excited; we are trying to get them interested and excited about the upcoming selection.

Building or Evoking Knowledge

Another extremely important part of preparing students to read is making certain they have the background knowledge they need to understand and enjoy the text. Background knowledge includes whatever concepts and experiences students have available to bring to a particular reading task. Obviously, background knowledge will vary from classroom to classroom, student to student. For instance, suppose you have a class of third graders in rural Arkansas and they are going to read a story in which a blizzard plays a central part. Their background knowledge for reading such a story will be quite different from that of a class of third graders in rural Minnesota. Similarly, the background knowledge of high-achieving fifth graders for reading a chapter on the Constitution will differ from that of low-achieving students in that same class. In fact, every students' background knowledge will be slightly different from that of every other student. We need to be aware of individual differences and provide for these in our instruction. However, since much of the time we are working with groups of students, we also need to make some generalizations and assumptions about the background knowledge of the groups of students we teach.

Building background knowledge might be something you do right before students read a specific selection, or it might be an ongoing activity that takes place over several days or weeks. For example, before your second or third graders read and compute story problems found in math texts, you might create opportunities to write story problems from situations that arise in the classroom during the days or weeks prior to students' reading commercially prepared story problems. Whenever students are involved with a situation that can be represented numerically, show them how to write it as a mathematical story: For instance, "Twenty students have returned their field trip permission slips. There are 28 students in our class. How many more students need to return their slips?" Or, "We're going to have a party next week. Katie is bringing a dozen chocolate chip cookies, David is bringing a dozen sugar cookies, and Jill is bringing a dozen peanut butter cookies. How many cookies will we have for our party?" Or, "If we have 36 cookies for our party and 28 students at the party, how many cookies will each student get to eat? How many more cookies would we need for each student to have two cookies?"

After you have spent time developing story problems as a class, provide opportunities for students to write their own story problems from similar experiences that arise. When it comes time to read and compute story problems found in texts, students will have the background knowledge to understand how to read and solve these problems.

The importance of background knowledge to students' understanding and enjoyment of what they read cannot be overstated. The more you know, the easier it is to understand and learn from text. If you know what a river is, how much easier to conceptualize creek, stream, and tributary. If your students are going to read a story about Ben Franklin, they will understand and enjoy it more if they know something about the time period in which he lived, something about his life, what inventors, philosophers and diplomats are, and so on.

In the following sections, we consider five types of activities that make use of and strengthen students' background knowledge.

Relating the Reading to Students' Lives

This is an extremely powerful approach for getting students to commit themselves to a text, to claim ownership of it. If we can see how something relates to our lives, we are making a personal connection. We suddenly have a vested interest. Let us say you have a class of third graders and you run across an engaging story about a boy and his new puppy. One of your students, Charlie, just got a puppy for his birthday, and you realize this would be a great book for Charlie. To prepare him to read the story, you might get him to talk about his puppy—what he feeds it, where it sleeps, who takes care of it, and how he feels about it. Getting Charlie to think about his own experiences with a puppy will help him better understand the events that take place in the story and the actions and emotions of the main character.

You can also relate the topics of expository material to students' lives. Say, for instance, your fifth-grade students are going to read about electricity in their science texts that day. As a prompt for their journal writing that morning, you might write on the board, "Write about the different ways you used electricity so far today." Or, "Imagine your electricity went out this morning. Describe what your morning would be like without it." Writing in general, and journal writing in particular, is an effective way to build or evoke background knowledge.

Relating reading to students' lives includes any kinds of activities that help students understand how what they read has meaning for their lives.

Relating the Reading to Students' Lives Sample Activity: *Common Threads*

Common Threads helps bridge the gap between the characters in a story and the students' experiences by having them think about experiences in their own lives that are similar to the ones faced by the story's protagonist.

Selection: *The True Confessions of Charlotte Doyle* by Avi. This historical novel is a gripping account of intrigue and murder on the high seas told by a 13-year-old girl who finds herself the lone passenger on a sailing ship bound from England to America in 1832. Because of the unusual situation Charlotte find herself in and the demands it places on her physically, mentally, and emotionally, she goes through a virtual metamorphosis. Charlotte begins her tale as a prim and proper school girl and ends up a seasoned sailor who runs away to crew on a sailing ship.

Students: Sixth graders of mixed abilities.

Reading Purpose: To read and enjoy an exciting, well-written piece of historical fiction.

Goals of the Activity: To bridge the gap between readers' lives and the story's main character and setting by helping them make meaningful connections to their lives. Also, to introduce the basic elements of plot—problem, solution, and change.

Rationale: The setting and situation described in this novel are very different from what young readers will have personally encountered. However, although the magnitude and nature of Charlotte's problems may be far removed from today's 10- to 13-year-old readers, what lies at the heart of her story remains the same—people adapt to difficult situations by drawing on inner resources and modifying their behavior and attitude as circumstances demand. Focusing on these universal themes and having students discover examples from their own experiences can help students bridge the gap between themselves and the main character and promote a deeper understanding of the text. The activity also helps students focus on some of the primary elements of fiction—a character with a problem, actions taken to solve the problem, and the character's change or reaction.

Procedure: Begin by asking students to think about a difficult, strange, or unusual situation they have found themselves in. For example, maybe they were babysitting and one of the children locked himself in the bathroom, or perhaps they moved to a new school and didn't know anyone, or maybe they had to take care of a sick sibling. Encourage students to talk about their difficult situations, what they did about them, and whether the experiences changed them in any way.

Tell students that the reason you're having them think about these ideas is that the main character in a book they will be reading faces an extremely difficult and unusual situation. They will learn just what that situation is when they read the book, but first you want them to think about their own experiences with unusual and difficult situations. Doing this will help them understand and enjoy the novel more.

Write these headings on the board.

Problem	Solution	How Changed?

Next, hand out sheets of paper and have students fold them into thirds and write each of the headings in a column.

Before asking students to write their responses in each of the columns, model the activity by giving an experience from your own life and recording your responses on the board. Elaborate orally on these responses as you write them. Tell students that you are writing quickly and not worrying about spelling or using complete sentences and that they can do the same with their responses. What you want them to get down is the just the gist of the idea.

Problem	Solution	How Changed?
Was asked to give a speech at a banquet	Worried at first and didn't want to do it, then wrote the speech and practiced giving it	Found I didn't mind talking in front of an audience, felt proud I had done something that I thought was hard for me

After this, have students write their own problems, solutions, and changes. After they have had a chance to record their own responses, let students share them with the rest of the class. You may want to record some on the board or a chart.

Problem	Solution	How Changed?
Got separated from parents in downtown San Francisco	Started roaming the streets, cried, eventually found a policeman who found my parents	More careful to stay with parents when in a strange place, no longer afraid of policemen
Came to live in a country where I didn't know anybody and didn't know the language. I hated it.	Went to school, listened to teacher and students, tried to be friendly	Not so afraid anymore, can speak new language have many friends. Now I like it.

After ample discussion, hold up a copy of *The True Confessions of Charlotte Doyle* and read the title and author. Explain that Charlotte Doyle is the main character in the story, and have students predict from the cover illustration—which shows Charlotte on the deck of a 19th century sailing vessel—where the setting for the story might be. Tell students that the story takes place on a sailing ship in 1832, and ask them to predict what difficult situations 13-year-old Charlotte might find herself in. Explain that Charlotte will indeed face a number of problems throughout the novel.

These will become obvious to them as they read. When they finish reading, you will talk about those difficulties, Charlotte's responses to them, and in what ways she changed.

Adapting the Activity: *Common Threads* can be used as a prereading activity for any novel or story in which the main character is faced with numerous problems to solve or obstacles to overcome. Literature abounds with these kinds of situations; realistic and historical fiction, biographies, and fantasies all contain numerous stories of heroes who triumph over difficulties. Examples include *Harriet Tubman, Call to Freedom* by Judy Carlson, *Hatchet* by Gary Paulsen, *Frozen Fire* by James Houston, *Rachel Chance* by Jean Thesman, *The Princess in the Pigpen* by Jane Resh Thomas, *Back Yard Angel* by Judy Delton, and *Maniac Magee* by Jerry Spinelli. Also, instead of their doing this as a whole group activity, you might have students work in groups of four to six.

Reflection: Most students are usually eager to talk about themselves, but some will have some tendency to ramble and need to be encouraged to stick to the main topics of problem, solution, and change. Also, an activity such as this one begins as a prereading activity but is continued through the other two phases of reading. While they read, students might record problems, solutions, and changes in the main character. Then, after they have finished the novel, they can discuss with each other what they discovered about problems, solutions, and change.

As in the case when motivating students, in relating a selection to students' lives, it is important to remember that the focus needs to be on those aspects of students' lives relevant to the targeted selection. As one reviewer pointed out, introducing a science selection about the ocean by asking whether students have ever been to the ocean and then presiding over a discussion of vacations at the seashore will be of minimal benefit to students' understanding the concepts in the chapter. At the same time, as Robert Calfee and his colleagues (Calfee, Chambliss, & Beretz, 1991) emphasize, establishing connections between the text and children's lives is essential to their comprehension of what they read.

Activating Background Knowledge

Students come to school with a vast repertoire of concepts that teachers can tap into. Some students have read widely or have been read to; many have traveled, lived in various locations, taken trips to museums, gone on nature outings, and belonged to groups such as Boy Scouts, Campfire Girls, and the YMCA that provide a variety of experiences. In addition, television and movies may be the nemesis for some parents and educators, but they also provide a significant supply of background knowledge for many students—knowledge that teachers can link into.

Activating prior knowledge means providing students with prereading experiences that prompt them to bring to consciousness information they already know. Sometimes students might write about what they know; other times they might talk about it. If this information is shared in a class discussion or in writing, it will be available for both the students who produced it and others in the class. Having this information readily available will help students make connections with similar ideas when they meet them in the text. The following activity shows one approach to helping students discover what they know about a topic and to share, refine, and use that knowledge.

Activating Background Knowledge Sample Activity: *1-2-3*

1-2-3. In this three-step PReP activity, students think about what they know about a topic and how to relate that knowledge to the information in the text. The PReP activity was developed by Langer (1981).

Selection: *The Tipi: A Center of Native American Life* by David and Charlotte Yue. *The Tipi* is an informational trade book that not only describes the function, structure, and furnishings of the sophisticated dwelling designed and built to meet the demands of life on the Great Plains but also takes a broader look at Native American life. It talks about Native Americans' dependence on the buffalo and their struggle against a harsh environment as well as their legends, social life, and spirituality.

Students: Third graders of mixed ability, two ESL students, one from Russia and the other from the Middle East.

Reading Purpose: To understand the importance of the tipi to Native Americans and to gain an understanding and appreciation of Native American culture and way of life.

Goal of Activity: To encourage students to think about what they know about tipis and to help them elaborate on their existing concepts as they read.

Rationale: Except perhaps for the two ESL students, most will probably have had some prior exposure to the concept of the tipi. By creating a link between students' past experiences and the concept they will be meeting in the text, you will be setting up appropriate expectations that in turn will aid students in comprehending the material.

Procedure: Write *tipi* on the chalkboard. (Since the class includes two ESL students, you might also want to display pictures of tipis or a model.) Next, have students give their **initial associations** with the concept. Ask them to tell anything that comes to mind when they see or hear the word *tipi*. Write down each student's response on the chalkboard. Some responses might include "Indians," "tent," "house," "made of skins and poles," "plains," "buffalo," "place to sleep," and "cone-shape."

After students have given their initial responses, have them **reflect** on the initial associations. Ask students to tell what made them think of their particular responses. For example, the student who gave the response "tent" might say, "A tipi looks kind of like a tent and it is put up and comes down like a tent." During this procedure they can weigh, reject, accept, revise, and integrate any of the ideas that come to mind.

The last phase of this prereading activity is **reformulating knowledge**. After students have had a chance to reflect on their reasons and discuss them, ask if they have any new ideas about tipis. Encourage them to talk about anything new they have learned about tipis through the discussion, and ask if any of their previously held ideas have changed.

Steps in the 1-2-3 Activity:

1. Brainstorm — (What does the target word make me think of?)
2. Reflect — (Why do I think the way I do?)
3. Reformulate — (Do I think any differently now?)

Adapting the Activity: This activity is readily adaptable to any selection that contains concepts students have some knowledge about. For example, before fifth- or sixth-grade students read Isaac Asimov's *How Did We Find Out About Pluto?*, they might tell what comes to mind when they hear the phrase "law of gravity." Next, they would state what made them give the responses they did. Then, you encourage them to reformulate their knowledge by asking if they have any new ideas about the law of gravity. Other materials this activity would work well with are biographies such as *Christopher Columbus: Voyager to the Unknown* by Nancy Smiler Levinson and *Columbus and the World Around Him* by Milton Meltzer. The target word with these biographies might be *explorer* or *Columbus*. You could also use the *1-2-3* activity targeting the word *immigrant* before students read *Immigrant Kids* by Russell Freedman, *In the Year of the Boar and Jackie Robinson* by Bette Bao Lord, *The Star Fisher* by Lawrence Yep, and any number of books that portray characters who come to the United States from other countries.

Reflection: Getting students to list initial associations with a concept is often fairly easy. However, at first you might have to do a lot of encouraging and probing to get students to reflect on why they made the initial responses they did. That encouraging and probing are well worth the effort, however, for by learning to reflect on their thinking students are taking a significant step toward becoming the sort of critical thinkers today's world demands. Moreover, after you have used this activity a few times and provided opportunities to practice this type of reflective thinking, it will become easier for them and for you. The reformulation phase may also prove difficult at first. Many students may not have had a great deal of practice in synthesizing ideas. When you are doing this activity for the first time, you may need to do some modeling of how you might go about reflecting on your initial associations and then reformulating that knowledge; in other words, revealing the thought process you go through as you come up with ideas. For example, you might say something like the following: "The word tipi makes me think of camping. I think of camping because a tipi is shaped like a tent, and it doesn't seem like a permanent house to me but one you can move from place to place and set up wherever you want to. After listening to what you have to say about tipis, you have given me some new ideas. Now I can see that for Native Americans a tipi probably meant a lot more than something to sleep in. It was very important for their way of life and survival. They had to be able to travel quickly to where the buffalo herds were."

Building Text-Specific Knowledge

In the previous activity, we assumed that the students had some background knowledge relevant to the topic of the upcoming selection and our task was to activate it. In building text specific knowledge, we assume that students might not possess some specific information they need to understand or appreciate the upcoming text. For instance, if they are going to read a chapter on electricity in a science text, they will probably have some general understanding of electricity but won't know the precise topics covered or how they are organized. In this situation, you might tell them what those topics are and how the author has organized and structured the text. Or, perhaps students are going to read the time-travel books, *The York Trilogy*, by Phyllis Reynolds Naylor. To fully understand and enjoy these stories, students will need to know something about the fantasy element of time travel as it is used in the stories. Giving them a few details about the sort of time travel that takes place in the stories can be easily accomplished in a brief prereading discussion.

One way to build text specific knowledge is to give students a preview of the material they are going to read. A preview of a reading selection is similar to previews of movies and TV shows and can be used with both expository and narrative texts. A preview of an article, textbook chapter, or informational book could include the topics, events, people or places covered, and unusual or difficult vocabulary. In a preview of a novel or short story, you might introduce the setting, characters, and something about the plot.

Building text specific knowledge can be achieved in a variety of different ways. Such knowledge includes any information students need in order to understand, learn from, and enjoy a text. Here we include three sample activities.

Building Text-Specific Knowledge Sample Activity 1: *In a Nutshell*

In a Nutshell uses an outline and deductive and inferential questioning to familiarize students with the content of the text.

Selection: "Waves" in *Science in Your World* (Hackett & Moyer, 1991). This chapter from an elementary science text discusses the physical phenomenon of waves as rhythmic disturbances that transfer energy—mechanical waves involve matter, and electromagnetic waves involve electric and magnetic fields. Some of the topics covered are how waves transfer energy, the properties of waves, and electromagnetic waves, which include radio waves, infrared waves, light, ultraviolet waves, X-rays, and gamma rays.

Students: Fifth-grade students of mixed abilities in a suburban setting.

Reading Purpose: To gain new understanding about the properties and functions of waves— both mechanical waves and electromagnetic waves.

Goal of the Activity: To give students information on the topics and structure of the text so that they will have a schema in place that includes both the concepts presented in the chapter and how the chapter is organized.

Rationale: Giving students an outline of the material they are going to read provides them with a conceptual framework for understanding and remembering what they read. Also, having them explain what information the outline reveals stimulates inferential and deductive reasoning—a kind of thinking that will serve them well in life as well as with many other texts.

Procedure: Before the lesson, either on a transparency or the chalkboard, outline the chapter title and subtitles.

WAVES

How Do Waves Transfer Energy?

Electromagnetic Waves

Radio Waves

Higher Frequency Waves

Infrared Waves

Light

Ultraviolet Waves

X rays and Gamma Rays

Lasers

Tell students that today you are going to take a look at the topics and subtopics from the chapter on waves before they read it. Tell them that noticing how a chapter is organized can help them understand the ideas the author is presenting.

Draw students' attention to the outline, and challenge them to pick out the three major topics. Call on a volunteer to read them. (*How Do Waves Transfer Energy?*, *Electromagnetic Waves*, *Lasers*) Ask students to explain how they determined that these are the main topics. (*They are written in large print and are not indented. Some have subtopics written below them.*)

Next, ask students to identify which of the main topics have subtopics. (*Electromagnetic Waves has the subtopics Radio Waves and Higher Frequency Waves. Higher Frequency Waves has the subtopics Infrared Waves, Light, Ultraviolet Waves, and X rays and Gamma Rays.*) If students are unable to come up with the correct responses, be sure to praise their efforts anyway, and then show them the correct responses and how you arrived at them. (*Main topics are in larger type than subtopics. Subtopics are indented under the main topic. Sometimes subtopics have subtopics of their own, which are also indented. Subtopics are details that explain more about a topic. For example, a main topic might be compared to a house, subtopics to the rooms in a house, and further subtopics to the objects in the room.*)

After this, explain to students that now that they have identified the topics and subtopics in the chapter on waves, they are going to see how much information the author has given on the topic in just these few words. Tell them that they may be surprised at just how much they already know. Starting with the first main topic, guide students to the following conclusions.

Q: What do we know about waves from the question "How Do Waves Transfer Energy?"
A: Waves transfer energy.

Q: What do we know about waves from the topic "Electromagnetic Waves"?
A: Some waves are electromagnetic.

Q: What do we know about waves from the subtopic "Radio Waves"?
A: Some waves are called radio waves.

Q: What do we know about waves from the subtopic "Higher Frequency Waves"?
A: Waves have different frequencies, some higher and some lower. Radio waves probably have a low frequency since they are not listed under the subtopic "Higher Frequency Waves."

Q: What do we know about waves from the subtopics "Infrared Waves," "Light," "Ultraviolet Waves," and "X rays and Gamma Rays"?
A: Infrared, light, ultraviolet, x-rays, and gamma rays are all names for high frequency rays because they are listed as subtopics under "Higher Frequency Waves." Infrared probably has the lowest frequency of these waves because it is listed first in the sequence and gamma rays probably has the highest because it is listed last. (This sequence from lowest to highest can be deduced from the fact that radio waves are listed as a separate topic before the higher frequency waves and, therefore, probably have a lower frequency than the others.)

Q: What do we know about lasers from the topic "Lasers"?
A: Lasers have something to do with waves since they are listed as a topic in the chapter on waves.

Keep the questioning lively. Encourage students to keep thinking and to make inferences from the information given. Praise their participation, and tell them that their efforts now will payoff in their understanding and learning from the chapter.

Adapting the Activity: This activity can be used prior to reading any material that outlines easily or in which the author has organized the material into topics and subtopics—textbook chapters, informational trade books, and articles. Chapter 1, for instance, from *Garbage! The Trashiest Book You'll Ever Read* by Suzanne Lord, would work well for this activity. The titles and subtitles for this chapter are:

Garbage: The Never-ending Story
>What Do We Mean by Garbage?
>How Long Has Garbage Been Around?
>A Short History of Garbage
>What Kinds of Garbage Are There?
>>Natural Garbage
>>Personal Garbage
>>Industrial Garbage
>>Hazardous Garbage
>>Space Garbage

There is, however, one thing to be on the lookout for in selecting material to outline in this way. Check to see that the headings and subheadings accurately reflect the material the text contains. In some cases, headings turn out not to be good guides to the content of selections.

Reflection: As you probably noticed, there are some difficult concepts presented in this outline. Sometimes the materials your students will be reading offer real challenges. When this is the case, you want students to know that material sometimes is challenging but not impossible. If they approach learning with the attitude that they can successfully understand new ideas and information if they put forth some extra effort, they will usually find that their efforts are rewarded. When you introduce students to difficult vocabulary and concepts, encourage them not to feel defeated if they don't immediately understand all the concepts. Explain that they will be learning fuller meanings of these terms when they read, that now they are just getting a head start in understanding the material. Also, some students may tend to be complacent and let their classmates do all the talking and all the thinking. Encourage the more reluctant participants, the drifters and dreamers, to participate in the activity by saying something like, "There are some good thinkers in this class we haven't heard from yet. Not everyone may get the chance to speak their answers, but everyone can think their answers. If you're thinking along with us, then you're doing your part."

In showing students the structure and content of the "Waves" chapter in In a Nutshell, *we used a standard outline. Alternately, we could have presented the information as a graphic organizer, a frequently recommended visual display for which Richard and Jo Anne Vacca (1993) provide a convenient description. A possible graphic organizer for the chapter is shown in Figure 4.1.*

There are at least two reasons why you might sometimes want to use a graphic organizer rather than a standard outline. One is that the graphic organizer may be more informative. In the case of the "Waves" example, the graphic organizer clearly shows that the topic of higher frequency waves receives a good deal of attention. Another reason you might want to use a graphic organizer occasionally instead of an outline is simply to provide some diversity. Sometimes varying the way you present information can spark interest in both you and your students.

Building Text-Specific Knowledge Sample Activity 2:
The Coming Attraction

In *The Coming Attraction,* the teacher provides a preview of the selection in which some of the main characters are introduced, a few words defined, and some interesting details

Figure 4-1   Graphic Organizer for "Waves" Chapter

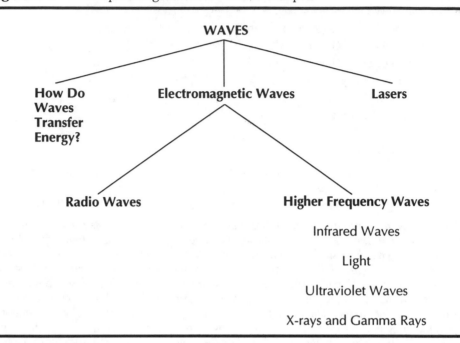

of the plot revealed. Previews of this sort have been described by Graves, Prenn, and Cooke (1985).

Selection: "The Signalman" by Charles Dickens, adapted by I. M. Richardson. In this eerie tale, a railroad signalman is visited by a ghostly figure who seems to warn of approaching tragedies along the track.

Students: Low-achieving sixth to eighth graders in an urban setting, three ESL students and one visually impaired student.

Purpose for Reading: To understand and enjoy an intriguing piece of literature by a well-known author.

Goal of Activity: To provide students with relevant information from the upcoming story to help establish a schema that will facilitate meaning-building as they read.

Rationale: The setting and situation in this story may be unfamiliar to many students. A preview that includes some of the important details will not only help establish a framework for understanding the selection but also serve to pique students' interest, introduce vocabulary, and set purposes for reading.

Procedure: Prior to the lesson, review the story to determine which details of setting, characters, plot, and unusual or colorful language will help your students understand and appreciate the story. Next create a preview—either written out in detail, in outline form, or on notecards, whichever style fits you best—that will pique students' interest, draw them into the story, and provide the essential details for a smooth and enjoyable reading experience. The following is a detailed preview for "The Signalman" based on one used by Graves, Cooke, and LaBerge (1983).

Danger. Think about what that word means to you. Have you ever been in a dangerous situation? Nearly every day an accident or disaster of some kind happens somewhere, doesn't it? A plane crashes, an earthquake or tornado occurs. Can you think of any accidents or disasters that have occurred lately?

Many times before a disaster strikes, a warning is given. For example, lights might blink on the instrument panel of an airplane, or instruments might pick up tremors in the earth that predict an earthquake is about to occur. Can you think of other types of warnings?

Some people think they are warned of dangers in supernatural ways. They believe that spirits, or voices, or maybe even ghosts warn them to do—or not do—something. Have you ever heard of someone being warned this way? What was the warning, and how did they receive it?

Maybe you've been warned about something. For example, have you ever awakened from a dream thinking that what you dreamed would happen? If so, did it? Have you ever had a feeling that something bad was about to happen? If so, did it?

The story you will read today is about a man who often gets warnings. The warnings this man gets don't come from dreams or his mind but from a ghost or *specter*. It seems that a ghost always appears before something terrible happens, as if he is trying to warn of danger.

The story takes place some time ago in a very lonely and gloomy spot, hidden away in the mountains. The man you will read about is a signalman for a railroad. He lives alone in a hut that is on a railroad line and near a tunnel. The hut has many things the man needs, such as a desk, a record book, an instrument to send telegraphs, and a bell.

The signalman's job is to signal the trains, watch for danger on the tracks, and warn passing trains of trouble ahead. The signalman works very hard at his job and is quite exact in all his duties. He is nervous, though, because he has seen many people die in train accidents near his post. He wants to be sure that he signals the trains of any danger.

The story is told by a man who visited the signalman at two different times and learned much about him. The story opens as the visitor calls, "Halloa! Below there!" to the signalman. He wants to know how to reach the signalman's hut from where he is at the top of a cliff. The signalman hears the man call to him but doesn't answer. He is afraid and looks down the railroad line instead of up to the man.

Strange, isn't it? What is the signalman looking for? And why is he afraid? When you read the story, you will find out.

Adapting the Activity: Previews can be used for many reading selections—poems, narratives, and informational pieces. The details and emphasis, of course, will be different with each selection, but the elements of piquing interest, bridge-building, and providing information that will help students understand and enjoy the selection will remain the same. Some reading selections in which previews may be helpful are stories in which the plot line or narrative execution veers from the predictable, such as *Maniac Magee* by Jerry Spinelli and *Canyons* by Gary Paulsen. Because both of these stories offer some challenges in terms of narrative style, readers with certain predisposed expectations of what constitutes "normal" plot structure may find these novels a bit confusing. A good preview can help students avoid such confusions.

Previews are also excellent vehicles for motivating students to read informational books and for providing background information on the treasures in these selections. For example, if your students are self-selecting books to read for a social studies unit on cultural diversity in the United States, you might give brief previews of a number of possible selections. A few of these might include *Happily May I Walk: American Indians and Alaska Natives Today* by Marlene Hirshfelder, Richard Ammon's *Growing up Amish*, Sheila Hamanaka's *The Journey*, and Virginia Hamilton's *Anthony Burns: The Defeat and Triumph of a Fugitive Slave*. An enticing preview can both motivate and provide a good beginning framework for the reading experience.

Reflection: Although the preview for "The Signalman" presented in this activity is quite detailed and perhaps sounds a bit formal, it is only one of a variety of ways of giving a preview of a reading selection. Shorter, more spontaneous previews of stories or expository material work well if students need a little information to ease them into the reading material. Previews can be presented with visuals as well. Without giving away too much of the story, you can show an illustration or two taken from an upcoming selection that reveals information about a story's setting and characters. Also, students themselves can develop previews of books or other kinds of material they've read to give to their classmates, either orally or in writing. Our experience (Cooke & Graves, 1993) indicates that students can do an excellent job of this and that they really appreciate what their classmates have to say about an upcoming selection. You might compile and index students' written previews in a loose-leaf notebook for other students to read, or you might have students develop a radio or TV show in which they preview a number of books and tape record or video tape the show for future listening or viewing. More generally, it is worth pointing out that students teaching other students can be one of the most effective forms of instruction (McKeachie, Pintrich, Lin, Smith, & Shafma, 1990; Rekrut, in press).

Like anything else, previews should be used only when students will benefit from them, and they should not be used so often that students become bored with them. We do want to point out, however, that previews are the most robust prereading activity for increasing comprehension we know of. A substantial body of research (for example, Chen, 1993; Dole, Valencia, Greer, & Wardrop, 1991; Graves, Prenn, & Cooke, 1985; Graves, Cooke, & LaBerge, 1983) has shown them to be effective with students of various age and ability levels and with ESL students as well as with native English speakers.

Preteaching Vocabulary

One important part of the background knowledge readers possess is their word knowledge. The words students encounter while they are reading may fall on a continuum from those they can read and understand easily to those they can't even pronounce, much less associate with a meaning. For instance, most third graders could decode and understand the meaning of the word *garden*, but very few would be able to pronounce *gargoyle*, much less understand its meaning.

In Chapter 2, we defined vocabulary instruction as instruction on words that are new labels for concepts that students already have; for example, teaching *gregarious* to students who already know what *friendly* means. That is the sort of learning task we deal with here.

Activities for preteaching vocabulary focus on helping students pronounce and define words as they are used in the upcoming selection. The purpose of such activities is to provide students with this information before they read so that when they meet these words in the text they don't have to focus on deciphering individual word meaning but can focus on the ideas the author is presenting. For example, before fourth graders read the "August" entries in Pam Conrad's *Pedro's Journal*, you might plan vocabulary activities that enable students to pronounce and learn a basic meaning for the words *mandarin, rosary, rudder, boatswain, chaukers, rigging, rudder,* and *trek.*

There are any number of vocabulary activities you can engage students in prior to their reading a selection. We include two samples here.

Preteaching Vocabulary Sample Activity 1:
Paired Questions

In *Paired Questions,* targeted words are presented in pairs of questions, one that can be answered affirmatively and the other negatively. This activity is based on vocabulary instruction suggested by Kameenui, Carnine, and Freschi (1982).

Selection: *Camper of the Week* by Amy Schwartz. At summer camp, Rosie Matthews is honored as "Camper of the Week." Rosie is pleased about the honor, but it also creates some tension between being true to this honor and loyalty to her friends. In time, Rosie finds a unique way of resolving the issue.

Students: Second and third graders of mixed abilities in an urban setting.

Reading Purpose: To understand and enjoy an engaging picture book.

Goal of Activity: To increase students' understanding and enjoyment of a story by preventing their stumbling over challenging words and to increase their knowledge and appreciation of word meanings.

Rationale: *Camper of the Week* is not a particularly challenging selection for the average second or third grader, but there are a few words that may pose difficulties—words that are in students' oral vocabularies but not their reading vocabularies or words for which they have an available concept but not a label. Having students pronounce, read, and think about some of the words used in an upcoming story makes reading easier and more enjoyable. Also, an activity such as this one, which requires students to apply their knowledge of words to novel situations, encourages critical thinking and appreciation of words.

Procedure: After reading through the story, select half a dozen or so words that might be stumbling blocks for some of your students and develop paired questions using these words: One question should yield an affirmative answer, the other a negative answer. We have chosen the words *courteous, considerate, smirk, minnow,* and *powwow.*

Write the paired sentences on the chalkboard:

Are you *courteous* to your parents and teachers?
Are you *courteous* to your bedroom wall?

Are you *considerate* of your friends' feelings?
Are you *considerate* of the dust balls under your bed?

Can you have a *smirk* on your shoe?
Can you have a *smirk* on your face?

Could you see a *minnow* in a lake?
Could a *minnow* invite you for supper?

Can you go to a *powwow?*
Can you eat a *powwow?*

Read the sentences to students or have volunteers read them. Have students think about these questions, answer them for themselves, and then discuss the answers together. As a whole group activity or in small groups, have students compose other sentences that can be answered "yes" or "no" for each word and write these on the board. For example, for *courteous*, students might suggest:

> Can we be *courteous* to each other?
>
> Are mittens and hats usually *courteous?*

Adapting the Activity: This activity is readily adaptable to any selection—narrative or expository—that contains words that are in your students' oral vocabularies but perhaps not in their reading vocabularies or words for which they have an available concept but not a label. For instance, you might introduce *independent, survive, sovereign, scoffed* and *legislature* in paired sentences before your fifth graders read the first few pages of Jean Fritz's *Shh! We're Writing the Constitution.*

Reflection: We have found that students really enjoy vocabulary activities, especially when they are fun and offer some challenges, too. Word pairs gives students a chance to be a bit silly and have some fun with words, while at the same time giving them new insights into word meaning and an appreciation of words themselves. Experimenting with word pairs also helps students realize that words are not just printed marks on a page but compact capsules of meaning that can be interesting and fun to work with.

Preteaching Vocabulary Sample Activity 2: *Word Clues*

Word Clues introduces potentially difficult vocabulary using context-rich sentences in teacher-created worksheets.

Selection: "Thomas Nast: Political Cartoonist Extraordinaire" by Lynn Evans. Bavarian-born Thomas Nast is responsible for creating some of our most notable and enduring political symbols—the Republican elephant, the Democratic donkey, and Uncle Sam. As a young student, Nast did poorly in all subjects except art, and at 15 he began work as a draftsman for *Frank Leslie's Illustrated Paper.* In 1859, he began his 30-year partnership with *Harper's Weekly,* and together they became a powerful force against political corruption. Fiercely Republican in his views, Nast is credited with the election of many Republican candidates, that is, until 1884, when Nast and *Harper's* supported a Democrat for the first time, presidential candidate Grover Cleveland. In 1886, Nast and *Harper's* ended their association, and the political influence of both declined.

Students: Sixth to eighth graders of average to low ability.

Reading Purpose: To understand and recall some of the important highlights of an historical figure's life and work.

Goal of Activity: To introduce potentially difficult vocabulary and to give students practice in using context clues to unlock word meaning.

Rationale: This piece, as will be the case with many content area selections, contains vocabulary that will prove difficult for some students. To give them practice in using context clues to unlock word meaning as well as learn the meanings of some key words, a worksheet activity that requires them to focus on context clues is a helpful aid.

Procedure: Before the lesson, select five to ten words you suspect some of your students may have trouble reading and that are important to understanding the selection.

From the Thomas Nast selection, we have chosen these words:

1. *draftsman*—This is a relatively easy word to decode, but because students may not be familiar with this occupation and because it is central to understanding the article, we have included it.

2. *emigrated*—This polysyllabic word is less easily decodable. Most students should probably have some idea of its meaning when seen in context.

3. *reform,*

4. *endorsed,*

5. *symbol*—These are probably fairly easily decodable words. However, understanding their meaning is critical to appreciating the substance and thrust of Nast's career.

6. *corruption,*

7. *critical*—These words may prove difficult at both the decoding and interpretation levels, although most students will have a basic notion of the concepts.

Present each of the words you select in a context-rich sentence or paragraph that provides clues to the word's meaning. Following this sentence or paragraph, create two items that will give students practice in using context clues for unlocking the word's meaning. Two examples are given below.

1. Target word—*draftsman*

   Mr. Jones called on his best *draftsman* to sketch plans for the new ice arena.

   - Based on the sentence above, a draftsman would probably use pencils and rulers in his or her job.

     true   false

   - A draftsman is probably someone who

     a. runs
     b. draws
     c. teaches
     d. rides

2. Target word—*emigrated*

   Thomas Nast *emigrated* to the United States in 1840 when he was just six years old. He and his mother and sister settled in New York City.

   - Based on the sentences above, Thomas Nast probably left his home country and came to live in the United States.

     true   false

   - Emigrated probably means

     a. took clothes and food to poor people
     b. left one country to settle in another
     c. ran a very difficult uphill race
     d. borrowed enough money to buy a house

Before giving students the worksheet, write all the target words and the first item from the worksheet on the board. Explain that these are some of the words they will be encountering in their reading selection. Read the words aloud. Tell students you will give them a worksheet that will help them unlock the meaning of these words, that knowing these words will make the article more interesting and understandable, and that the items on the worksheet will look something like what you have printed on the board. Read the target word and the sentence. Ask what words or phrases provide clues to the underlined word's meaning. After a brief discussion, complete the true-false and multiple-choice items, explaining the thought processes you go through in deciding which is the correct choice.

Ask if there are any questions and then distribute the worksheets. After students have completed the worksheet, briefly discuss their answers.

Adapting the Activity: Because almost all selections contain some context-rich sentences, *Word Clues* can be used with almost any reading selection. For example, it would work well with both Amy Schwartz's *Camper of the Week* and Jean Fritz' *Shh! We're Writing the Constitution*, the two selections we mentioned as also appropriate for the *Paired Question* activity. As a modification, instead of using individual worksheets, you could present the material to the whole class using a transparency and overhead projector. Also, after students have become familiar with the activity, you could choose less difficult words and let students create their own worksheet items that help unlock word meanings and try out their items on each other.

Reflection: On the one hand, since this type of activity takes quite a bit of teacher preparation time, you will probably want to use it primarily with those students who need practice in using context clues. On the other hand, since using context clues to unlock word meanings is such a useful skill and since many students would profit from becoming more adept with context clues, you might choose to use it fairly frequently. As we noted, students can learn to create instructional items like these themselves. Moreover, letting them do so gives them practice with specific words, practice with context clues, and a chance to write for a real audience—other students. Sometimes you might want to take advantage of these benefits by having your students write vocabulary items of this sort for students in lower grades or by asking teachers with upper grade classes if their students would be interested in developing "word clue" vocabulary items for your class.

As we mentioned in Chapter 2, SREs are not designed to teach strategies, and our suggestions for work with context clues here are not an exception to that rule. Although the above activities provide students with some excellent practice in using context clues, they do not give them explicit instruction in doing so. For detailed information on providing students with explicit instruction on using context clues, we recommend the procedures suggested in Buikema and Graves (1993) or Ryder and Graves (1994).

Preteaching Concepts

The major feature that distinguishes the preteaching of vocabulary and the preteaching of concepts is that while vocabulary instruction teaches new labels for known concepts, concept instruction focuses on words that represent new and difficult ideas. *Metamorphosis,* for example, is a word that would probably represent a new and difficult idea for most third graders, and *recession* is a word that fifth and sixth graders are likely to find challenging.

Concepts do not remain static but are ever changing according to our own particular experiences. Our concept for *friend,* for example, will be quite different at age 40 than it was at age 4. *Mountain* will not have the same meaning, nor will *beauty.* And certainly Colorado students' concept of *mountain* will differ from that of many students who have spent their lives living on the prairie or in inner-city New York or Chicago.

Providing students with opportunities to grow in their understanding and knowledge of words and concepts can help them better understand and enjoy what they read and interpret and appreciate themselves and the world they live in. While preteaching vocabulary activities focus on pronouncing, defining, and doing some manipulating of the potentially difficult words in a selection, activities designed to preteach concepts focus on establishing, embellishing, refining, and expanding students' knowledge of words and associated concepts.

Ideally, your students will be reading material that primarily includes vocabulary they can handle comfortably yet at the same time offers some opportunities to learn new words as well as a chance to add to the depth of knowledge of words and concepts they already know. For example, much of the vocabulary in *Number the Stars* by Lois Lowry is within the reach of competent fifth or sixth graders, yet these same readers might need help with such terms as *Nazi occupation* and the *Resistance*. Also, the vocabulary of Beverly Cleary's "Ramona" books is probably in the comfort zone of competent fourth graders yet offers opportunities to add to their knowledge of concepts such as *responsibility, thoughtful, indignant,* and *reassurance,* to name a few.

In deciding when to preteach concepts, what you need to do is decide when it is appropriate to do so. If your students are going to read *Number the Stars,* they are going to need some prior knowledge of the Nazi occupation and the Resistance to understand and appreciate the events in the story and the motivations and emotions of the characters. In this situation, you will need to supply the necessary information by explaining these terms. Or, perhaps your students could benefit from expanding their knowledge of the concept *responsibility.* Maybe *responsibility* has even become an issue in your classroom because of certain behaviors of your students. In this situation, presenting the word before students read, brainstorming on its probable meanings, and then having students notice how the word is used in *Ramona Forever* will help them understand the concept more fully.

Building students' knowledge and understanding of concepts is often a worthwhile prereading activity. The way you will go about presenting concepts before students read will depend on how familiar they are with the concepts and how well they need to know them in order to achieve their reading goals. Additional information on preteaching concepts and the differences between various word-learning tasks is presented in Graves (1985, 1992). On the next several pages, we give two detailed examples of activities for preteaching concepts.

Preteaching Concepts Sample Activity 1: *Multimedia*

Multimedia uses a combination of tactile stimuli, photographs, and simple diagrams to preteach the concept of a *glacier* and some of the formations glaciers create—*cirques, aretes,* and *horns.*

Selection: *Glacier* by Phyllis Root. This well-written book about Glacier National Park, amply illustrated with full-color photographs, provides interesting and useful information about the park. Some of the topics covered include the formation of Glacier's mountains, its history as a national park, its geographic features, and its flora and fauna.

Students: Fourth graders of mixed abilities in an urban setting, two ESL students.

Reading Purpose: To understand and appreciate a geological phenomenon, specifically, Glacier National Park.

Goal of Activity: To provide students with a hands-on activity that will either introduce the concept of a glacier to them or help expand on the concept they already have.

Rationale: To appreciate this national park's namesake and the impact glacial activity has had on the topography and geological features of the 1,500 square miles of park land, students need some understanding of the ways in which glaciers were able to shape the land. Providing students with visual and tactile stimuli—photographs, diagrams, and models—can help them in understanding the extraordinary sculpting power of a glacier.

Procedure: Before the lesson, locate photos that illustrate cirques, aretes, and horns. (The book itself provides examples of each.) Then draw a simple diagram on the chalkboard to illustrate each formation. Provide a small container of play dough or hunk of modeling clay for each student.

At the beginning of the lesson, ask students if they know what a glacier is. Write the word *glacier* on the board. Let students give their answers; then write the following terms on the board and have student volunteers read them.

> **three million years ago**
>
> **snow and ice packed tightly together**
>
> **layers piled up thousands of feet deep**
>
> **the piles became so heavy they slid down the mountains and through the valleys**

Tell students that each phrase reveals something about glaciers. Then ask students what they think these huge, heavy, moving rivers of snow and ice might do to the land they slide over and discuss their responses. (Students may come up with some fairly far-out responses at this point, but they also are likely to include a few more "on target" responses such as, *crush it, bury it, change it, shape it.)* Next, discuss the influence of glacial action on mountains. Show students the photographs of a cirque, a horn, and an arete. Tell students that a *cirque* is a hollowed-out mountainside caused by a glacier resting against it. An *arete* is a knife-edged ridge caused by glaciers pushing against two opposite sides of a mountain, and a *horn* is a three-sided mountain formed by glaciers scraping away from three different sides. Remind students that this sort of sculpting took place over many thousands of years.

Ask students to identify each of these three formations from the diagrams you have drawn on the chalkboard. Write each name (*cirque, arete, horn*) next to the corresponding diagram. Tell students that they are going to make their own formations out of clay and that sculpting their own cirques, aretes, and horns will help them better understand and appreciate these formations and what the movement of glaciers can do.

Distribute the clay, and when all students have something to work with, tell them to first sculpt a mountain with a single peak and gently sloping sides. If you think it is necessary, draw a simple illustration on the board.

Allow the students a few minutes to do their initial sculpting. Then tell them to use their fingers to simulate the force and sculpting action of a glacier to make one of the three glacial formations—a horn, an arete or a cirque. Remind them that a horn is formed by glaciers scraping away at three sides of a mountain; an arete, when glaciers wear away a mountain from two sides; and a cirque, when a glacier rests on one side, carving out a huge hollow basin. Tell them they will have about five minutes to complete what in real life it would take a glacier thousands of years to do. Answer any questions students have before they begin.

While the students are working, give encouragement and feedback on their progress and praise their creativity and resourcefulness.

When students have completed their models, let each show his or her formation to the rest of the class and explain which glacial formation it represents and why. Alternately, you might have the class guess which glacial formation each model represents.

Adapting the Activity: *Multimedia* can be used for a wide variety of fiction and expository selections, particularly those that include objects which your students haven't experienced first hand. For example, if students who live in rural Kansas are going to read a piece where the ocean plays an important role, you might want to show them photographs of the sea, play audio recordings of sea sounds, or bring in shells or driftwood from the seashore. Before students read *Life in the Rainforests* by Lucy Baker, you might show the National Geographic video "Rainforests" or have students make terrariums to simulate a rainforest.

Reflection: *Although an activity such as sculpting with a clay-type medium takes time to prepare and implement, students can benefit from such hands-on experiences. When reading, students need concrete images they can bring to mind in understanding what is being described. Kids need to know that often the things they read about are those that can be touched, smelled, heard, seen, and tasted. Through hands-on experiences, words are connected to the real world—they express and describe a tangible world.*

Preteaching Concepts Sample Activity 2: *Is It, Or Isn't It?*

With *Is It, Or Isn't It?*, students use their prior knowledge to expand, elaborate, and refine a concept by identifying and creating examples and non-examples of that concept.

Selection: "The Walrus and the Carpenter" by Lewis Carroll. In the middle of the night when the sun is "shining with all his might," the Walrus and the Carpenter are walking along a vast sandy beach when they come upon an oyster bed. The Walrus asks the Oysters to come and walk with them. Eldest Oyster declines, but the young ones eagerly hop "through the frothy waves, scramble to the shore," and follow the two. After walking for "a mile or so," the Walrus and the Carpenter rest on a low rock, while "all the little oysters stood and waited in a row." The Walrus begins a discourse ("The time has come to talk of many things"); the oysters ask if they might rest before conversation; and the Walrus and the Carpenter proceed to eat the oysters with polite civility, hypocritical empathy, and satiric denial.

> "I weep for you," the Walrus said:
>   I deeply sympathize."
>
> With sobs and tears he sorted out
>   Those of the largest size,
>
> Holding his pocket-handkerchief
>   Before his streaming eyes.
>
> "O Oysters," said the Carpenter,
>   "You've had such a pleasant run!"
>
> "Shall we be trotting home again?"
>   But answer came there none—

And this was scarcely odd, because
>   They'd eaten every one.

Students: Fifth graders of mixed abilities.

Reading Purpose: To visualize, understand, and enjoy the satirical humor in a poem.

Goal of the Activity: To help students enjoy the humor in "The Walrus and the Carpenter" by expanding on their concept of *nonsense.*

Rationale: To appreciate the humor in this poem, it would be worthwhile to activate and build up students' prior knowledge of what constitutes humor by focusing on the concept *nonsense.* Students probably know what nonsense is even if they don't have a label for it.

Procedure: Say to your students, "Would you please take out a paper and pencil so we can bake a cake. It's Ms. Goodman's (your principal's name) birthday yesterday, and we want to be sure to forget it." Your statements will probably create some confusion, a few odd looks, and a couple of snickers. Good. Your students are listening. Talk about what you said and why some people laughed. (*It didn't make sense; It sounded silly; You can't bake with a pencil and paper! etc.*) If the word *nonsense* doesn't come up, write it on the chalkboard. Explain to the students that what you were telling them was nonsense; it did not make any sense. Have students come up with their own examples of nonsense and write these on the chalkboard. (*For example, a florist arranging hot dogs in a vase; a teacher telling her student, "Please stand on your head so I can hear you better"; or a dog that meows.*) After some examples have been given, write a few non-examples on the chalkboard and have students suggest how you might turn them into nonsense.

a tree with blossoms—a tree with hats ; a car with blossoms

a baby crying —a baby shaving; a lamppost crying

"Please enter through the front door and exit through the backdoor."—
"Please enter through the keyhole and exit through the chimney."

Tell students that Lewis Carroll, the author of *Alice in Wonderland* and of the poem they will read, "The Walrus and the Carpenter," loved to write about nonsense in his stories and poems. When they read the poem, they will discover many examples of nonsense.

Adapting the Activity: This activity can be modified to use before reading almost any selection with an important central concept. For example, before reading Bruce Brooks' *Everywhere* , Nina Ring Aamundson's *Two Short & One Long*, or Margaret Wild's *The Very Best of Friends,* students could create examples and non-examples of the concept *friend.* Giving examples and non-examples of *tragedy* could help to increase students' perceptions and understanding of the novel *Cousins* by Virginia Hamilton or *Bridge to Terabithia* by Katherine Paterson. Before reading an informational article on drug abuse, students might list examples and non-examples of drugs. Sometimes the concepts you choose to have students work with will appear in the piece itself, and sometimes they won't. For example, the word *nonsense* doesn't appear in "The Walrus and the Carpenter," and such words as *discrimination, freedom,* and *justice* may or may not be used in a story that illustrates those ideas.

Reflection: Having students engage in this kind of activity where they are giving examples and non-examples of a concept not only provides students with an opportunity to expand their understanding of that concept but also gives them the chance to practice using their analytical and critical thinking skills. First they must think about the attributes of a concept (analyze it) and then come up with some examples that clearly represent or illustrate that particular concept and others that clearly do not. Additionally, as Dorothy Frayer (Frayer, Fredrick, & Klausmeier, 1969) has shown in her excellent model for teaching concepts, truly understanding what something is entails understanding what it is not. Thus, giving students opportunities to consider both examples and non-examples of concepts will sharpen their understanding of key concepts and begin to give them a sense of what it means to know a concept well.

Focusing Attention

This category of prereading activities includes **Prequestioning**, **Predicting**, and **Direction Setting**. These activities serve to direct readers' attention to a particular aspect or several aspects of the text. As an example, let us say you pick up the newspaper to read an article titled "The Great Debate" that discusses presidential candidates' views on a number of issues. You read the article looking for certain questions to be answered: "How does candidate A's stance on education differ from Candidate B's?" "Do the candidates really have concrete plans?" "Do the candidates give any concrete examples on how they will implement their ideas? If so, what are their plans?" Wanting answers to these questions causes you to focus your attention on these issues. You also might have some predictions in mind before you read—"I bet candidate A has nothing new to say." As you read, your attention is focused on whether your predictions are confirmed or contradicted. Or you might set directions for your reading rather than make predictions—"I'll read this article to see which candidate has the most concrete ideas for improving education. Then I'll decide whether those ideas seem likely to be effective."

Prequestioning, predicting, and direction setting are closely related activities that focus our attention and give us a definite purpose for reading. There are any number of focusing activities you can involve students in before they read a selection. In such activities, students combine their prior knowledge with any specific information they have about the text. In the classroom setting, this text knowledge might come from another person (you or a classmate), from students' previous experience with the topic or text, or from students' looking at illustrations, titles, subtitles, and the like.

Prequestioning

Posing questions before reading a selection gives students something to look for as they read. Thus, questions both direct attention and prompt students to be active, inquisitive learners. For example, one student might pick up the novel *Miracles on Maple Hill* by Virginia Sorenson, read the title, and ask himself, "I wonder what kind of miracles could happen on Maple Hill? What's Maple Hill anyway? A hill? A town? What?" Of course, others students might pick up the same novel and begin reading without posing any questions. Initially, teachers need to prompt these students with questions, partly to help them deal with the upcoming selection and partly to model the process of asking questions. The long-term goal, of course, is to get students in the habit of asking questions.

In Chapter 6 on postreading activities, we discuss in detail the various kinds and levels of questioning you might involve students in after they read a selection—questions that prompt students to demonstrate understanding of what they read, questions that ask students to apply, analyze, synthesize, or evaluate information or ideas, and questions that encourage creative, interpretive, or metacognitive thinking. Questions posed *before* students read a selection can also prompt them to think on these various levels. In the sample activity that follows, questions asked before students read a selection encourage them to think analytically, critically, and creatively.

Prequestioning Sample Activity: *What Do YOU Think?*

In *What Do YOU Think?* students generate their own questions about a story and then write their personal responses to a teacher-generated question on a reader response chart.

Selection: *Journey* by Patricia MacLachlan is a compact, well-crafted novel about an 11-year-old boy whose anger and grief over his mother's abandonment is eventually replaced by acceptance and trust. When Journey's mother leaves him and his sister Cat to live with their grandparents, he is deeply hurt by her abandonment and struggles to understand her motivation. With the help of his grandfather's photography, as well Journey's own detective work with a box of torn photographs, Journey is able to piece together his past. These photographs help him understand the present and give him hope for the future.

Students: Fifth and sixth graders of average to high ability.

Reading Purpose: To read and enjoy a sensitive, well-crafted piece of literature and to make personal connections with the thoughts and emotions of the main character.

Goal of the Activity: To focus students' attention by having students generate their own questions about the text and to consider a specific question for the reader response chart that will help them connect with the thoughts and emotions of the main character.

Rationale: Having students generate their own questions about a story establishes a strong, well-motivated purpose for reading. Encouraging students to give their personal responses to a teacher-posed question about a piece of literature can serve a number of purposes, but there are three primary objectives of this particular activity. One is to help students feel secure in their response to a particular work and not be dependent on someone else's response. Another is to encourage students to respect the unique responses of others. A third is to help students recognize the common elements in people's responses to the same piece of literature.

Procedure: Prior to students' reading the novel, bring in a camera and some pictures of yourself and your family. Show the camera and photos to your students and explain that a camera and photographs play a significant role in Patricia MacLachlan's novel, *Journey*. Mention also that you will be using both a camera and photographs for a classroom literature project.

Explain that two of the main characters in *Journey* have unusual names. The protagonist, an 11-year-old boy, is named Journey, and his older sister's name is Cat. They live on a farm with their grandmother and grandfather. Ask students to speculate on why a camera and family photographs might be important to the characters in the story. After students have discussed their ideas, tell them that when they go home that day you want them to look through their family photos and bring a favorite picture of themselves to school. Tell them that you also will be taking their picture at school. Explain that the photos they bring in and the pictures you take will be used for a special project. At this time display the reader response chart shown in Figure 4.2.

Tell students that the chart will give them an opportunity to share their responses to *Journey* and to other stories and poems they read. The chart will also let them see how other people respond. The question they are going to consider is "How did photographs help Journey?"

Figure 4-2   Reader Response Chart

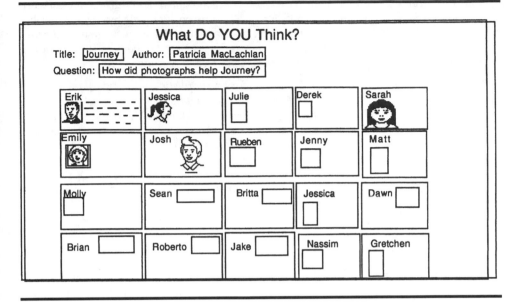

Next, read the following two quotes found at the beginning of the novel.

> It is our inward journey that leads us through
> time—forward or back, seldom in a straight line,
> most often spiraling.

> Eudora Welty,
> *One Writer's Beginnings*

> Photography is a tool for dealing with things every-
> body knows about but isn't attending to.

> Emmet Gowin, in
> *On Photography*
> by Susan Sontag

After you read the quotes, read the one-page introduction that precedes the first chapter. This describes the scene in the barn in which Journey's mother leaves Cat and Journey. She tells Journey that she will be back, but after she has gone, Journey's grandfather tells him that his mother won't return. Journey then hits his grandfather.

Have students generate questions from this scenario that they hope will be answered in the story. Write their questions on the board. Some of these might include: "Why was Journey's mother leaving? Why did Journey hit his grandfather? How did Cat feel? What is grandfather going to do?"

Adapting the Activity: Having students generate their own questions prior to reading is an activity that can be used before reading any kind of selection—narrative or expository. The reader response chart can also be used to publish student responses to any kind of reading material. Questions can focus on feelings—"What part of the story made you feel saddest, and why?" "How do you think the character felt when . . .?"; or speculation—"Why do you think the author . . . ?" "If there were another chapter in the book, what do you think the main character would do?"; or interpretation—"What do you think is the story's main theme?" The questions, whatever they are, should function to get students to *think* and respond.

Reflection: As you may have noticed, this activity accomplishes a number of prereading functions that lead up to the question-generating activity and the reader response chart. First, you do a bit of motivating with props (photos and a camera), and then you give a short preview of the book and ask students to predict how a camera and photographs might be important in the story. Next, you relate the reading to the students' lives by asking them to bring photos of their own family to school to share. And, by introducing the reader response chart, you are also preparing the foundation for during-reading and postreading activities. As we noted at the beginning of the chapter, when planning and implementing SREs, this kind of overlapping will very often occur.

Predicting

Consider again the novel *Miracles of Maple Hill*, which we mentioned in discussing prequestioning. Let us say the student who selected this novel from your library shelf reads the title and looks at the cover illustration. "Hmmn," he thinks to himself. "*Miracles of Maple Hill* . . . I bet the miracles have something to do with maple syrup." That student, of course, is making a prediction about the story. When he reads, he will be looking to see if he is correct, if the miracles do indeed have something to do with maple syrup.

Predicting activities encourage students to speculate about the text based on various prompts—illustrations, titles or subtitles, key words from the text, character names or descriptions, or short excerpts from the text. After students make their predictions, one of their reading purposes will be to see if their predictions are accurate.

Encouraging students to make predictions about an upcoming selection is a worthwhile prereading activity. Not only does it focus their attention and give them a purpose for reading, but it also models a useful reading strategy, one they can employ on their own with a variety of texts. Of course, the goal is to encourage reasoned predictions based on the information available, not wild guessing. Thus, predicting should often be accompanied by thoughtful discussion of what prompted the predictions and how certain or speculative the predictions are.

Predicting Sample Activity: *I Predict*

I Predict uses visuals to stimulate students' curiosity and assist them in making predictions about a text's content and in setting purposes for reading.

Selection: "Koalas—Just Hanging Around Under," *National Geographic World*. This article focuses on the Lone Pine Koala Sanctuary in Brisbane, Australia, and tells almost everything anyone might like to know about koalas. It touches briefly on their history, habitat, physical characteristics, diet, and behavior, as well as the sanctuary's role in protecting and maintaining this appealing marsupial.

Students: Third graders of mixed abilities.

Reading Purpose: To understand and appreciate wildlife sanctuaries generally and the Lone Pine Koala Sanctuary in particular.

Goal of Activity: To pique students' interest and to encourage them to make predictions about the article so they will have some definite purposes for reading.

Rationale: Predicting content is a natural and very appropriate prereading strategy for many informational selections. This article is no exception. Students' inherent curiosity about animals can be easily channeled toward the selection's content by asking appropriate questions and leading students to make their own predictions. These predictions then become the purposes for students' reading.

Procedure: Before students read the article, hold up the picture on the first page of the article showing a mother and baby koala nestled in eucalyptus branches. Ask students to predict what the article is about (*koalas*). Then say something similar to, "You can easily recognize this animal, but I wonder if you also know what kind of tree this koala mother and her baby are in and what other animals they are related to?" Let students volunteer answers. Write the words *eucalyptus* and *marsupial* on the board. Explain that a *eucalyptus* is a tree with very fragrant leaves (If possible, bring in eucalyptus leaves for students to smell.) and a *marsupial* is a kind of animal. Tell students that mother marsupials raise their young in a pouch in their body, and ask if they can think of other marsupials (*kangaroo, duck-billed platypus*).

Next, ask students what they might expect to learn in an article about koalas and what they predict this article will deal with. Write students' responses on the board under the heading WHAT WE MIGHT FIND OUT ABOUT KOALAS. Here are some possible responses:

WHAT WE MIGHT FIND OUT ABOUT KOALAS:

What they eat

Where they live

What they like to do

How big they are

After students have made several predictions, tell them that the koalas they see in the picture live in the Lone Pine Koala Sanctuary in Brisbane, Australia. Find Brisbane on a globe or map. Write WHAT WE MIGHT FIND OUT ABOUT THE LONE PINE KOALA SANCTUARY on the board, and again let students volunteer their predictions. Write these on the board also. Some of their predictions may be similar to the following:

WHAT WE MIGHT FIND OUT ABOUT THE LONE PINE KOALA SANCTUARY:

What a sanctuary is

Why the koalas are in a sanctuary

What they do in a sanctuary

After several predictions have been made, ask students what they would most like to know about koalas. Give them a few minutes to think about this, and then have each student write at least one prediction on a sheet of paper.

Collect the predictions, take a quick look at them, and tell students that they have done some good thinking and made lots of predictions about what the article might deal with. Review some of these predictions with students. Then, tell them to read to find out how accurate their predictions were. Explain that, after everyone has finished reading, you will discuss what they found out.

Adapting the Activity: Using visual aids to stimulate students' curiosity about a reading selection in order to make predictions about that selection is a technique that can often be used effectively. If appropriate illustrations don't accompany the selection itself, you can provide other types of materials—magazine illustrations, slides, photos, and concrete objects. For example, before students read Paul Goble's *Her Seven Brothers*—the Native American tale of a quill-working girl and her seven brothers who make bags, furniture, and clothing beautiful with embroidery of dyed porcupine quills—you might want to bring in porcupine quills or perhaps even an actual example of something embroidered with porcupine quills. The students might then predict why porcupine quills might be important to the story or why anyone would want to beautify objects with porcupine quills. Or students might look at the jacket cover of *The Great Gilly Hopkins* by Katherine Paterson (which pictures Gilly with a huge bubble gum bubble about to burst and cover her face) and predict what kind of a person Gilly is.

Reflection: Ideally, predicting activities such as this one will prompt students to make similar kinds of predictions when reading on their own. You can encourage such predicting by saying things such as "making predictions before reading and while you read can make reading more fun because predicting is kind of like playing a guessing game. Maybe you are reading a story in which the author shows a character running a lot. When it comes to a point in the plot when a race is about to take place, you make a prediction based on what you know. 'I bet that character will win the race because she's had so much practice.' After she does win, you can congratulate yourself. 'Nice job. I was right!' "

Direction Setting

Direction setting is a focusing activity that comes at the end of your prereading activities. It functions as one of the final words of direction and encouragement you give readers. Direction setting activities tell students what it is they are to attend to while they read. Sometimes they will be oral instructions—"Read the story to find out if your predictions are correct." Sometimes they will be written on the board, a chart, or a handout so students can reflect on them or refer back to them.

As the following two activities illustrate, direction setting activities often follow other prereading activities and are typically brief and to the point.

Direction Setting Sample Activity 1:
Looking for Old, Looking for New

Looking for Old, Looking for New is used following the *Share and Tell* activity (pp. 49–50) and focuses students' attention on finding examples of topics they discussed in their groups and examples of other information presented in the chapter.

Selection: "Exploring the Ocean" in *Science in Your World* (Hackett & Moyer, 1991). This chapter discusses features of the ocean floor such as the continental shelf, rift zones, trenches, and various forms of life in the ocean. It concludes with the issue of protecting the ocean.

Reading Purpose: To add to old knowledge and gain new information about the ocean's features, ocean life, and how to protect our ocean.

Students: Fourth graders of average to high ability.

Goal of the Activity: To increase comprehension by having students connect what they have learned in the *Share and Tell* prereading activity to what is presented in the text.

Rationale: After having engaged in the *Share and Tell* activity, students are aware of the topics discussed in this chapter. However, they will still benefit from an additional reminder of what to attend to as they read. Giving students specific directions as to what they should look for *just before* they begin reading will serve to reestablish a purpose for reading and focus their attention on salient aspects of the text. Doing so will help improve both understanding and recall.

Procedure: After you have completed the *Share and Tell* activity, give each student a sheet of lined paper and tell them to fold it in half, making two columns. At the top of the left-hand column, have them write "Old Information." At the top of the right-hand column, have them write "New Information." Tell students that when they read the first section of the chapter, "Ocean Features," they are to look for those features they discussed in their groups and ideas that are new ones, ones they didn't discuss. Encourage them to jot information down in the appropriate column as they read—previously discussed ideas in one column and new information in the other. Tell them they will have a chance to discuss their findings when they finish reading the section.

Proceed in a similar manner with the remaining two sections of the chapter, discussing what students discovered in their reading and evaluating the importance of the features and issues they discussed beforehand and those found in the selection.

Adapting the Activity: *Looking for Old , Looking for New* can be used as a direction-setting activity any time the prereading activities include having students discuss or write about what they know about the topics of a selection before reading it. As is the case with *Share and Tell* activity, you could also use *Looking for Old, and Looking for New* when your ethnically diverse fifth graders read Russell Freedman's *Immigrant Kids,* your California fourth graders read *Earthquakes* by Seymour Simon, or when curious and scientifically inclined third graders read *Insect Metamorphosis: From Egg to Adult* by Ron and Nancy Goor.

Reflection: This activity provides a good opportunity for students to work on critical thinking skills. When you discuss what students have recorded, they should be encouraged to look carefully and thoughtfully at the information they have chosen to record, identify what is more and less important in what they have recorded, and discuss why some information is more important than other information.

As you may have recognized, Looking for Old, Looking for New *incorporates parts of the K-W-L procedure, a well known instructional procedure developed by Donna Ogle (1986). Using K-W-L, students consider what they* Know, *what they* Want *to know, and what they* Learn. *Thus, the procedure includes both prereading and postreading components. We have included a complete K-W-L example as one of the comprehensive SREs presented in Chapter 7.*

Direction Setting Sample Activity 2:
Looking for Answers

Looking for Answers follows the *What do YOU Think?* activity (pp. 72–74) and serves to focus students' attention on finding answers to the questions they generated prior to reading the story and toward considering the question posed for the reader response chart.

Selection: *Journey* by Patricia MacLachlan is a compact, well-crafted novel about an 11-year-old boy whose anger and grief over his mother's abandonment is eventually replaced by acceptance and trust. When Journey's mother leaves him and his sister Cat to live with their grandparents, he is deeply hurt by her abandonment and struggles to understand her motivation. With the help of his grandfather's photography as well his own detective work with a box of torn photographs, Journey is able to piece together his past. These photographs help him understand the present and give him hope for the future.

Students: Fifth and sixth graders of average to high ability.

Reading Purpose: To read and enjoy a sensitive, well-crafted piece of literature and to make personal connections with the thoughts and emotions of the main character.

Goal of the Activity: To improve understanding and enjoyment of the story by focusing on finding answers to student-generated questions and to focus student thinking along the lines of the story's theme.

Procedure: After you have finished the *What Do YOU Think* activity, tell students to read the first chapter of *Journey* to find out the answers to their questions (which you have written on the board). Ask them to jot down answers as they run across them in the text. After students have finished the first chapter, give them the chance to discuss whether or not their questions were answered and if they were answered in the way they expected them to be. This discussion might take place in a large group, small groups, or pairs.

At the end of the discussion on the first chapter but before students begin to read the remainder of the novel, remind them that as they read the novel they should be thinking about the question, "How did photographs help Journey?" so that when they finish they can write a short response for the reader response chart. Tell them to pause after each chapter and reflect on that question, writing down any ideas they have, either in journals or on a sheet of paper you provide for that purpose.

Adapting the Activity: *Looking for Answers* can be used any time questions—either student generated or teacher generated—have been posed prior to reading a selection. Sometimes, you may want to give general directions such as having students pause at the end of a section or chapter to think about or write down their answers. Other times, you may want to give more specific guidance by giving page numbers or even specific paragraphs that contain the information that students are looking for. The more difficult or abstruse the text, and the less open to interpretation the questions, the more helpful specific directions will be.

Reflection: *You probably have noticed that while this activity is simple and straightforward it overlaps, not only with another prereading activity but with during-reading (silent reading) and postreading (discussion after reading the first chapter) as well. While all pre-, during-, and postreading activities are tied to each other in one way or another, it is particularly difficult to describe direction setting activities without also describing what precedes and follows. Also, as we mentioned at the beginning of this section, direction setting activities are often quite brief. One purpose they serve is to remind students of what they have done previously, whether it is to find out how the questions they posed are answered, whether or not their predictions are accurate, or how a selection's topic or theme relates to their lives. If they have asked the questions "Why was Journey's mother leaving? Why did Journey hit his grandfather? How did Cat feel? What is Grandfather going to do?", a direction setting activity will encourage them to look for answers to these questions in the text.*

Suggesting Strategies

In the past several years, a number of reading strategies have been identified as valuable for understanding, remembering, and enjoying text. Some of these include *using prior knowledge, asking and answering questions, determining what is important, imaging, summarizing, making inferences, dealing with graphic information, surveying,* and *monitoring comprehension.* As we noted in Chapter 2, teaching students to use reading strategies is an important part of reading instruction, but it is not a topic we discuss in this book.

However, sometimes as a prereading activity you will want to review strategies that students have already learned and suggest that they employ these while reading a specific selection. Such activities encourage students to engage in strategies while they read. Already, we have alluded to several strategies in our prereading activities—using prior knowledge, making inferences, determining what is important, using context clues to unlock word meanings, asking and answering questions, and making predictions.

Prereading activities that we have labeled as *suggesting strategies* simply remind students to use strategies that they have been taught before. For instance, you might suggest that students use imaging as they read, consciously creating pictures in their minds of the people and events in the story, or if there are illustrations in the text to look carefully at those. If they are reading material that is going to be important for them to remember, you might have them summarize after each paragraph or subtopic. You might also have them look for the most important point in each section of an article or textbook chapter.

Suggesting strategies is by no means meant to take the place of strategy instruction. Teaching students about strategies, what they are, and when and where to use them, and providing practice in their use requires in-depth, long-term instruction. However, once students have learned strategies, they should be encouraged to apply them when appropriate. The next sample activity encourages students to use a strategy they have been taught previously.

Suggesting Strategies Sample Activity: *Sum it Up* (or *A Title's Worth a Thousand Words*)

In *Sum it Up,* students create their own titles for each paragraph of a selection as they read.

Selection: *Immigrant Kids* by Russell Freedman. With photos and prose, Freedman captures the conditions turn-of-the-century immigrant children faced during their voyage to America, in their new homes and schools, at work, and at play.

Students: Fourth to sixth graders of mixed abilities.

Reading Purpose: To understand and appreciate the experiences of the children who immigrated to the United States during the late 1800s and early 1900s.

Goal of the Activity: To encourage students to summarize information by jotting down a title for each paragraph in the first chapter of an informational trade book.

Rationale: Having students create a title for each paragraph as they read encourages them to reflect on what they read in order to determine the most important idea. Such analysis will help them better understand and remember what they read.

Procedure: Show students the photograph on page 3 of *Immigrant Kids*. It pictures two immigrant children, a pouting little girl of about four clutching a doll and a stoic little boy of about six. Both children hold a ticket. Ask students to summarize what they see in the picture in just a few words so that their summary is like a title or a headline. Write their suggestions on the board. Some of these might include: *Unhappy Children, Old-fashioned Kids, Children of Long Ago, Waiting for Mom, Lost Children, Orphans* or even *Immigrant Kids*. Have students discuss why they came up with the titles they did.

> Eric: *Waiting for Mom . . . The way the kids are standing and the looks on their faces makes me think they're waiting for someone. Since they're so little, I bet it's their mom they're waiting for.*

> Sabrina: *Children of Long Ago . . . They're dressed in old-fashioned clothes like from a long time ago.*

> Tyler: *Orphans . . . The little girl looks so sad, and the boy kind of looks, by the expression on his face and the way he's standing, like he's in charge of his little sister. I bet they're orphans.*

Next, discuss how they came up with these thumb-nail summaries, then synthesize students' statements about how they came up with their titles in a sentence or two. (*You created summaries by looking at the details in the photograph, making some inferences, then condensing the information into a few words.*)

Show them the actual title, *Immigrant Kids*, on the cover of the book and some of the photographs in the book, and then read the first paragraph of the Preface to them.

> *The boys and girls in these old photographs were born nearly a century ago. They grew up during the late 1800s and early 1900s, when millions of immigrants arrived in the United States from every corner of Europe.*

Next, write these titles on the board:

Growing up in Europe

Old Photographs

Immigrant Kids of a Century Ago

Ask students to pick a title that best captures the main idea of the paragraph you just read and explain why they chose it. (*"Immigrant Kids of a Century Ago " is the best title for that paragraph because that is what the paragraph talks about. It mentions "growing up in Europe" and "old photographs," but these are not the main ideas or the only ideas in the paragraph.*)

There are six paragraphs in the Preface. For the first three, have students choose among three possible titles that you have composed. For the final three, let students suggest their own titles, reminding them that the title should summarize or at least give a general idea of what the paragraph is about in a few words.

After you have finished reading the Preface and students have come up with titles for the six paragraphs, ask them to tell some things about the book from the information given in the Preface. Explain that the reason you were creating titles for the paragraphs is that putting the author's ideas in your own words and forcing yourself to be brief is a good way to understand

and remember what the author is writing about. Remind them also that when they read informational books like *Immigrant Kids* remembering information is often an important goal.

Tell students that as they read through the first chapter titled, "Coming Over," you want them to write a title for each paragraph in the chapter. The title should tell what the paragraph is about in just a few words. After they have finished reading the first chapter, they will get the chance to share their titles with the rest of the class and talk about whether or not the activity helped them understand and remember what they read.

Adapting the Activity: *Sum It Up* can be used whenever you think students will benefit from writing very short summaries—titles. Short articles or textbook chapters are possibilities, as well as some informational trade books such as *The King's Day: Louis XIV of France* by Aliki, *Going Green: A Kid's Handbook to Saving the Planet* by John Elkington, et al., and *Shh! We're Writing the Constitution* by Jean Fritz. Newspapers offer another opportunity for creating summary titles. With newspapers, you can actually cut off headlines and let students create their own. Then they can compare their headlines with those actually used in the newspaper and discuss the strength and weaknesses of each.

Reflection: Competent and creative readers enjoy doing this kind of activity with expository material. However, some kids will need extra help coming up with viable titles. Working in pairs or groups can provide support and encouragement to those youngsters who need extra help in reading and synthesizing information. While we have included this as a prereading activity, as you may have noticed, the strategy also includes activities undertaken during and after reading.

If Sum It Up *looks like the sort of active learning strategy your students need to really understand and learn from informational text, we suggest you give careful consideration to Merlin Wittrock's concept of generative learning and to how you can involve students in generating meaningful relationships involving the ideas in the informational texts they read. We discussed the concept briefly in Chapter 3, and the references to Chapter 3 contain several of Wittrock's articles explaining the concept more fully. We have highlighted the notion here because we believe that it is an important one in fostering students' ability to learn from expository material.*

• Prereading: A Final Word •

As we said at the outset, prereading activities serve to motivate and prepare students to read. Sometimes, just one brief prereading activity will be sufficient to ensure a successful reading experience for your particular group of students with the specific selection they will be reading. Other times, you may want to provide your students with several prereading activities. What you plan will be determined by the overall purpose for reading the selection (information, enjoyment) and coordinated with the activities students will be doing during and after reading.

The more students *want* to read, have *real purposes* for reading, the more *background information* they have to bring to a text, the more *strategies* they have to use, the more they will both contribute to and take from what they read. Their reading experience will be easier, more enjoyable, and more memorable if students are motivated and prepared.

References

Buikema, J.L., & Graves, M.F. (1993). Teaching students to use context cues to infer word meanings. *Journal of Reading, 36,* 450–457. Provides detailed information on a validated procedure for teaching students to make use of context cues.

Calfee, R.C., Chambliss, M.J., & Beretz, M. (1991). Organizing for comprehension and composition. In R. Bowler & W. Ellis, *All language and the creating of literacy* (pp. 79–93). Baltimore, MD: Orton Society. Describes an approach to fostering growth in comprehension and composition for all students and ways of supporting teachers in achieving this goal.

Chen, H.S.. (1993). *Effects of previewing and providing background knowledge on Taiwanese college students' comprehension of American short stories.* Unpublished doctoral dissertation. University of Minnesota. Minneapolis, MN. Documents the effects of previewing and providing background knowledge for ESL students.

Cooke, C.L., & Graves, M.F. (1993). *Writing for an audience—For fun.* Manuscript submitted for publication. Describes a junior high school writing project in which students wrote and published reviews of their favorite self-selected books.

Dole, J.A., Valencia, S.W., Greer, E.A., & Wardrop, J.L. (1991). Effects of two types of prereading instruction on the comprehension of narrative and expository text. *Reading Research Quarterly, 26,* 142–159. Shows positive effects of previews with both narrative and informational texts.

Frayer, D.A., Fredrick, W.C., & Klausmeier, H.J. (1969). *A schema for testing the level of concept mastery* (Working Paper No. 16). Madison, Wisconsin Research and Development Center for Cognitive Learning. The original source of the Frayer model for teaching concepts.

Graves, M.F. (1992). The elementary vocabulary curriculum: What should it be? In M.J. Dreher & W.H. Slater (Eds.), *Elementary school literacy: Critical issues* (pp. 101–131). Norwood, MA: Christopher-Gordon. An examination of what a comprehensive vocabulary program might contain.

Graves, M.F. (1985). *A word is a word. . . Or is it?* New York: Scholastic Book Services. An introduction to a variety of approaches for teaching vocabulary.

Graves, M.F., Cooke, C.L., & LaBerge, M.J. (1983). Effects of previewing difficult short stories on low ability junior high school students' comprehension, recall, and attitudes. *Reading Research Quarterly, 18,* 262–277. One of the most compelling studies supporting the effects of previewing on students' comprehension.

Graves, M.F., Prenn, M.C., & Cooke, C.L. (1985). The coming attraction: Previewing short stories to increase comprehension. *Journal of Reading, 28,* 549–598. A clear description of how to write previews and a summary of much of the research on previewing.

Kameenui, E.J., Carnine, D.W., & Freschi, R. (1982). Effects of text construction and instructional procedures for teaching word meanings on comprehension and recall. *Reading Research Quarterly, 17,* 367–388.

Langer, J.A. (1981). From theory to practice: A prereading plan. *Journal of Reading, 25,* 152–156. A concise and useful description of this plan for assessing and activating background knowledge.

McKeachie, W.J., Pintrich, P., Lin, Y., Smith, D. A., & Shafma, R. (1990). *Teaching and learning in the college classroom* (2nd Ed.). Ann Arbor: University of Michigan, National Center for Research to Improve Postsecondary Teaching and Learning. Comprehensive review of the research on college teaching.

Ogle, D. (1986). K-W-L: A teaching model that develops active reading of expository text. *The Reading Teacher, 39,* 564–570. Initial description of the K-W-L procedure.

Rekrut, M.D. (in press). Peer and cross-age tutoring. *Journal of Reading.* Concisely presents the instructional implications of research on peer and cross-age tutoring.

Ryder, R.J., & Graves, M.F. (1994). *Reading and learning in content areas.* Columbus, OH: Merrill. A comprehensive content area reading text dealing with comprehension, critical thinking, vocabulary, cooperative learning, writing to learn, and assessment.

Vacca, R.T., & Vacca, J.A.L. (1993). *Content area reading* (4th ed.). New York: HarperCollins. Provides a clear and concise description of structured overviews with quite a few examples.

Children's Books Cited

Aamundsen, N.R. (1990). *Two short, one long.* Boston: Houghton Mifflin.

Aliki (1989). *The king's day: Louis XIV of France.* New York: Crowell.

Ammon, R. (1989). *Growing up Amish.* New York: Atheneum.

Asimov, I. (1990). *How did we find out about Pluto?* New York: Walker.

Avi. (1990). *The true confessions of Charlotte Doyle.* New York: Orchard.

Baker, L. (1990). *Life in the rainforests.* London: Two-Can Publishing Ltd.

Brooks, B. (1990). *Everywhere.* New York: HarperCollins.

Carlson, J. (1989). *Harriet Tubman, call to freedom.* New York: Fawcett Columbine.

Carroll, L. (1963). "The Walrus and the Carpenter," in *Oxford book of poetry for children.* New York: Franklin Watts.

Cleary, B. (1984). *Ramona forever.* New York: William Morrow and Company.

Conrad, P. (1991). *Pedro's journal.* Honesdale, PA: Boyds Mills Press.

Delton, J. (1983). *Back yard angel.* Boston, MA: Houghton Mifflin.

Dickens, C., adapted by Richardson, I.M. (1982). *The signalman.* Mahwah, NJ: Troll Associates.

Elkington, J. et al. (1990). *Going green: A kid's handbook to saving the planet.* New York: Viking.

Evans, L. (1988). "Thomas Nast: Political Cartoonist Extraordinaire," *Cobblestone,* Volume 9, No. 11, November.

Freedman, R. (1980). *Immigrant kids.* New York: E.P. Dutton.

Fritz, J. (1987). *Shh! We're writing the Constitution.* New York: G. P. Putnam's Sons

Goble, P. (1988). *Her seven brothers.* New York: Bradbury.

Goor, R., & Goor, N. (1990). *Insect metamorphosis: From egg to adult.* New York: Atheneum.

Hackett, J.K., & Moyer, R.H. (1991). "Exploring the Ocean," *Science in Your World,* Level 4. New York: Macmillan/McGraw-Hill.

Hackett, J.K., & Moyer, R.H. (1991). "Waves," *Science in Your World,* Level 6. New York: Macmillan/McGraw-Hill.

Hamanaka, S. (1990). *The journey.* New York: Orchard.

Hamilton, V. (1988). *Anthony Burns: The defeat and triumph of a fugitive slave.* New York: Knopf.

Hamilton, V. (1990). *Cousins.* New York: Philomel.

Hirschfelder, A. (1986). *Happily may I walk: American Indian and Alaska natives today.* New York: Scribners.

Houston, J. (1977). *Frozen Fire.* New York: Margaret K. McElderry.

Landon, L. (1989). *Meg Mackintosh and the mystery at the medieval castle.* Boston: Joy Street.

Levinson, N.S. (1990). *Christopher Columbus: Voyager to the unknown.* New York: Lodestar.

Lobel, A. (1979). *Days with frog and toad.* New York: Harper & Row.

Lord, B.B. (1984). *In the year of the boar and Jackie Robinson.* New York: Harper & Row.

Lord, S. (1993). *Garbage! The trashiest book you'll ever read.* New York: Scholastic.

Lowry, L. (1989). *Number the stars.* Boston: Houghton Mifflin.

MacLachlan, P. (1991). *Journey.* New York: Delacorte.

Meltzer, M. (1990). *Columbus and the world around him.* New York: Franklin Watts.

National Geographic World. (1988). "Koalas—Just hanging around under." National Geographic, Dec.

Naylor, P.R. (1980–81). *The York trilogy.* New York: Macmillan.

Paterson, K. (1977). *Bridge to Terabithia.* New York: Crowell.

Paterson, K. (1978). *The great Gilly Hopkins.* New York: Crowell.

Paulsen, G. (1990). *Canyons* . New York: Delacorte.

Paulsen, G. (1987). *Hatchet.* New York: Bradbury.

Root, P. (1988). *Glacier.* Mankato, MN: Crestwood House.

Schwartz, A. (1990). *Camper of the week.* New York: Orchard.

Sharmat, M.W. (1972). *Nate the great.* New York: Dell Publishing Co.

Sharmat, M.W. (1989). *Nate the great goes down in the dumps.* New York: Coward-McCann.

Simon, S. (1991). *Earthquakes.* New York: Morrow.

Sorenson, V. (1956). *Miracles on Maple Hill.* New York: Harcourt.

Spinelli, J. (1990). *Maniac Magee.* Boston: Little Brown.

Thesman, J. (1990). *Rachel Chance.* Boston, MA: Houghton Mifflin.

Thomas, J.R. (1989). *The princess in the pigpen.* Boston, MA: Clarion.

Wild, M. (1990). *The very best of friends.* San Diego: Harcourt Brace Jovanovich.

Yep, L. (1991). *The star fisher.* New York: Penguin Books.

Yue, D. & C. (1984). *The tipi: A center of Native American life.* New York: Knopf.

5

During-reading Activities

After you have motivated and prepared students to read with prereading activities, the next step is to read. Here students will meet and interact with the text. They will begin to construct meaning from the text by reading or, occasionally, by being read to. During-reading activities include things that the students do as well as the things you might do to assist them in their reading. We have broken down the during-reading phase of SREs into five categories.

During-reading

1. Silent Reading
2. Reading to Students
3. Guided Reading
4. Oral Reading by Students
5. Modifying the Text

These categories, of course, reflect only one of many ways to organize and think about during-reading activities. The activities themselves might also fit into pre- or postreading experiences. For example, reading to students could work as a prereading activity or oral reading by students as a postreading activity.

During-reading activities involve students with the text in a way that best suits the students, the text, and their purposes for reading it. Some questions you might ask before designing during-reading activities are: "How might the reading task best be accomplished? What might I do to involve students actively with the text? What can I do to help make this material come alive for students as they read? What would make this material more accessible to students? What might students do as they read that will make the text more understandable, or memorable, or enjoyable?"

Guide to Activities for Chapter 5

Reading to Students:	*Poetry to Prose*
Guided Reading:	*Problem, Solution, Change*
	What Does It Mean?
	I Didn't Know That!
	Word Round-Up
	Who? What? When?
Oral Reading by Students:	*Two Voices*
	On the Air!
	Flag It
Modifying the Text:	*Focusing*

Silent Reading

Silent reading will be the most frequent during-reading activity. Reading, obviously, is the primary activity of the scaffold, the *raison d'etre*, and most often students will be doing this reading by themselves, silently. The other activities in the scaffold are designed to support students' reading—to prepare them for it, to guide them through it, and to take them beyond it.

Reading to Students

As we just noted, most of the time students will be reading a selection silently. Sometimes, however, it is appropriate for students to have the material read to them. If the material cries out to be heard, for whatever reasons—because the language is beautiful and inspiring, because students need a good send-off for a lengthy or challenging selection, because the concepts are new and need interpretation—hearing the words may help students grasp the material so that when and if they do read it on their own, it will hold more meaning, pleasure, and interest for them.

Reading aloud to your students not only makes certain texts accessible but it also provides a model for expressive reading. By reading aloud, you can show your enthusiasm for information, ideas, and language. As story teller and author Bill Martin Jr. (1992) has said, "A blessed thing happened to me as a child. I had a teacher who read to me."

Because this book deals with helping students read specific selections, the reading to students we present here is done in conjunction with their doing some reading on their own. However, we do not want to miss this opportunity to emphasize the importance of reading to children as one critical component of a complete reading program. As Jim Trelease (1989) has pointed out so powerfully in *The New Read-along Handbook*, "A large part of the educational research and practice of the last 20 years confirms conclusively that the best way to raise a reader it to read to that child—in the home and in the classroom." In fact, Trelease continues, "This simple, uncomplicated 15-minute-a-day exercise is not only one of the greatest intellectual gifts you can give a child; it is also the cheapest way to ensure the longevity of a culture." We most emphatically agree: Reading to children builds their vocabularies, their knowledge of the world, their knowledge of books and many of the conventions employed in books, and—probably most important—their interest in reading.

Reading aloud to students is one way to demonstrate the beauty and power of language, and for students who struggle with reading on their own or have had little exposure to books, it may be the most significant way. The activity that follows demonstrates both of these functions.

Reading to Students Sample Activity:
Poetry to Prose

In *Poetry to Prose*, a prose selection is introduced by reading aloud a poem that reflects its theme or topic.

Selections: The poem, "Weather is Full of the Nicest Sounds," by Aileen Fisher and the informational trade book, *Weather Words and What They Mean,* by Gail Gibbons.

Students: Second graders of mixed abilities.

Reading Purposes: To understand and enjoy a playful piece of poetry; to learn weather words and concepts.

Goal of the Activity: To pique students' interest in weather words and demonstrate how ideas can be communicated in a fun and playful way.

Procedure: If readily available, assemble some weather props on a table—an umbrella, galoshes, sun glasses, suntan lotion, a pinwheel, a kite, and a wool scarf and mittens—and perhaps don a bright yellow macintosh.

Write "_____ is Full of the Nicest Sounds" on the board and read it aloud to students. Tell students that this is the title of a poem you are going to read with the most important word left out. You left it out because you want them to guess what the topic of the poem is. Tell them to listen carefully for word clues as you read. Read the poem, "Weather is Full of the Nicest Sounds," leaving out the word *weather.*

Weather is full
of the nicest sounds:
it sings
and rustles
and pings
and pounds
and hums
and tinkles
and strums
and twangs
and whishes
and sprinkles
and splishes
and bangs
and mumbles
and grumbles
and rumbles
and flashes
and CRASHES.
I wonder
if thunder
frightens a bee,
a mouse in her house,
and bird in a tree,
a bear
or a hare
or a fish in the sea?
Not *me*!

Ask students to raise their hands if they think they know the word. If some students don't raise their hands, read the poem again. If you have weather-word props on a table, tell the class that these props are also clues. When you think all students probably know the word, let them say it out loud together. Talk about when (under what circumstances) weather makes the sounds suggested in the poem—"When does weather sing? rustle? pound? hum? tinkle? and so on."

Tell students that poetry can get us thinking about how weather affects us and that there are also many informational books about weather, books that can help us understand weather words and what they mean. Explain that Gail Gibbon's book, *Weather Words and What They Mean,* is filled with lots of weather words. Show students the book. Leaf through it and read some of the words aloud: *temperature, air pressure, moisture, wind, dew, frost, cloudy, rain, thunder, lightening,* and so on.

Either read *Weather Words and What They Mean* aloud to students or have them read it silently.

Adapting the Activity: Reading poems aloud to introduce prose selections is something that can be done for a variety of selections. You might introduce Russell Freedman's *Lincoln: A Photobiography* by reading the poem "Nancy Hanks" by Rosemarie and Stephen Vincent Benet. Nancy Hanks didn't live to see her son grow up and the poem ends with the questions "Did he grow tall?/ Did he have fun?/ Did he learn to read?/ Did he get to town?/ Do you know his name?/ Did he get on?" Similarly, to introduce Russell Freedman's *Buffalo Hunt,* you might read "Buffalo Dusk" by Carl Sandburg.

The buffaloes are gone.
And those who saw the buffaloes are gone.
Those who saw the buffaloes by thousands and how they
pawed the prairie sod into dust with their hoofs,
their great heads down pawing on in a great pageant
of dusk,
Those who saw the buffaloes are gone.
And the buffaloes are gone.

Reflection: *As we have said before, pre- and during-reading experiences lead naturally to postreading activities. These two selections—"Weather is Full of the Nicest Sounds" and* Weather Words and What They Mean—*suggest all sorts of wonderful postreading activities in art, music, dance, drama, and writing. Students might create a bulletin board that displays a potpourri of weather words illustrated with student drawings or clippings from magazines. Students might create weather dances and instrumental pieces to accompany those dances—a rain dance, perhaps, or a sun dance or wind dance. Students could gather in groups to produce weather dramas depicting various kinds of days—windy days, stormy days, sunny days, wintry days, rainy days, and so on. Students might write a story or poem about their favorite kind of weather or go on a weather word hunt and try to find as many words as they can that tell something about weather. Or they might write a poem titled "Weather is Full of the Nicest Smells" or "Weather is Full of the Funniest Sights." Students could also make a graph that charts the number of cloudy, partly cloudy, rainy, and sunny days for a month's time. Or students might make up weather story problems that need to be solved using a mathematical equation. For example, "In March there were 6 sunny days and 7 rainy days. How many more rainy days were there than sunny days?" or, "If March has 31 days in it and 25 days were either rainy, cloudy or partly cloudy, how many days were sunny?"*

Guided Reading

Much of the time, particularly with narratives, students will read the material from beginning to end without stopping to record or reflect on what they are reading. The interactions that take place as students read narratives are often personal ones between the reader and the text. As Louise Rosenblatt (1978) has explained, the primary concern with narratives is likely to be with what happens to students as they read rather than what they remember afterward. Responses to what they have read might be shared after they have read or perhaps not at all. Sometimes, however, it is appropriate to guide students' reading—to help them focus on, understand, and learn from certain aspects of the text. *Guided reading* means just that—guiding the thought processes that accompany reading. Guided reading activities encourage the sort of generative learning that Merlin Wittrock (1990) sees as promoting real learning; they lead students to make connections among ideas in the text and between their existing experience and knowledge and what is presented in the text.

Although guided reading activities are most often used to help students read expository material, they can also be used for narratives. Perhaps you feel students would understand and enjoy a story more if they focused their attention on certain aspects of character, setting, plot, or theme. Or maybe you want them to be aware of colorful or unusual language. Maybe you want to encourage students to make personal responses to what they read, make predictions, or consider how they or the characters in a selection are feeling. These are all good reasons for designing guided reading activities. Some general kinds of guided reading activities for narratives might include:

- informal writing that elicits personal responses such as journaling or writing letters
- reading with a partner and pausing to reflect out loud
- using reading guides, which might include answering questions, or completing charts or outlines that focus on character, plot development, point of view, or various aspects of language or style

As we mentioned earlier, guided reading activities are most frequently used to help students understand and remember the information presented in expository materials. Some general kinds of guided reading activities for expository texts might include:

- having students focus on various organizational patterns of text, such as sequencing, cause and effect, or comparison/contrast
- encouraging critical thinking by having students note examples of fact and opinion, make inferences, draw conclusions, or predict outcomes
- leading students to manipulate the text in ways that will help them better understand and retain key concepts. For example,

  recording main ideas and their supporting details
  outlining
  summarizing
  semantic mapping
  constructing time-lines

- having students monitor their understanding of what they read

Guided reading activities can be effective scaffolds for students while they read in any genre. Again, the value and effectiveness of any sort of activity will depend on your students, the material they are reading, and the purposes for reading it. When designing guided reading activities you might ask, "What is it that students should be attending to as they read? Should they be looking for key concepts? Cause and effect issues? The author's biases or perspective? Colorful language? Motives of characters? Sequence of events?" Or you might design guided reading activities to encourage students to be metacognitive as they read. "What do I know about this topic?" is the type of question that you would like them to ask frequently as they approach an informational piece. Guided reading activities can also lead students to consider particular points or questions that come up at various junctures in their reading— "Does what the author says about clouds make sense in terms of what I know about clouds, water vapor, rain, etc.?"

What guided reading should do is get students thinking about and manipulating the ideas and concepts in the material in a way that will help them understand, enjoy, and remember it better. The five activities that follow are designed to do just that.

Guided Reading Sample Activity 1:
Journal Writing: *Problem, Solution, Change*

In *Problem, Solution, Change,* students record in journals what they feel are any problems the main character faces, solutions to those problems, and changes that took place in the main character because of the problem and solution.

Selection: *The True Confessions of Charlotte Doyle* by Avi. *The True Confessions of Charlotte Doyle* is the gripping account of intrigue and murder on the high seas told by a 13-year-old girl who finds herself the lone passenger on a sailing ship bound from England to America in 1832. Because of the unusual situation Charlotte finds herself in and the demands it places on her physically, mentally, emotionally and spiritually, Charlotte goes through a virtual metamorphosis. She begins her tale as a prim and proper school girl and ends up a seasoned sailor who runs away to crew on a sailing ship.

Students: Sixth to seventh graders of mixed abilities.

Reading Purpose: To read and enjoy an exciting adventure story by focusing on the basic plot elements of problem, solution, and change.

Goal of Activity: To focus students' attention on the elements of plot as they develop and unfold throughout the novel and to encourage students to make connections between ideas in the text and their knowledge of the world.

Rationale: Having students think about the problems a main character faces, how he or she solves those problems, and what changes take place within the character because of the problems and resolutions, can help students discover one of the most salient features of fiction—characters encounter problems, find ways to solve them, and are changed in the process. Because of the number and magnitude of the dilemmas young Charlotte faces, *The True Confessions of Charlotte Doyle* is an outstanding vehicle for this process.

Procedure: (Ideally this activity would follow the *Common Threads* prereading activity in which students have recorded problems, solutions, and changes in their own lives.) Begin by reading the prologue to the novel aloud. These three pages are titled "AN IMPORTANT WARNING" and begin "Not every thirteen-year-old girl is accused of murder, brought to trial and found guilty." The narrator warns the reader, "If strong ideas and action offend you, read no more. For my part I intend to tell the truth as *I* lived it." In this prologue, the reader learns that Charlotte began her story as a proper young lady about to embark on a voyage from England to America. However, the reader is also forewarned that the events that transpired on Charlotte's journey change her drastically and that keeping a journal is what enabled her to relate "in perfect detail everything that transpired during that fateful voyage across the Atlantic Ocean in the summer of 1832."

If you have done the *Common Threads* prereading activity, remind students of some of their responses and then have them predict what sorts of problems a 13-year-old girl might encounter on a voyage such as Charlotte took, how she might go about solving those problems, and how she might be changed because of them.

Explain that part of the pleasure and purpose of reading literature is to experience adventures and make discoveries through the actions and thoughts of the main characters in a story. In most fiction they read, students will find a character who is faced with a problem. *The True Confessions of Charlotte Doyle* by Avi is no exception. This is an adventure-packed novel in which Charlotte is faced with numerous and very difficult problems that she must solve on her own. In the process of dealing with each of these dilemmas, she is changed a bit, until by the end of the novel she is a very different person.

Remind students that Charlotte kept a journal of her experiences and they will be keeping a journal as they read the novel. Their journal, however, will focus on Charlotte's problems, solutions, and changes. Explain that keeping their own journal will help them keep track of these events and that in doing so they will be able to extend and enrich their own knowledge and explore new ideas along with the main character.

Next, provide students with several sheets of lined paper to serve as their journal. Have them fold the paper in thirds to form three columns and label the three columns as shown below. This will enable students to record their ideas regarding Charlotte's problems, solutions, and changes.

Problem	Solution	How Changed?

After this, have students bind the pages together in some manner—a simple staple would do or you might want students to create a front and back cover that they can embellish later.

Before students begin reading the novel and recording Charlotte's problems, solutions, and changes, you might want to read the first chapter aloud and then demonstrate how to make the journal entries. After reading the chapter aloud, have students suggest problems, solutions, and changes. Write these suggestions on the board.

Remind students that there are no right or wrong responses. Anything they feel constitutes a problem, solution, or change should be recorded. Also, sometimes a problem may not have an immediate solution, or any change in Charlotte may not be recognizable at the moment. They may need to read further in the novel to discover solutions and changes, and of course they may identify some problems that aren't resolved in the novel.

When students are clear as to what they will be doing, have them begin reading the novel and recording problems, solutions, and changes in their journals. Tell them that when they finish they will have an opportunity to share and discuss what they discover about Charlotte and her adventures.

Adapting the Activity: This type of activity is appropriate for almost any novel in which the main character is faced with numerous problems to solve or obstacles to overcome. Just a few examples include *Cousins* by Virginia Hamilton, *Everywhere* by Bruce Brooks, *Hatchet* by Gary Paulson, *Dixie Storms* by Barbara Hall, *A Hand Full of Stars* by Rafik Schami, *Maniac Magee* by Jerry Spinelli, *Number the Stars* by Lois Lowry, and *Rachel Chance* by Jean Thesman. It is probably harder to find novels or short stories that do not lend themselves to such an analysis than to find those that do.

Reflection: While most students will probably have little trouble identifying the problems that come up in the novel, some may find it difficult to identify Charlotte's solutions, and even more will have a hard time finding the change that took place in Charlotte. It's a good idea to encourage students not to become bogged down looking for precise answers. They should realize that not everyone will see Charlotte's problems, solutions, and changes in the same way and that some solutions may not come until the end of the novel, and some not at all. The idea of the activity is for them to see how problems cry out for solutions and that change is a big part of the problem-solving process. Since fiction mirrors life, it provides an interesting and convenient way to take a look at this process.

It is worth noting the general function this guided reading activity serves because it is a very useful function and one that guided reading activities can serve fairly frequently. What we have done is focus students' attention on an aspect of the text that both helps them understand and appreciate this text and that will aid them in appreciating a number of texts they read in the future. We have given them a mini-lesson like those Nancie Atwell recommends (1987). This certainly has not been a full-blown lesson in which we have attempted to give students a definite strategy for identifying problems, solutions, and changes that often occur in narratives; and you may at some time want to provide a more substantial strategy lesson on this topic—a matter we consider at some length in Graves, Watts, and Graves (1994). However, at the very least, the mini-lesson will give students a start in learning to look for such patterns in literature.

This response activity is only one of many types that might be implemented for this selection. Another procedure, a two-column response journal described by Hilda Ollmann (1992), could be used for this novel, as well as for many other stories, poems, or expository pieces. When following this procedure, students write quotes from the text in one column and their personal responses to the quotes in another. For example, an entry for chapter one in The True Confessions of Charlotte Doyle *might look like this:*

In The Text	In My Head
p. 15. " 'But . . . that would be all men, Mr. Grummage! And . . . I am a girl. It would be wrong!' I cried, in absolute confidence that I was echoing the beliefs of my beloved parents."	I know I would feel horrified too if were in Charlotte's place. To be the only girl with all those men. I'm sure I would have not gone on that ship!

Response journals like this are one way to involve readers actively with text and to encourage analytical, evaluative, and creative thinking.

Guided Reading Sample Activity 2:
Reading Guides: *What Does It Mean?*

In *What Does It Mean?*, students interpret colorful or figurative language in order to understand the text better as well as appreciate the subject of the text.

Selection: *I Have A Dream, The Story of Martin Luther King, Jr.* by Margaret Davidson. This biography traces the emergence of Martin Luther King, Jr. as a powerful civil rights leader and pacifist, from his youth in Atlanta, Georgia, through his assassination at age 39 in Memphis, Tennessee. The biography stresses King's compassion, intelligence, and eloquence as well as his unquenchable spirit and commitment to justice, equality, and peace.

Students: Fifth to seventh graders of mixed abilities and from various ethnic backgrounds.

Reading Purpose: To understand and appreciate Martin Luther King, Jr. as a person and to learn about his accomplishments as a civil rights leader.

Goal of Activity: To introduce or reintroduce the concept of figurative language and to have students focus on this language to better understand Martin Luther King, Jr.

Rationale: Martin Luther King, Jr. was, of course, an eloquent speaker with a passion for words and ideas. King often spoke in colorful and figurative language, examples of which are sprinkled throughout the biography. Calling the reader's attention to these and interpreting their meaning will help the reader to better understand the text and to appreciate King as a person.

Preparation: Before the lesson—either on the chalkboard, a transparency, or handouts—write the following phrases and page numbers.

Page 54:   "My feet is tired, but my soul is at rest."

Page 59:   "Cold fingers of fear creeping up my soul."

Page 63:   "I want it to be known in the length and breadth of the land."

Page 66:   "The clock said it was noon, but it was midnight in my soul."

Page 67:   "We got our heads up now, and we won't ever bow down again."

Page 73:   "It's an idea whose time has come."

Page 74:   "The weapon that cuts without wounding. It is the sword that heals."

Page 77:   "We do not want freedom fed to us in teaspoons over another 150 years."

Page 80:   Find the figurative statement about *God's companionship*.

Page 87:   Find the figurative statement about setting something in motion that can't be stopped.

Procedure: At the beginning of the lesson, write "I may *smell* like a mule, but I don't *think* like one" on the chalkboard. Ask a volunteer to read the sentence; then encourage students to explain what it means. Tell them that Martin Luther King, Jr. spoke those words to his friends when he was just about their age (King was 10 at the time.). Also, tell them that King loved words and ideas and often spoke in colorful and figurative language. If students don't know what a figurative statement is, give them some examples and non-examples.

Literal (non example)	**Figurative** (example)
I'm hot.	I'm burning up.
I'm cold.	I'm frozen.
I'm tired.	I'm dead.

Ask student to explain how figurative statements are different from literal ones. Then let them give examples of their own.

Show students a copy of the book, *I Have a Dream*. Tell them that it is a biography of Martin Luther King, Jr. and that it is filled with King's language. Explain that to understand and appreciate the ideas in the book, it is helpful to understand the meaning of King's colorful and figurative statements.

Direct students' attention to the sentences on the chalkboard or worksheet. Ask volunteers to read these aloud. Explain that while they are reading the biography, they are to write in their own words what each of these sentences means. (For pages 80 and 87 only, they need to also identify the figurative statements. They should write down the statements and explain what each means.)

Tell students that language was one of King's most effective tools. By really thinking about the meaning behind King's words, they will better understand Martin Luther King, Jr. and what happened in his short but powerful life.

Adapting the Activity: This activity can be used with any text that contains colorful or figurative language. Cynthia Rylant's *A Couple of Kooks and Other Stories About Love* and *Appalachia: The Voices of Sleeping Birds;* Gregory Alexander's interpretation of Kipling's *The Jungle Book;* Richard Kennedy's *Amy's Eyes,* a fantasy-mystery rich in metaphor and colorful language; Patricia Pendergraft's *Miracle at Clements' Pond,* or Steve Sanfield's African American folk tales, *The Adventures of High John the Conqueror,* all contain language worthy of pondering and savoring.

Reflection: It is very likely that students will become so caught up in the drama of King's life that they may pass by the figurative phrases and have to back track to find them. Giving them 10 colored strips of construction paper to mark the pages on which the figurative language is found is one way to remind them. You might mention something about the colorful paper also symbolizing the colorful language King used.

Obviously, this is only one of many guided reading activities that could be implemented with this book, and ideally it would be used in conjunction with literature activities in which students are introduced to the concepts of simile and metaphor. Also, as students are focusing on and pondering over the colorful language King used, they could at the same time take a look at the figurative language they hear on television or in music lyrics, or even phrases they use themselves. Additionally, seeing a film or video of King's "I Have a Dream" speech is a powerful way to illustrate the effectiveness of language in general and King's rhetorical style in particular.

This activity prompts us to make three generalizations. One is that although the activities we have mentioned here all focus on figurative language that occurs throughout a selection, it is often appropriate to focus on just one use of figurative language in a selection, a particularly vivid or informative instance. Another general point is that the brief listing of examples and non-examples of figurative language is another instance of a mini-lesson, a brief segment of instruction imbedded within an authentic reading experience. The third general point is that this focus on figurative language is just one example of our commitment to providing a variety of activities designed to get students interested in language. Other focuses—for example, focusing on the clarity or power with which an author makes a point—are frequently useful.

Guided Reading Sample Activity 3:
Reading Guides: *I Didn't Know That!*

In *I Didn't Know That!,* students record in their own words interesting facts from the topics and subtopics in a science chapter.

Selection: "Waves" from *Science in Your World* (Hackett & Moyer, 1991). This chapter from a science text discusses the physical phenomenon of waves as rhythmic disturbances that transfer energy—mechanical waves involve matter and electromagnetic waves involve electric and magnetic fields. Some of the topics covered are how waves transfer energy, the properties of waves, and electromagnetic waves, which include radio waves, infrared waves, light, ultraviolet waves, X-rays, and gamma rays.

Students: Sixth graders of average to high ability.

Reading Purpose: To build upon existing knowledge and gain new information about the properties of mechanical and electronic waves and how they transfer energy.

Goal of Activity: To encourage students to focus on interesting information that is new to them to help them better understand and remember what they read.

Rationale: This text is a not a particularly dense one, but it does have a number of concepts that will be new and possibly challenging for students. Having them interact with the text ideas as they are reading by thinking about what information is new or particularly interesting to them will increase both students' understanding of the material and their memory of what they learn.

Procedure: Before the lesson, duplicate the following outline on a handout or the chalkboard. If a handout is used, be sure to leave enough space between topics and subtopics for students to write their information.

WAVES

How Do Waves Transfer Energy

Wave Properties

Electromagnetic Waves

Radio Waves

Higher Frequency Waves

Infrared Waves

Light

Ultraviolet Waves

X-rays and Gamma Rays

Lasers

At the beginning of the lesson, say something like this: "When I first read this chapter on waves, I found out some really interesting things I didn't know before. For instance, in the section on How Do Waves Transfer Energy?, I learned that there are two kinds of waves—mechanical and electromagnetic—and that both types transfer energy. With mechanical waves, the energy is transferred as the wave travels through matter. For example, in a wave created by a rock thrown in the water, the water moves up and down but isn't carried along with the wave. But electromagnetic waves don' t have to travel through matter. They can transfer energy through empty space.

"I know you will discover some information in this chapter that is new to you also. To help you better understand and remember the ideas in the chapter, write down one interesting piece of information from each topic and subtopic in the chapter. After everyone has finished reading the chapter and recording their facts, you can share the new pieces of information you have learned."

Before students begin reading, review the topics and subtopics for the chapter and ask if there are any questions. With some groups, you may want to read the first topic and subtopics aloud before students tackle the chapter on their own. This chapter contains heady concepts, so be sure to offer students encouragement and praise their participation. Tell them that they are improving their reading and thinking skills all the time and they should be pleased with their progress.

While students are reading the chapter silently, be available to answer questions and give feedback, or read the chapter yourself while students read, recording new or interesting information you discover.

Adapting the Activity: Having students record the interesting facts they encounter while reading can be done whenever you want them to focus on new and interesting information. This activity would work well with informational tradebooks such as Russell Freedman's *Immigrant Kids*. With this book, students could record new and interesting information they find in each of the five chapters in the book, writing down a few interesting facts about the immigrants' journey to America while reading the chapter titled "Coming Over," about their home life while reading "At Home," and about immigrants' school, work, and play experiences while reading "At School," "At Work," and "At Play." Also, while reading Lisa Westberg Peters' *Water's Way*, students could record three or four interesting facts they learn about the different forms that water can have. To turn this into a cooperative endeavor, as a postreading activity students might meet in five different groups and make charts for each chapter. The charts would list all the interesting facts students from each group found in their particular chapter. Students could then use the chart information to develop skits, compose songs or poems, or paint murals.

Reflection: For this to be a truly generative learning activity, the sort that Wittrock (1990) has shown to be effective in promoting learning and understanding, students will need to do more than just copy information verbatim from the text. They will need to think about what information is new to them and be encouraged to write that information in their own words. To learn to recognize when they have succeeded in recasting an author's thoughts—in paraphrasing—they are likely to need your feedback. Thus, at least when students are first learning to paraphrase, you will want to read their paraphrases and give them feedback on whether they have successfully captured the author's ideas and on whether they have done so in their own words.

Guided Reading Sample Activity 4:
Semantic Mapping: *Group and Label*

In this semantic mapping activity (Heimlich & Pittelman, 1986; Pearson & Johnson, 1978), students, working in pairs or groups, read a selection and sort the information in it into various categories.

Selection: *Inside and Outside You* by Sandra Markle. In this 38 page informational book about the human body, the author begins by discussing the make-up and function of skin and then proceeds to give readers a close look at the inner workings of the human body.

Students: Third graders of mixed abilities; three ESL students.

Reading Purpose: To learn about, appreciate, and remember the various parts of the body and their functions.

Goal of Activity: To help students understand and remember the names and functions of various parts of the human body by identifying and categorizing those parts and writing them on a chart.

Rationale: Since this book contains a myriad of labels and concepts, having students organize these to show how they are related may be needed to help them understand the concepts and remember them.

Procedure: Give each student two sheets of paper and tell them you are going to conduct an experiment. Next, tell them to put their heads on their desks and close their eyes while you place several items on the table (a flower, a dish, a button, a fork, a chalk eraser, a hat, a ball, a small mirror, a comb, a pencil, a toothbrush).

Have students gather around the table and look at the objects, giving them 20 seconds to do so. Tell them to return to their seats while you scoop the items back in the paper bag. Then tell students to write down on one of their sheets of paper as many items as they can remember, advising them not to worry about spelling at this time. Give them a minute to record their answers, then collect the papers.

Tell students to once again close their eyes. Take several different items from another bag, but this time arrange them on the table in three groups: Group 1—a small paint brush, a tin of paints, a pack of colored chalk, crayons; Group 2—a measuring cup, a cookbook, a spatula, a wooden spoon; Group 3—a piece of lined paper, a pencil, an eraser, a dictionary.

While students still have their eyes closed, tell them you have arranged the items into three groups—drawing and painting items, cooking items, and writing items. Tell them that they will have as much time as before to look at the items, and should again try and remember as many items as they can.

Have students return to the table. Point to each group of items and say, "drawing and painting items, cooking items, and writing items." Again, give students 20 seconds to look at the items before you put them away. Then give them a minute to write down as many as they can remember on their second sheet of paper. Collect the papers and tally the number of correct guesses for each set on the chalkboard.

Without Groups	With Groups
𝍸𝍸𝍸 𝍸𝍸𝍸 𝍸𝍸𝍸	𝍸𝍸𝍸 𝍸𝍸𝍸 𝍸𝍸𝍸 𝍸𝍸𝍸
𝍸𝍸𝍸 𝍸𝍸𝍸 𝍸𝍸𝍸	𝍸𝍸𝍸 𝍸𝍸𝍸 𝍸𝍸𝍸 𝍸𝍸𝍸
	𝍸𝍸𝍸 𝍸𝍸𝍸 𝍸𝍸𝍸 𝍸𝍸𝍸

Barring some bizarre result, students will remember considerably more of the grouped items than the ungrouped ones. Encourage them to deduce why they remembered more of the grouped items. Explain to students that it is almost always easier to understand and remember information if you group it into sets of things that have common characteristics. For example, if they were reading a book about games to find some suitable to play at their birthday party, they might group the games in their mind into these sorts of categories:

Games for four or more people

Games that use the equipment I have

Games that my mom would let us play in the house

Games you have to play outside

Games that sound the most fun to me

After they finished reading, they might add a final category: Games I want to play at my birthday party.

Show them the book *Inside and Outside You* by Sandra Markle, and explain that it is a good book with which to practice the grouping technique because it has lots of names of things in it. Remind students that the names will be easier to remember if they group them together.

Give students copies of the semantic map shown in Figure 5-1 without the individual items filled in and explain the categories to them.

After explaining how to complete the semantic map, have students work in pairs or groups, taking turns reading the text aloud and completing the map. After students have finished reading and completing their maps, bring the whole class together again. As a group, complete the same map which you have drawn on the chalkboard.

Attending to two matters can make this a particularly rewarding experience for the three ESL students in the class, as well as for the native English speakers, who may know very little about other languages. First, be sure that each of the ESL students is in a group with native speakers and ask one native speaker in each of those groups to assist the ESL student. Second, let the ESL students label some of these parts of the body with words from their own language, and have

Figure 5-1   Semantic Map for *Inside and Outside You*

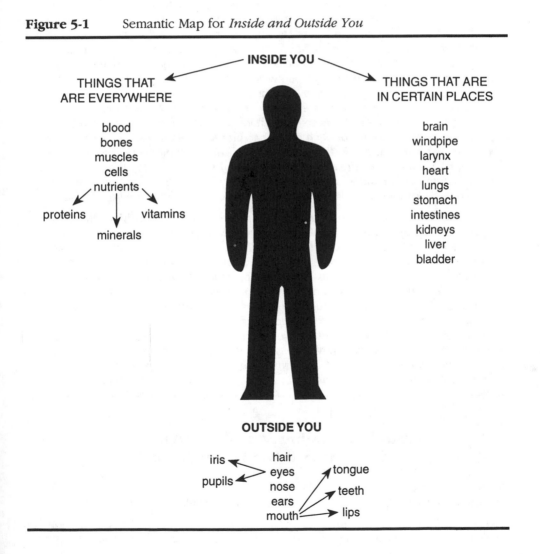

them teach at least some of these words to the native English speakers. These two steps ensure that the ESL students learn, give the ESL students an opportunity to demonstrate their knowledge to the native English speakers, and give the native English speakers a taste of another language.

Adapting the Activity: This activity can be used whenever a text lends itself to grouping information. For example, this technique would work well with Joanna Cole's *The Magic School Bus* series. In these books, Ms. Cole provides a great deal of information on a variety of subjects (the human body, the solar system, inside the earth, at the waterworks) in a narrative style. Even though these books are packed with information, children love them because they are humorous and have plots and characters with whom youngsters can identify. Using semantic maps can help students organize the information to better understand and retain it.

Reflection: Obviously, semantic maps that are designed to serve as reading guides will vary from selection to selection, since they will reflect the information contained in each particular selection. Also, while semantic mapping can sometimes be useful as a during-reading activity, it is also a worthwhile prereading or postreading activity. As a prereading activity, semantic mapping can be used to activate prior knowledge and as a postreading activity to recall and organize information contained in the reading material. For example, before students read any number of books about pioneers—such as Pioneer Children of Appalachia, Spanish Pioneers of the Southwest, *and* Pioneer Settlers of New France *all by Joan Anderson—you might develop a semantic map for the concept* pioneers. *Write* pioneer *on the board along with categories such as* People Who Were Pioneers, Pioneer Activities, Reasons for Being Pioneers, *and* Characteristics of Pioneers, *and have students suggest words and phrases for each category. After students have read a specific book about pioneers, you could do this same activity. The word* pioneers *would still be the target word, but the categories you select and students' responses to those categories will reflect the information that was presented in the text. This postreading activity works well for any number of selections whose topics or themes might range from frogs to friendship.*

Considered more generally, the matter of grouping items is frequently worth taking into account as you plan instruction. As George Miller (1956) pointed out in an article with the rather catchy title "The Magic Number Seven Plus or Minus Two," our mind's capacity to remember ungrouped items is severely limited. Specifically, we can generally remember only five to nine ungrouped items—seven digit phone numbers are a good example. If, however, we group items into meaningful categories, each category functions more or less like a single item, and the total number of items we can remember is greatly increased. Thus, for example, if we head off to the supermarket with 20 ungrouped things to buy and no list, we are likely to be in trouble. If, on the other hand, we take those 20 things and group them as three vegetables, two fruits, two dairy products, and the like, we stand a good chance of remembering all 20 them. It's exactly the same with students' learning from text;. to remember information, they need to group it in meaningful categories.

Guided Reading Sample Activity 5:
Time Line: *Who? What? When?*

In this activity, students record on a time line the important names, events, and dates from a chapter in a trade book that chronicles the history of a scientific discovery.

Selection: *Neptune* from the *How Did We Find Out About?* series by Isaac Asimov. *How Did We Find Out About Neptune?* by Isaac Asimov chronicles the years of observation by astronomers that led to the discovery of Neptune's existence. It also describes many fascinating and unusual things about the eighth planet from the sun, including its rings, its giant moon, and a tornado called the Great Blue Spot. Asimov challenges his readers to think about the questions that astronomers asked prior to making their discoveries and to pose new questions that might lead to a more complete understanding of the planet.

Students: Sixth graders of average to high ability.

Reading Purpose: To gain new knowledge about the discovery of Neptune and to understand and appreciate the people, times, and places involved in the discovery process.

Goal of Activity: To help students conceptualize and remember important events that led up to Neptune's discovery by recording these events in chronological order.

Rationale: This text is filled with numerous dates, persons, and events that led to the discovery of the planet. Having students record these facts on a time line will help fix names and events in their minds.

Procedure: Before students begin reading, provide them with five 2 × 18-inch strips of paper, one for each chapter in the book.

At the end of whatever prereading activities you do, explain that *Neptune* contains many dates, persons, and events that led to the planet's discovery. Each of these in some way serves as a link or clue to the ultimate discovery of Neptune and our present-day knowledge of the planet. To help themselves visualize the path to Neptune's discovery, students will record these facts on time lines.

You may want to review the procedure for constructing a time line. One way would be to have students skim the first chapter, "Uranus," for names and dates while you record these on a time line you have made on the board or a strip of butcher paper.

1543	1608	1610	1665
Copernicus claimed planets revolved around sun	telescope invented	Galileo discovered 4 satellites that circled Jupiter	Huygens discovered a satellite that circled Saturn

Since some students might be tempted to skim the chapter for names and dates and not do a thorough reading, tell them that after they have read the chapter and recorded the persons, dates, and events on their time line, they should reread the chapter to make sure they have understood how these persons and events are related and how they are likely to influence what happens in subsequent chapters. As their time lines will reveal, the discovery of Neptune occurred because of the questions and discoveries of many different people over many years, and newer discoveries were built on older ones. Tell students that this process is not unlike one they go through every day—adding to and building on to their own storehouse of knowledge.

Adapting the Activity: Time lines can be used whenever the reading selection includes a number of persons, dates, and events that can be understood and recalled better if visually presented in chronological order. For example, time lines might be used with any one of the books from Asimov's *How Did We Find Out About?* series and other informational selections, such as Milton Meltzer's *Bill of Rights* and Olga Litowinsky's *The High Voyage: The Final Crossing of Christopher Columbus*. Since narratives also have a chronological structure, time lines can be used with them, too. However, most students will be able to follow the chronology of narratives without using a time line.

Reflection: How Did We Find Out About Neptune? *is a fairly dense text, and to read it successfully many students may need various kinds of during-reading help, a time line being only one possibility. After reading the text yourself, you will discover the ideas and information that you want your students to focus on, to manipulate and retain. These then will determine the make-up of your reading guide.*

Rather than having students note sequence, as the time line does, perhaps you feel your students' purposes might be better served by having them focus on cause and effect—this event happened because of this, and, as a result, this happened. Your reading guide then will reflect this goal. Reading guides are scaffolds designed to help students reach reading goals. They are also, as we have pointed out, opportunities for mini-lessons; and one topic very appropriate for mini-lessons is that of organizational patterns. Thus, when the text students are going to read exemplifies a particular pattern—simple listing, sequence, cause and effect, compare and contrast, and the like—you have the teachable moment for a mini-lesson on that pattern.

Oral Reading by Students

Having students read aloud can achieve some of the same purposes that reading to students accomplishes—students' experimenting with and enjoying the sound of language as well as focusing on meaning. Additionally, if done in a supportive, non-threatening way, students' read-aloud activities can enhance their interest and enjoyment of reading, improve fluency, increase vocabulary, and add to their storehouse of knowledge and concepts.

Two popular read-aloud activities are choral reading and Readers Theatre. In choral reading—by using contrasts such as high and low voices, different voice combinations and contrasts, sound effects, movements, gestures, or different tempos—students combine their voices to convey and construct the meaning of a text. Choral reading can accomplish several purposes. It gives students the opportunity to hear printed language, and because choral reading requires repeated readings, the chances for adding words to their reading vocabularies and becoming increasingly fluent in reading also increases. Choral reading has been traditionally used with poetry, but some narratives lend themselves to this activity as well. Primary grade students might enjoy doing a choral presentation of Michael Rosen's *We're Going on a Bear Hunt*—a repetitive tale with wonderful rhythmic lines, imagery, and alliteration—and third or fourth graders studying Japan might enjoy making a choral presentation out of David Wisniewski's picture book, *The Warrior and the Wiseman*, a Japanese folk tale.

Readers Theatre, in which students take turns or assume roles in reading portions of a text aloud, can be used effectively with poetry and narratives and has even been done successfully with expository materials (Young & Vardell, 1993). In Readers Theatre students present drama, prose, or poetry by "reading the text out loud using their voices, reading fast or slow, loudly or softly, emphasizing certain words or phrases to reading rate, intonation, and emphasis on the meaning-bearing cadences of language to make print come alive" (Hoyt, 1992). Fifth- or sixth-grade students studying United States history could turn Julius Lester's *To Be A Slave* into a powerful

Readers Theatre presentation. In this book, Lester chronicles the tragedy of slavery through many eloquent and provocative voices—the slaves themselves and the comments from various newspaper editors of the times. With Readers Theatre, students could make this piece of history come to life.

Choral reading and Readers Theatre provide an entertaining, cooperative, non-threatening atmosphere in which students can build meaning from text and learn more about language—its purpose, beauty, and power. They are outlets for oral interpretation and opportunities for students to perform and to gain confidence in speaking and reading.

In addition to performance activities such as choral reading and Readers Theatre, reading text aloud can be used in conjunction with what Linda Hoyt (1992) has described as "oral interactions"—dialogue that is stimulated by the ideas and information students discover as they read in various texts. As students read through material silently, they mark certain passages as "hot spots"—ideas they liked, didn't understand, or disagreed with, or ones that answered a question they had, or another student had, or that the teacher posed. In pairs or groups, students share their hot spots by reading the passages aloud and talking about them.

Choral reading, Readers Theatre, and oral interactions are only three of the many kinds of oral reading activities you might use in your classroom. Here, we describe how you might implement each of these.

Oral Reading Sample Activity 1: Choral Reading: *Two Voices*

In *Two Voices,* students are organized into two groups that alternately read and dramatize the lines of a poem. This activity is adapted from McCauley and McCauley (1992).

Selection: "I'm Thankful" from *The New Kid on the Block* by Jack Prelutsky. This light-hearted poem lists the many things a young boy or girl might be thankful for, but with a humorous twist.

Students: Third and fourth graders, several of whom are ESL students.

Reading Purpose: To enjoy the humor and satire in a piece of light verse.

Goal of the Activity: To provide an entertaining, low-stress situation in which students can expand their reading vocabularies, improve fluency and diction, gain language proficiency, and gain confidence in reading aloud.

Rationale: Because much of the meaning and effect of poetry relies on auditory devices such as repetition of sounds, cadence, and rhythm, it needs to be heard to be truly appreciated. Many of Jack Prelutsky's poems are ideal for choral presentation. Children will delight in Prelutsky's humor and love hearing and reciting poems that so succinctly express the topics and emotions of childhood. Choral reading also provides a safe environment for less able readers to practice their reading skills and for ESL students to grow in their understanding of English words and phrases.

Procedure: Briefly discuss with students some of the things they are thankful for. Then tell them you would like to share a poem with them titled "I'm Thankful," by Jack Prelutsky. Explain that the poet has a humorous way of looking at all the things he's thankful for. Ask students to listen for the funny lines in the poem, then read the poem aloud.

I'm thankful for my baseball bat,
I cracked it yesterday.
I'm thankful for my checker set,
I haven't learned to play.
I'm thankful for my mittens,
one is missing in the snow.
I'm thankful for my hamsters,
they escaped a month ago.

I'm thankful for my basketball,
it's sprung another leak.
I'm thankful for my parakeet,
it bit me twice last week.
I'm thankful for my bicycle,
I crashed into a tree.
I'm thankful for my roller skates,
I fell and scraped my knee.

I'm thankful for my model plane,
it's short a dozen parts.
I'm thankful for my target game,
I'm sure I'll find the darts.
I'm thankful for my bathing suit,
it came off in the river,
I'm thankful for so many things,
except, of course, for LIVER!

Read the poem again, this time holding up the object (or a picture of the object) the poet is writing about and dramatize the italicized lines. The italicized lines are asides, so you might cup one hand next to your mouth and lean toward the audience as if letting them in on a secret, then do a dramatization. For example, for the lines "I'm thankful for my baseball bat, *I cracked it yesterday,*" you might hold up a baseball bat, lower your voice when you say, "*I cracked it yesterday,*" then act out what might have happened to the bat by acting mad, sad, disgusted, surprised, whatever.

For the third reading, display the poem on a chart or overhead. Read the poem slowly and have students read along with you. Let a volunteer hold up the items or pictures of them as they are read, while another volunteer acts out the asides and dramatizations.

Read the poem aloud a few more times, increasing the tempo a bit with each reading. With these readings, have students stand and read along with you while they dramatize the italicized lines.

When you feel students are comfortable with the words and movements, divide the class into two groups (January-July birthdays and August-December birthdays, or curly hair and straight hair, or divide class down middle of the room). Have one group stand on one side of the room and read the lines that tell what they are thankful for and the other group stand on the opposite side and say the asides with gestures and dramatizations, with you as the audience. Let students practice reading the poem this way a few times, then have students switch lines. However, continue only if students express interest. The purpose for the activity is not to achieve a polished performance but for the students to read and have fun. Be sure to applaud your students' efforts.

While you do not want to do much of this if students aren't very interested, if students do show interest in the poem, you might want to have them prepare it to perform for another class.

Adapting the Activity: *Two Voices* may be done with any number of poems and even some prose material. *The Whipping Boy* by Sid Fleischman, for example, lends itself to a two-part choral reading, with the two groups reading alternating paragraphs aloud or one group taking the role of Jemmy and the other that of Prince Brat. *Joyful Noise, Poems for Two Voices* by Paul Fleischman is particularly suited for a two-part choral reading activity.

For choral reading in general, some good choices are *Hail to Mail* by Samuel Marshak and *Country Crossing* by Jim Aylesworth to use with primary students, *Where the Sidewalk Ends* by Shel Silverstein and *If I Were in Charge of the World and Other Worries* by Judith Viorst to use with middle graders, and Victoria Forrester's *A Latch Against the Wind* to use with older readers.

Reflection: *Dividing students into two groups is only one way to implement a choral reading experience. Some selections lend themselves to solos, ensembles, or whole group work. Because the lines in "I'm Thankful" are written as declarative statements followed by asides, it lends itself well to a two-part reading. We chose also to add dramatization to this piece, but the asides would work well with a simple gesture and a lowering of the voice.*

Be cautious of trying to have students recite lengthy passages that may result in mottled production or expressionless sing-song. Successful and enjoyable experiences are often those in which students have only simple, single phrases to recite, such as "except, of course, for LIVER!"

We have already noted that choral reading can be effective with bilingual students; we want to emphasize this point. Choral reading gives students repeated exposure to English words, it leads them toward automaticity in recognizing English words, it gives them practice with English structures and intonation patterns, it gives non-native speakers an opportunity to participate and succeed in the same activity native speakers are engaged in, and it does all of this in a non-threatening environment.

Oral Reading Sample Activity 2:
Readers Theatre: *On the Air!*

With *On the Air!*, students create Readers Theatre tapes, which both the creators and other students can listen to and enjoy.

Selection: *The Whipping Boy* by Sid Fleischman. When the obnoxious Prince Brat decides to run away from the palace, he takes his whipping boy, Jemmy, with him. In a series of adventures in which the two lads meet up with all manner of low life outside the castle and end up trading identities, the two come to know themselves and each other better and in the end become friends.

Reading Purpose: To understand and enjoy the setting, language, and characterization in an award-winning piece of historical fiction.

Students: Fourth or fifth graders of average to high ability.

Goal of the Activity: To help students interpret and appreciate a piece of literature by using oral language to help make print come alive. To foster an understanding of life in England in a time gone by and to help students appreciate the enduring value of friendship.

Rationale: As the story suggests, life is more fun when its shared; so, too, with literature. Performing this tale not only gives students a chance to practice and hone their interpretive reading skills but also exposes them to the effective use of language and the insights we can gain about ourselves through literature.

Procedure: Background information: Students in this class have performed works using Readers Theatre a number of times prior to this activity. They have also made a collection of story tapes they call "Radio Show," tapes for students to listen to in their spare time. The best of these have been duplicated and given to the media center for other students in the school to listen to.

Read the first few chapters aloud to students, delivering the dialog of the two main characters, Jemmy and Prince Brat, with the pizazz you would like to inspire in students for their own oral readings. After you have finished reading, discuss with students whether or not they think this would be a good story to perform as a Readers Theatre activity and to add to their collection of radio show tapes. If they show interest, divide the class into groups of three or four students, and assign each group two or three chapters from the novel to prepare to read orally. (There are 20 short chapters in this 90-page book.)

After students have prepared their chapters, make tape recordings of their readings, complete with sound effects or other embellishments they have come up with.

Adapting the Activity: As mentioned earlier, Terrell Young and Sylvia Vardell (1993) have reported Readers Theatre's success with nonfiction materials across the curriculum—in math using David M. Schwartz's *How Much is a Million?* and in science using Joanna Cole's *The Magic School Bus Lost in the Solar System* and Billy Goodman's *A Kid's Guide to How to Save the Planet.* For the latter selection, a seventh-grade teacher turned the text into a Readers Theatre script by creating a radio call-in show hosted by Earthman Jack and other DJs. Other possible nonfiction texts for creating Readers Theatre tapes are Tomie dePaola's *The Popcorn Book,* Ina Chang's *A Separate Battle: Women and the Civil War,* and Russell Freedman's *Buffalo Hunt.* Also, Shelbey Anne Wolf (1993) has used Readers Theatre successfully with Arlene Mosel's *Tikki Tikki Tembo* with ESL students.

Reflection: Students typically enjoy performing, and because a part can be made as brief as necessary for a particular student to succeed with it, every student can experience success in reading a part. Still, if some students are reluctant to participate as readers, they can be assigned to create sound effects, introduce the readers, or be in charge of production (operating and caring for equipment). In time, and with encouragement, these reluctant readers might eventually risk taking a reading part, but until then they will learn about language by listening to others and gain confidence in their abilities by contributing to the group project. Students can experience success in a myriad of ways. It is up to us as teachers to create conditions that guarantee all students successful experiences.

Oral Reading Sample Activity 3:
Oral Interactions: *Flag It*

In *Flag It,* students use self-stick notes to mark passages in the text. *Flag It* combines teacher oral reading, guided silent reading, and student oral reading to stimulate discussion on certain aspects of a text. This activity is based on one suggested by Hoyt (1992).

Selection: *Shadows on the Wall* by Phyllis Reynolds Naylor. *Shadows on the Wall* is the first of three books about Dan Roberts and his time-travel adventures that take him to York, England in various periods of its history. In this first book, Dan is visiting present-day York with his mother and father, who have come there to trace their family's history. Dan's paternal grandfather had

Huntington's disease, and they want to find out what other family members also had the disease. As Dan roams the fortress at York, he sees visions of Roman soldiers and experiences unsettling sensations he cannot explain. Dan becomes friends with Joe Stanton, a local cab driver and tour guide, and learns that Joe has visions similar to his own. Joe introduces Dan to a family of Gypsies, the Faws. Dan will meet Joe and the Faws again in different periods of York's history in subsequent books. In this story, Dan is whisked back to the time when the Romans had built a fortress at York, then called Elboracum. One of the younger Faws gives Dan an ancient Roman coin that plays a significant part in the next two books.

Students: Fifth graders of average to high ability.

Reading Purpose: To enjoy a well-written fantasy with the secondary purpose of considering how the author develops the theme of courage through the main character, Dan.

Goal of Activity: To help students better understand the characters and events in the story and to appreciate literature's capacity to portray universal themes; to give students an opportunity to practice oral reading and provide a forum for sharing ideas and listening to the ideas of others.

Rationale: *Shadows on the Wall* is a story with both external and internal conflict. Having students look for examples of outward action that reflects what a character is experiencing inwardly—intellectually, spiritually, and emotionally—can help them see the connection between what we do and who we are. Also, reading aloud gives students a chance to hear well-written material and practice their oral reading skills. Discussion gives students the opportunity to think more carefully about their responses, practice defending and justifying a viewpoint, and hear and learn from others' interpretations.

Procedure: Begin by reading and discussing the quote by Plutarch at the beginning of Chapter One, "I am whatever was, or is, or will be . . . ."

Explain that there are many things about Dan, the main character in *Shadows On the Wall* by Phyllis Reynolds Naylor, that he has no control over—things such as his build, the color of his eyes, his intelligence, his ancestry, the past, and the fact that he is spending the spring with his parents in York, England. Have students discuss those things about themselves and their lives over which they have no control. Explain that although there are many things about Dan's life that he can't change, there is one thing that he can control—how he chooses to respond to the circumstances of his life. For example, he might have chosen to spend his days in York watching TV or reading magazines but instead decides to find out as much as he can about the place. In choosing this course of action, Dan encounters both fascinating and frightening situations, some of which require small amounts of courage and some a good deal.

Tell students they are going to read the novel using an activity called Flag It. In this activity they will use self-stick notes to keep track of the incidences in the story in which Dan showed courage. Then, after they have finished reading the novel, they will get the chance to read these portions aloud and discuss how they illustrate courage.

Demonstrate how students will do this activity by reading the first chapter aloud, pausing at those places that you think illustrate courage, showing students how you would mark these passages with a self-stick note, and telling them what you might write on the note. For example, for your flag on page 4 where Dan is jogging around York, you might comment, "It takes courage to jog in a strange place, especially when you think someone might be following you!"; for pages 11 and 12 where Dan wanted to gain access to the Treasury House cellars, "Dan went to the Treasurer's House to try and see the ghosts of the Roman soldiers!"; and for page 17 when Dan finally gathers courage to ask his Dad the question he'd been dreading, "It took courage for Dan to ask his dad if he were sick because Dan was afraid of what his answer might be."

After you have modeled this procedure and students understand what they are to do, give them pads of self-stick notes and have them read the novel on their own, flagging those passages they feel illustrate Dan's courage.

When students have finished reading, have them get together in pairs or small groups to read their passages aloud and discuss how they illustrate courage. Before the groups begin their discussions, we recommend you lead a demonstration of the oral reading and discussion procedures they are to use. This might consist of calling on volunteers to read their flagged passages for Chapter Two and explain why they think the passages illustrates courage. Doing this will allow you to clear up any misunderstandings before students work on their own. While students are meeting in their groups, you might sit in on a group as a participant or circulate among the groups giving support and encouragement.

The activity might conclude with a whole group discussion focusing on those passages in which students feel Dan showed the greatest amount of courage. Students can read these passages aloud and tell why they think they demonstrate great courage. In addition, some sort of evaluative discussion is in order, with students answering such questions as:

- Was this a worthwhile activity? Why or why not?
- Did the group work go smoothly? Why or why not?
- If we use this activity again, what might we do differently?

Adapting the Activity: Flag It can be used with narrative or expository materials in which you want students to focus on a certain aspect of the text. For example, you might use Flag It to have students flag those incidents in Jerry Spinelli's *Fourth Grade Rats* in which Suds exhibits "rat-like" characteristics. In the discussion, students can tell how Suds feels about his rat-like behavior in each of these incidences. Flag It might also be used with an informational book such as *Inside and Outside You* by Sandra Markle for students to flag the five most interesting things they learned about their insides. Or, while students read the biography, *I Have a Dream* by Margaret Davidson, they might flag the five most important events in Martin Luther King, Jr.'s life. Their individual responses, which are likely to reflect some interesting differences, will make for lively discussions.

Reflection: As you can see, Flag It is a guided reading activity with an oral reading component. Typically, an activity such as this is preceded by prereading experiences that could include a number of different activities but definitely should include a discussion of the elements of fantasy and time-travel. Some students may have a fairly well-developed schemata for fantasy and time-travel from other books they have read or from movies or television. However, others may need additional information to make the narrative more understandable and enjoyable. Also prerequisite to this activity is having students think about courage, the trait they will be focusing on in this particular Flag It activity. To encourage this engagement, students could either write about or discuss, in small groups or as a whole class, incidences from their own lives that exemplify difficult circumstances and that have called for courage on their part.

We presented this activity as if this were the students' first encounter with the novel; however, you might introduce this activity after students have read through the novel once for pure pleasure. This will depend on you and your students' preferences. Some students do better reading a story from beginning to end without having to stop and physically interact with it. Others profit from stopping and considering matters from time to time.

Modifying the Text

The central purpose of SREs is to ensure that students have success in reading—that they are able to engage in meaning making and will gain new knowledge, new insights, and a sense of accomplishment from a reading selection. For some students, achieving success requires your presenting a selection in a form that is a variation of the original. Sometimes because of what is either required by your school district or what is available, the material may be too challenging for some students. In these cases, modifying or shortening the selections is a viable option.

Let us say, for instance, you are a fifth-grade teacher and your school district requires that students learn the concepts presented in the state-adopted U. S. history text. While the text is written at a fifth- to sixth-grade reading level, the reading ability of the students in your class ranges from second grade to twelfth grade. If the material in this text is going to be made accessible to the students reading well below fifth grade level, something may need to be done to the material. This might mean tape recording some sections, assigning only certain portions of the text to read, or writing (or having students write) simplified versions or summaries of the most important concepts.

As another example, suppose your second-grade class contains a number of ESL students and the social studies curriculum includes selections on families and community workers. Most of the trade books and pamphlets included in the prepackaged unit supplied by your school demand English reading skills. In this situation, you might pair your ESL second graders with sixth-grade students and have the older students help the second graders write books of their own, one on community workers and the other on families. The sixth graders could then write a simplified version of the community workers booklet based on the topics in the social studies selections. For the booklet on the family, the ESL students could dictate information about their own families that the sixth graders write down in a booklet for the second graders to read. Obviously, the ESL second graders will not be reading the same words as the students who read the trade books and commercially prepared pamphlets, but the ideas will be similar and they will be *reading*.

Sometimes, it isn't feasible or even advisable for students to read an entire selection. When lack of time or other constraints make reading an entire selection impractical, shortening the reading assignment is one workable option. In doing this, you have students read only selected portions of a chapter, the topics you feel are most important for them to understand. Of course, students will miss some of the information presented in the chapter, but assuming they cannot or will not read all of it, success in reading part of it is certainly preferable to failure in reading all of it. Moreover, as Walter Kintsch and Tuen van Dijk (1978) have emphasized, what readers typically remember after reading a text is its gist; by no means do they remember everything.

As mentioned previously, another way to make difficult material accessible to your students is to tape record a selection for students to listen to as they read along silently in the text. You, or competent students, can make the recordings, or you can purchase commercial tapes. Recordings can make material accessible to less able readers as well as provide models of good oral reading.

Recent work done by Margaret McKeown and her colleagues (McKeown, Beck, & Worthy, 1993) on Questioning the Author suggests another possibility for modifying text. Readers sometimes blame themselves for not understanding text when, in fact, the fault may lie with the writer. The writer, perhaps, has assumed too much background knowledge on the part of his or her audience or simply has not presented ideas clearly or with sufficient elaboration to make them understandable. When you run across texts like these, you might have the students themselves rewrite short segments of the text so that it makes sense to them. "How would you write this paragraph," you might ask them, "to make it more understandable?"

Students should acknowledge the author's expertise and knowledge but not be intimidated by it or believe that printed text is beyond reproach. If they aren't building meaning with a text, the fault may not lie with them but with the author. Grappling with the ideas—rewording, rearranging, and embellishing—may be the only way meaning building will take place. Students at all levels of reading ability can grapple with and rewrite problemetic sections of texts in order to understand them. Students might do this rewriting in groups or pairs, with their main question being "How can we rewrite this—rephrase, reorganize, add, subtract—to make it more understandable?" Alternately, you and the students might discuss these problematic sections with the goal of clarifying the author's meaning.

Doing something with the reading material to make it more accessible to students is yet another way to help ensure that students both understand and enjoy what they read. The following example represents one possibility.

Modifying the Text Sample Activity: *Focusing*

In *Focusing*, instead of assigning an entire chapter or selection, you choose certain portions of the material for students to read.

Selection: "Electricity" from *Science in Your World* (Hackett & Moyer, 1991). In this science text chapter, static electricity, current electricity, and circuits are discussed. Other topics covered are electricity in the home, electric motors, and measuring electric usage. A special section on pacemakers is also included.

Students: Sixth graders of low to average ability.

Reading Purpose: To expand students' knowledge of electricity—what it is and its uses.

Goal of Activity: To focus on certain key concepts in the text and make these ideas more accessible to students by creating a reading experience of a length that they can handle successfully.

Rationale: In deciding what portions of this chapter on electricity students will read, we take into account what students already know about the topic, the difficulty of the material, and how much time could reasonably be spent covering the chapter. If students had studied static and current electricity previously, it is appropriate to briefly review these topics in a group discussion and then have students read the sections on circuits, electricity in the home, electric motors, and measuring electric usage on their own.

Procedure: Prior to the lesson, write the following outline on the chalkboard:

ELECTRICITY

Static Electricity—Discuss

Current Electricity—Discuss

    Circuits—Read pages 82–84

Electricity in Your Home—Read pages 86–89

    Electric Motors—Read pages 90–91

    Measuring Electric Usage—Read pages 92–93

    Pacemakers—Page 96, optional

Draw students' attention to the outline on the chalkboard. Tell them that since you have discussed static and current electricity already, they are only to read the sections on circuits, electricity in the home, electric motors, and measuring electric usage. The section on pacemakers is optional reading. Explain that after they have finished reading, the class as a whole will discuss the required sections, and volunteers can discuss the section on pacemakers.

Adapting the Activity: Shortening selections by assigning only certain portions of a piece works best for expository material that contains previously covered information, text that is too lengthy and too challenging to be read in its entirety by your students, or material that contains information you feel your students don't need to deal with at the present time. If you want your students to get the information in Russell Freedman' book *Immigrant Kids,* for example, but don't feel they could handle the book alone in the time they have, you could assign reading specific chapters to groups of students, who would be responsible for writing a summary of their chapter, and make these available for other students to read. Or, instead of every student reading each of the folk tales included in Virginia Hamilton's collection of African American folk tales called *The People Could Fly*, groups of students could choose one of the tales to read and then present a dramatization of their chosen tale. In this way, although students read only one story, they are able to learn about and enjoy each of them.

Reflection: The purpose of students' reading the chapter is to add to their knowledge of electricity. An activity such as this one reduces the amount of information students have to deal with, thereby increasing the chances of their successfully understanding and retaining the most crucial concepts they need for further understanding electricity and related topics. Reducing the amount of text students need to read is an extremely simple task, both conceptually and practically. However, it can pay enormous dividends in terms of students successfully building meaning with those parts of the text you do ask them to read.

• During-reading: A Final Word •

How do you decide what sort of during-reading activities will benefit your students? First of all, as is the case with any of the three phases of SREs—pre-, during- or postreading—the kinds of activities your students engage in will depend on their needs, interests, and abilities; the material they are reading; and their purposes for reading. Are they reading for pleasure or information? What is it they need or want to get from the text? If they are reading primarily to enjoy a well-told tale, then preparing a study guide for them would almost certainly be a waste of time. However, if their purpose is to read and understand the salient features of the industrial revolution as they are described in a social studies text, they might be able to benefit from a reading guide designed to help them focus on cause and effect. As is the case with prereading, the purpose of during-reading activities is to provide a scaffold that will help students achieve their reading goals. As is also the case with prereading, as well as with postreading, there is the matter of your time to consider. There simply is not time for you to create all of the activities you might like to, and so you must focus on creating those that will best help your students succeed in the reading they do.

References

Atwell, N. (1987). *In the middle: Writing, reading, and learning with adolescents.* Portsmouth, NH: Boynton/Cook. In this popular book, Atwell discusses her concepts of reading and writing workshops, mini-lessons, and a number of other contemporary pedagogical approaches to literacy instruction.

Graves, M.F., Watts, S., & Graves, B.B. (1994). *Essentials of classroom teaching: Elementary reading methods.* Needham Heights, MA: Allyn and Bacon. This concise text contains a thorough discussion of how to teach comprehension strategies as well as information on how to teach most of the other components of a comprehensive elementary reading program.

Heimlich, J.E., & Pittelman, S.D. (1986). *Semantic mapping: Classroom applications.* Newark, DE: International Reading Association. A very practical guide to using semantic mapping for a variety of purposes.

Hoyt, L. (1992). Many ways of knowing: Using drama, oral interactions, and the visual arts to enhance 'reading comprehension. *The Reading Teacher, 45,* 580–584. This brief article does just what the title indicates.

Kintsch, W., & van Dijk, T. (1978). Toward a model of text comprehension and production. *Psychological Review, 85,* 363–394. A technical and challenging yet very insightful discussion of how we understand and remember text.

Martin, B. (1992). Afterword. In B.E. Cullinan (Ed.), *Invitation to Read: More children's literature in the classroom* (pp. 179–182). Newwark, DE: International Reading Association. A heartfelt statement on the importance of reading aloud by a leading children's author.

McCauley, J.K. & McCauley, D.S. (1992). Using choral reading to promote language learning for ESL students. *The Reading Teacher, 45,* 526–533. Clearly explains the value of choral reading for students learning English as a second language.

McKeown, M.G., Beck, I.L. & Worthy, M.J. (1993). Grappling with text ideas: Questioning the author. *The Reading Teacher, 46,* 560–566. A very clever approach to getting students deeply involved with text.

Miller, G.A. (1956). The magical number seven, plus-or-minus two: Some limits on our capacity for processing information. *Psychological Review, 63,* 81–97. A true classic, significant for its contributions to both theory and practice.

Ollmann, H.E. (1992). Two-column response to literature. *Journal of Reading, 36,* 58–59. Suggests a format for students to use in interpreting and responding to literature.

Pearson, P.D., & Johnson, D.D. (1978). *Teaching reading comprehension.* New York: Holt, Rinehart and Winston. Probably the first text to present a view of teaching reading consistent with cognitive psychology, this book contains one of, if not *the*, earliest treatments of semantic mapping.

Rosenblatt, L. (1978). *The reader, the text, the poem: The transactional theory of the literary work.* Carbondale, IL: Southern Illinois Press. One of several presentations of Rosenblatt's very influential response theory.

Trelease, J. (1989). *The new read-aloud handbook* (2nd ed.). New York: Penguin. This bestseller contains a wealth of insights for both teachers and parents.

Wittrock, M.C. (1990). Generative processes of comprehension. *Educational Psychologist, 24,* 345–376. A concise overview of generative comprehension processes.

Wolf, S.A. (1993). What's in a name? Labels and literacy in Readers Theatre. *The Reading Teacher, 46,* 546–551. Discusses the potential of Readers Theatre for students labeled at risk.

Young, T.A. & Vardell, S. (1993). Weaving Readers Theatre and nonfiction into the curriculum. *The Reading Teacher, 46,* 396–406. Presents many ways for using Readers Theatre with informational trade books.

Children's Books Cited

Alexander, G. (1991). *The jungle book.* New York: Arcade.

Anderson, J. (1989). *Spanish pioneers of the Southwest.* New York: Lodestar.

Anderson, J. (1986). *Pioneer children of Appalachia.* New York: Lodestar.

Anderson, J. (1990). *Pioneer settlers of New France.* New York: Lodestar.

Asimov, I. (1990). *How did we find out about Neptune?* New York: Walker.

Avi. (1990). *The true confessions of Charlotte Doyle.* New York: Orchard.

Aylesworth, J. (1991). *Country crossing.* New York: Atheneum.

Benet, R. & S.V. (1965). "Nancy Hanks," in *Arrow book of poetry* selected by Ann McGovern. New York: Scholastic.

Brooks, B. (1990). *Everywhere.* New York: HarperCollins.

Chang, I. (1991). *A separate battle: Women and the Civil War.* New York: Lodestar.

Cole, J. (1990). *The magic school bus lost in the solar system.* New York: Scholastic.

Davidson, M. (1986). *I have a dream, the story of Martin Luther King, Jr.* New York: Scholastic.

dePaola, T. (1978). *The popcorn book.* New York: Holiday House.

Fisher, A. (1965). "Weather is Full of the Nicest Sounds," in *Arrow book of poetry* selected by Ann McGovern. New York: Scholastic.

Fleischman, P. (1988). *A joyful noise: Poems for two voices.* New York: Harper & Row.

Fleischman, S. (1986). *The whipping boy.* New York: Greenwillow.

Forrester, V. (1985). *A latch against the wind.* New York: Atheneum.

Freedman, R. (1988). *Buffalo hunt.* New York: Holiday House.

Freedman, R. (1980). *Immigrant kids.* New York: E. P. Dutton.

Freedman, R. (1987). *Lincoln: A photobiography.* New York: Clarion.

Gibbons, G. (1990). *Weather words and what they mean.* New York: Holiday House.

Goodman, B. (1990). *A kid's guide to how to save the planet.* New York: Avon Books.

Hackett, J.K., & Moyer, R.H. (1991). *Science in Your World.* New York: Macmillan/McGraw-Hill.

Hall, B. (1990). *Dixie storms.* San Diego: Harcourt Brace Jovanovich.

Hamilton, V. (1990). *Cousins.* New York: Philomel.

Hamilton, V. (1985). *The people could fly.* New York: Knopf.

Kennedy, R. (1985). *Amy's eyes.* New York: Harper & Row.

Lester, L. (1968). *To be a slave.* New York: E. P. Dutton.

Litowinsky, O. (1991). *The high voyage: The final crossing of Christopher Columbus.* New York: Delacorte.

Lowry, L. (1989). *Number the stars.* New York: Dell.

Markle, S. (1991). *Inside outside you.* New York: Bradbury.

Marshak, S. (1990). *Hail to mail.* New York: Henry Holt.

Meltzer, M. (1990). *Bill of Rights.* New York: HarperCollins.

Mosel, A. (1968). *Tikki tikki tembo*. New York: Henry Holt.

Naylor, P.R. (1980). *Shadows on the wall*. New York: Atheneum.

Paulsen, G. (1987). *Hatchet*. New York: Bradbury.

Pendergraft, P. (1987). *Miracle at Clement's Pond*. New York: Philomel.

Peters, L.W. (1991). *Water's way*. New York: Arcade.

Prelutsky, J. (1984). *The new kid on the block*. New York: William Morrow.

Rosen, M. (1989). *We're going on a bear hunt*. New York: McElderry Books.

Rylant, C. (1990). *A couple of kooks and other stories about love*. New York: Orchard.

Rylant, C. (1991). *Appalachia: The voices of sleeping birds*. San Diego: CA: Harcourt Brace Jovanovich.

Sandburg, C. (1965). "Buffalo Dusk," in *Arrow book of poetry* selected by Ann McGovern. New York: Scholastic.

Sanfield, S. (1989). *The adventures of high John the conqueror*. New York: Orchard.

Schami, R. (1990). *A hand full of stars*. New York: Dutton.

Schwartz, D.M. (1985). *How much is a million?* New York: Lothrop, Lee & Shepard.

Silverstein, S. (1974). *Where the sidewalk ends*. New York: Harper & Row.

Spinelli, J. (1991). *Fourth grade rats*. New York: Scholastic.

Spinelli, J. (1990). *Maniac Magee*. Boston: Little Brown.

Thesman, J. (1990). *Rachel Chance*. Boston: Houghton Mifflin.

Viorst, J. (1983). *If I were in charge of the world and other worries*. New York: Atheneum.

Wisniewski, D. (1989). *The warrior and the wiseman*. New York: Lothrop, Lee & Shepard.

6

Postreading Activities

Why engage students in postreading activities? What function do these sorts of activities serve in the scaffold? Why, after reading a selection, shouldn't students just go on to something else?

As Francis Bacon observed, "Some books are to be tasted, others to be swallowed, and some few to be chewed and digested." Not every reading experience needs to be followed by some activity. There will be times when students will read, reflect, and respond in their own personal way. When students are just "tasting" a selection, their reflection and response may be quite brief. Sometimes, however, it is appropriate to provide activities that encourage students to do something with the information and ideas in a selection after they have read it—to chew and digest. To determine the appropriateness and the type of activity called for, we turn once again to our model: Do the students, selection, and purpose suggest or require postreading activities?

Postreading activities encourage students to do something with the material they have just read, to think—critically, logically, and creatively—about the information and ideas that emerge from their reading, and sometimes to transform their thinking into action. We often perceive information or an idea from a text without much effort or involvement, but until we do something with it, it isn't really ours.

Read → Think and Elaborate ↔ Respond

As the model illustrates, in some cases we read, think and elaborate, and then respond; and that response may foster further thought and elaboration, which may, in turn, foster further response. Response can take a variety of forms—speaking, writing, dramatics, creative arts, construction, or application and outreach activities. In postreading activities, students recall what they've read and demonstrate understanding. They apply, analyze, synthesize, evaluate, and elaborate the information and ideas in a text and connect that information and ideas in a way that makes sense to themselves and to others. Postreading activities also provide opportunities for students to extend ideas, to explore new ways of thinking, doing, and seeing—to invent and create, to ponder the question "What if?"

We have divided postreading activities into seven categories.

Postreading

1. Questioning
2. Discussion
3. Writing
4. Drama
5. Artistic, Graphic, and Nonverbal Activities
6. Application and Outreach Activities
7. Reteaching

The activities in the first six categories encourage students to think in the ways we just suggested—to recall, understand, apply, analyze, synthesize, evaluate, and elaborate information and ideas; to make logical connections between and among ideas; to go beyond given information or ideas; and to explore new ways of thinking and of expressing themselves.

To these we have added a seventh category, reteaching. Reteaching is the safety net in the reading scaffold. You don't want students leaving a reading selection without a sense of accomplishment, of a job well done. Sometimes, if that goal hasn't been achieved, it means retracing steps to find out what didn't work and why, and then perhaps trying a different approach. You and your students are jointly account-able for a successful reading experience.

Obviously, this list is not the only way postreading activities might be described or categorized. As with the pre- and during-reading categories, our postreading categories are options. Although not all reading selections are meant to be "digested," some sort of postreading experience is often appropriate. Not engaging in postreading activities is a bit like taking a trip and promptly forgetting about it. If you want to keep that vacation memory alive, you need to do something further with it— perhaps put together a scrapbook or organize your slides, videos, and photographs and share them with friends. Postreading activities allow students to relive the read-ing adventure and to discover new insights to take from it, explore ways to act upon those discoveries, and build bridges to other experiences, whether those experiences come from their lives or from other texts.

Guide to Activities for Chapter 6

Questioning:	*Yellow Brick Road Story Map*
Discussion:	*Three's a Charm!*
	Both Sides: Discussion Web
Writing:	*Compare/Contrast*
	What If?
Drama:	*History Comes to Life*

Artistic, Graphic, and Nonverbal:	*Worth a Thousand Words*
Application and Outreach:	*Getting to Know You*
Reteaching:	*Play it Again, Sam*

Questioning

Questioning activities encourage students to think about and react—either orally or in writing—to the information and ideas in the material they have read. Questions might be designed to have students recall what they have read, show that they understand what was read, and apply, analyze, synthesize, or elaborate information and ideas. Questions might also encourage creative, interpretive, or metacognitive thinking. As an example of these various levels of thinking, here are some questions students might be asked to answer after reading *Shh! We're Writing the Constitution* by Jean Fritz:

Recalling: How many delegates were supposed to attend the grand convention in 1787?

Understanding: How did the delegates keep the proceedings a secret?

Applying: What are some things you might do to keep a secret meeting secret?

Analyzing: Why did the delegates decide to keep the proceedings a secret?

Synthesizing: What do you think might have happened if the public had found out what was going on in the meetings?

Evaluating: Do you think it was a good idea to keep the meetings a secret? Why or why not?

Elaborating: What do you think were the most effective features of the delegates' plan to keep the proceedings secret?

Creating: What if the delegates had decided there should be three presidents presiding over the nation instead of one? What might have happened?

Interpreting: How do you think Benjamin Franklin felt being the oldest delegate at the convention?

Thinking Metacognitively: Did you understand the author's description of the three branches of government on page 14? If not, what might you do to make this explanation clearer to you?

Questions that stimulate these various kinds of thinking are appropriate for either expository or narrative material. After they read narratives, questions can be developed that prompt students to focus on elements of theme, plot, and setting, or character traits, motives, and development. In Jerry Spinelli's *Fourth Grade Rats*, to please his best friend the protagonist, Suds, tries hard to make the transition from being a third-grade "angel" to a fourth-grade "rat." In doing so, he acquires some pretty obnoxious behavior. Questions such as "At first, why didn't Suds want to become a rat?" "What happened to make him change his mind?" and "What did he finally decide about being a rat and why?" can help lead students to discover the story's theme.

Questions that involve feelings are also appropriate for narratives. Students can be guided to examine the feelings of the characters in the story and their own emotional reactions as well. "How do you think Suds felt when he started saying 'no' to his Mom?" "Why do you think he felt this way?" "How do you think Suds' Mom felt when he said "no" to her?" "Why do you think she felt this way?" and "How did you feel about Suds' behavior toward his mother?"

Questions that lead students to think about universal themes and feelings help them make the connection between literature and real life. As Dianne Monson (1992) has pointed out, if students can see themselves and their situations in the story characters, they may come to understand and appreciate art as a vehicle for expressing our common humanity.

Questions can also guide students toward becoming metacognitive readers: "Were there parts of the text you didn't understand?" "Why didn't you understand these?" "What might you do to better understand the ideas?" "Should you reread parts of the text, take some notes, draw a map, do some background reading, or ask a friend for assistance?" These kinds of questions encourage students to monitor their own understanding and focus their attention on considering and implementing fix-up strategies.

In responding to questions, students should generally be aware of their audience. For whom are they answering them? Themselves? Their teacher? Other students? The author? In the questions listed above for *Shh! We're Writing the Constitution*, the audience was a teacher. However, questions might also be constructed from the point of view of the author, as if the author were asking questions of the readers. For example, for the novel, *The Star Fisher*, by Lawrence Yep, author-asked questions might be "What do you like best about the character Emily?" "What is your favorite scene in the story and why do you like it?" "Did Emily say or do anything that helped or inspired you? If she did, what was it?" Students would answer these questions as if they were writing to Lawrence Yep himself. Or, for the informational book *Touch, Taste, and Smell* by Steve Parker, author-asked questions might be "What did you find most interesting about how you perceive a smell?" "Why did you find this part interesting?" "When you came across a word you didn't understand, what did you do?" and "How could I have helped you better understand what the word meant?"

Also, students might ask and answer their own questions. For example, after reading a chapter on California missions in their social studies text, they might write five questions they still have about the issues or topics in the chapter. To answer the questions, they might refer back to the text or look for the answers in other sources. Another possibility is to have students develop questions for the books they read that other students will answer. These questions can be written on a sheet of paper and placed in the book. Whoever reads the book next would write answers to the questions and give them to the student author. Together, the two students could discuss the questions and answers.

Another line of questioning, Questioning the Author, has been suggested by Margaret McKeown and her colleagues (McKeown, Beck, & Worthy, 1993). As we mentioned in Chapter 5 when talking about modifying text, students are often under the impression that if they do not understand what they read, the fault lies with them and certainly not with the author. This may or may not be the case. Students need to realize that authors are not infallible; they are not always the lucid communicators they attempt to be. Asking questions such as "What was the author trying to tell you?" "How could the author have expressed the ideas in a clearer way?" and "What would you want to say instead?" can prompt students to participate actively in building meaning from text.

Although postreading questioning activities sometimes serve to assess students' reading comprehension and their ability to think at various levels, the primary purpose of the postreading questioning we have described is to allow and encourage students to delve more deeply into the texts they read. Questioning activities tap into students' innate curiosity about the world and provide opportunities for them to think about and respond to information and ideas on a variety of levels. On the following pages is one example of a questioning activity.

Questioning Sample Activity: *The Yellow Brick Road*

In *The Yellow Brick Road*, questions are developed that follow in sequential order the information that is central to understanding the selection. These questions create what Isabel Beck and Margaret McKeown (1981) call a Story Map, a set of questions that, when answered, constitute the essence of the story.

Selection: *Vasilisa The Beautiful*, translated from the Russian by Thomas P. Whitney, illustrated by Nonny Hogrogian. On her deathbed, Vasilisa's mother gives her a magical doll to protect and guide her. After her mother dies, Vasilisa's father marries a widow with two daughters, who treat Vasilisa cruelly. One day while doing needlework with her stepsisters, their candle light goes out and Vasilisa is forced to get a light for their candle from Baba Yaga. Baba Yaga lives deep in the forest and devours any living things that bother her. Vasilisa is very frightened by the task, but the magical doll tells her that she will protect and help her. Because of the doll, Vasilisa is able to perform all the duties Baba Yaga demands, and the witch sends her back home with a light that destroys the evil stepmother and sisters. Vasilisa then goes to live with a kindly widow in town and, again with the help of the doll, weaves an incredibly fine cloth that the widow presents to the king as a gift. Next, Vasilisa makes shirts for the king out of the cloth, and when he meets her and sees how beautiful she is, he asks her to marry him. Finally, in traditional folk tale style, they live happily ever after.

Students: Fourth graders of mixed abilities.

Reading Goal: To understand and enjoy a traditional folk tale.

Goal of Activity: To focus students' attention on the important events of the story in the order in which they take place.

Rationale: As do most folk tales, *Vasilisa The Beautiful* includes a number of events that follow a predictable order. Having students answer questions about important story events in the sequence in which they occur can help promote comprehension of this particular story as well as help develop a general schema for story sequence.

Procedure: Decide first what the starting point for the story is. Next, list briefly the major events that reveal the essence of the story in the order in which they occur. Write a question for each event. Below are the major events and matching questions for *Vasilisa The Beautiful*.

Event 1: Vasilisa's mother gives her a magical doll just before she dies. *What did Vasilisa's mother give her before she died?*

Event 2: Vasilisa's father marries a widow with two daughters. *How did Vasilisa get a new mother and two stepsisters?*

Event 3: When Vasilisa's father's business takes him away for a long time, the stepmother moves her two daughters and Vasilisa to a house on the outskirts of a deep forest where the horrible witch Baba Yaga lives. *Where did Vasilisa's stepmother move Vasilisa and the two stepsisters?*

Event 4: While Vasilisa and her stepsisters are working one night, their candle light goes out, and they tell Vasilisa she must fetch a light from Baba Yaga. *Why did the stepsisters make Vasilisa go fetch the light from Baba Yaga?*

Event 5: When Vasilisa finally gets to Baba Yaga's, the witch tells her she must live with her. If she does all the work Baba Yaga tells her to do, she will give Vasilisa a light and not eat her up. *What did Baba Yaga tell Vasilisa she had to do?*

Event 6: With the help of the doll, Vasilisa is able to do all the difficult work Baba Yaga assigns her. *How was Vasilisa able to do all the work Baba Yaga gave her?*

Event 7: When Baba Yaga asks how Vasilisa was able to do all the work and Vasilisa tells her, "Mother's blessing helped me," Baba Yaga tells her to leave. The witch doesn't want anyone around her who has been blessed. *Why did Baba Yaga tell Vasilisa she didn't want her around anymore?*

Event 8: Baba Yaga gives Vasilisa a lighted skull and Vasilisa returns home. *What did Baba Yaga give Vasilisa to take home?*

Event 9: When she arrives at her stepmother's, the skull casts burning rays on the stepmother and sisters and pursues them everywhere until they are eventually only ashes. Vasilisa, however, is unharmed. *What happened to the stepmother and sisters when Vasilisa returned? Do you think it was fair? Why or why not?*

Event 10: Vasilisa goes to live with an old woman in the city, where she weaves a fine linen thread and makes a beautiful cloth. The old woman brings the cloth to the king as a gift. The king falls in love with Vasilisa and they are married. *How does weaving a cloth help Vasilisa at the end of the story?*

After constructing the questions, write a number for each on the "yellow brick" spaces as shown in Figure 6-1. Have students work in pairs of differing abilities to write the answers to the questions on a separate sheet of paper, or put the questions on a transparency and have students answer them as a group activity.

Adapting the Activity: This activity can be used for any story in which the events proceed in chronological order. Simply identify the events of the story that reveal its basic meaning and write a question for each. *Yellow Brick Road* might be used with *How the Ox Star Fell From Heaven*, a simply and clearly told Hmong folk tale by author-illustrator Lily Toy Hong; the Zimbabwean folk tale *Mufaro's Beautiful Daughters*, written and illustrated by John Steptoe; Aesop's fable *Androcles and the Lion*, retold and illustrated by Janet Steven; and many other folk tales, fables, and fairy tales.

Another way to use the story map is to laminate the yellow brick road (without the questions on it) to a manila file folder to use as a game board for the folk and fairy tales students read. Write two questions for each event in the individual stories on separate index cards. Number one set

Figure 6-1   The Yellow Brick Road Story Map

1. What did Vasilisa's mother give her before she died?

2. How did Vasilisa get a new mother and stepsisters?

3. Where did Vasilisa's stepmother move Vasilisa and the two stepsisters?

4. Why did the stepsisters make Vasilisa go fetch the light from Baba Yaga?

5. What did Baba Yaga tell Vasilisa she had to do?

6. How was Vasilisa able to do all the work Baba Yaga gave her?

7. Why did Baba Yaga tell Vasilisa she didn't want her around anymore?

8. What did Baba Yaga give Vasilisa to take home?

9. What happened to the stepmother and sisters when Vasilisa when Vasilisa returned? Do you think it was fair? Why or why not?

10. How does weaving a cloth help Vasilisa at the end of the story?

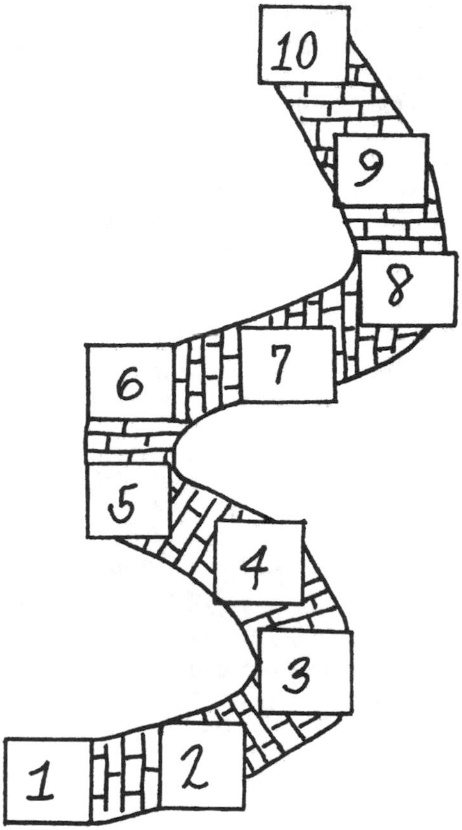

of cards 1A, 2A, 3A, etc. and the other set 1B, 2B, 3B, etc., and put possible answers on the back of each card. Players take turns answering from either set A or B in chronological order. If a player answers to his or her partner's satisfaction, he or she can move up to the next space. The other player then has the chance to move forward by answering the other question correctly. The first person to reach "The End" is the winner. The story board game and folder can be used for many different selections; simply change the questions to coincide with the story. The answers for open-ended questions such as #9, "Do you think it was fair?" will have no right or wrong answer. Some rules will need to be established beforehand to determine acceptable answers.

Reflection: You may have noticed that most of the questions in our story map are largely literal ones dealing with specific events of the story. Beck and McKeown define a story map as a sequenced list of important events and ideas in a story, and they note that story maps include some inferential questions, since fully understanding a story requires at least some inferences. We certainly agree. Nevertheless, we have found that our story maps for simple stories, such as Vasilisa The Beautiful, contain largely literal questions. For this reason, as Beck and McKeown note, story map questions are not the only questions to ask on reading selections. Once students understand the essence of the story, then interpre-

tive, analytical, and creative questions are appropriate and important to pursue. However, in Beck and McKeown's judgment and in our's, these are best considered after the story map has been established in students' minds.

Although the Story Map was developed for narratives, similar guidelines can be followed when constructing questions for informational material by creating questions that coincide with the organizational approach taken by the author. For example, questions for texts that present lists of details and concrete examples can reflect that organization, "What are three words that describe the Vietnam Memorial?" Of course, in such instances you would want to ask only questions that deal with important details and examples, even if, as is too often the case, the text presents many unimportant details (Beck & McKeown, 1988).Other organizational patterns can also be paralleled with questions. Cause and effect questions can be developed for text that presents issues using that format, "What were the effects of the Boston Tea party?" Compare and contrast questions can be written for selections employing that organization, "In what three ways are lizards and snakes alike. In what three ways they different?' Whatever organizational scheme the author has chosen to develop his or her topic can be used and underscored by posing questions that parallel that organization.

Also, students themselves can be taught how to develop questions for selections for other students to answer. As a during-reading activity, students can compose questions while they read a selection that a partner or group members will answer as a postreading activity. Before students develop questions, however, they will need instruction on how to develop questions and the various kinds of questions they might ask.

Questioning activities encourage students to think about what they have read and to probe more deeply. By asking the appropriate kinds of questions, you can channel students' thinking and improve their comprehension and recall, as well as foster critical and creative thinking.

Discussion

Almost every classroom reading experience will include some sort of discussion—exchanging ideas out loud. The key word here is *exchanging*—some like to use the term *dialog* to describe the give-and-take nature of discussion. The intent of discussion is to explore ideas freely, to learn something new or gain a different perspective because of the information or insights more than one person has to give. Discussion fosters an active exchange of ideas, ideally one in which everyone has the opportunity to participate equally. Discussion provides an opportunity to solidify, clarify, or modify knowledge. Discussion activities give students a forum in which to talk about the meaning *they* constructed from texts, listen to the insights of *others,* and weigh their responses in light of those of their classmates. Here, they can think about, ponder, consider, analyze, evaluate, and make connections between the text and their own lives and among the ideas in the text, their personal experiences, and the thoughts and experiences of their classmates.

Discussion groups can be teacher led or student led. They can involve the entire class, small groups, or pairs. Whatever format is used, here are a few guidelines for implementing discussions:

- Develop a clear purpose or purposes—What is it the discussion is to accomplish? Are students examining two or more sides of an issue? Are they looking to discover a book's theme? Are they trying to solve a problem? Master the content of a text? Discussion should not be rigidly structured, but without clear purpose or focus it runs the risk of deteriorating into meaningless chit-chat.
- Discussion leaders (as well as participants) should be supportive, non-critical, and open-minded. Leaders should encourage response from all members of the group and be sparing with their own comments and suggestions.
- Discussion prompts might include or begin with literal level questions but should go beyond these to stimulate critical and creative thinking. Discussions should incorporate a number of levels of thinking—recalling, applying, analyzing, synthesizing, evaluating, and interpreting.
- When differences of opinions arise concerning literal or recall questions, the text should be consulted in order to verify or refute positions.
- Encourage group members to evaluate discussions. Was the purpose achieved? Did everyone get a chance to participate equally? What were the strengths of the discussion? Weaknesses? What might be done differently in the future?

A sample activity is shown below.

Discussion Sample Activity: *Both Sides*

Both Sides is a Discussion Web activity (Alvermann, 1991) in which students use a graphic aid to help them look at both sides of an issue before drawing conclusions. In this activity, students meet in pairs and then as groups of four to reach a consensus about a question raised by their reading.

Selection: *Frozen Fire* by James Houston. *Frozen Fire* is the story of Matthew Morgan and his Eskimo friend Kayak, who battle to stay alive in the harsh Canadian wilderness close to the Arctic circle while attempting to rescue Matthew's father and a helicopter pilot.

Students: Sixth graders of mixed abilities.

Reading Goal: To understand and enjoy an exciting survival story.

Goal of the Activity: To help students understand how literature can be a medium for learning about the various ways people respond to similar situations and issues and to provide all students with the opportunity to voice their opinions and work toward coming to a group consensus.

Rationale: *Frozen Fire* poses a number of questions worth pondering. One in particular arises from an incident in which Matthew discovers gold nuggets at a frozen waterfall. The boys have given up their search for Matthew's dad and are desperately trying to make their way back to Frobisar. Their food supply is nearly gone, and death is imminent if they don't reach Frobisar soon. However, overjoyed at the fortune within his grasp, Matthew loads his pockets and backpack with the precious metal against Kayak's warning that the gold will be only a hindrance to their struggle to get home. Since most students this age are intrigued by the idea of instant fortune, the question "Should Matthew have taken the gold nuggets?" should make for a lively discussion.

Procedure: On the chalkboard, a transparency, or individual worksheets duplicate the following chart.

Reasons

———				———
———				———
———	**NO**	Should Matthew have taken	**YES**	———
———		the gold nuggets?		———
———				———
———				———

Conclusions

Pair students and explain that they are to discuss the pros and cons of Matthew's taking the gold nuggets. Encourage them to come up with good reasons for both sides of the issue and to write these down on a sheet of paper. Stress that initially the goal is to get down all possible reasons for and against taking the gold, *not* to support one position or the other. Explain that they might want to refer to their books but need only write key words or phrases in the appropriate column. They should try to give an equal number of reasons in each column.

Below are some sample responses.

Reasons

Didn't belong to him	Didn't belong to anybody
Were worthless in Arctic	Would make him rich
Kayak told him not to	Would have made his dad happy

NO   Should Matthew have taken   YES
the gold nuggets?

Would slow Matthew down	Could buy things for Kayak's family
Could cost him his life	If took only a few, would have been a little richer

Conclusions

After the partners have had a chance to jot down their reasons, pair one set of partners with another set. Ask the new groups of four students to compare their reasons why Matthew should or shouldn't have taken the gold nuggets. Explain to students that while the goal is to work toward a consensus, it is perfectly acceptable for members to disagree with that conclusion. Tell them that you will have a large group discussion at the end of the period in which dissenting views will be heard.

When the groups of four have reached their conclusions, select a spokesperson for each or have students select their own. Give each group about three minutes to choose the one reason that best supports the group's conclusion, and have the spokesperson jot it down. When each group has chosen its reason, call on the different spokespersons to report their group's decision. At this time, ask the spokesperson to also give any dissenting viewpoints and the support for these positions.

As a follow-up activity to the Discussion Web, you might want to have students write their individual answers to the question "Should Matthew have taken the gold nuggets?" and post these in the classroom for others to read.

Adapting the Activity: The *Both Sides* activity can be used any time students read material that raises a question that might evoke dissenting viewpoints. For example, in *In the Year of the Boar and Jackie Robinson* by Bette Bao Lord, Emily, the sixth-grade class president, is supposed to present Jackie Robinson with the key to P.S. 8 but gives the honor instead to Shirley Wong, the protagonist in the story. Students might use the Discussion Web to decide the answer to the question, "Should Shirley have allowed Emily to give her the honor of making the presentation to Jackie Robinson?" Or after reading *The Kids from Kennedy Middle School: Choosing Sides* by Ilene Cooper, students might discuss the question, "Should Jon have quit the basketball team?" Also, the Discussion Web can be modified to use across the curriculum. Suppose students have read a selection on the Civil War that discusses Stephen A. Douglas and Abraham Lincoln and their opposing views on the slavery issue. As a postreading activity, you might substitute the names DOUGLAS and LINCOLN for the YES and NO columns of the Discussion Web, write *slavery* in the box where the question usually goes, and have students discuss the two men's differing views on the issue.

Reflection: Although the primary purpose of this activity is to discuss the pros and cons of an issue before drawing conclusions, in many cases this activity could generate further discussion leading to a consideration of a story's theme. Such a discussion might be prompted by a question such as "Why did the author include this episode?" This in turn might lead to these considerations: "Was he trying to show the contrast between what has value in a wilderness survival situation contrasted to the values of civilization?' or "Was he making a statement about the cost of individual greed on collective survival?"

Quality literature and non-fiction serve the purpose of generating and communicating ideas—ideas humans need to survive, to make strides personally and collectively. Discussion provides not only a forum to make ideas accessible to students but also a way to take sparks and create flames.

Writing

E. M. Forster said, "I don't know what I think until I see what I said." For many of us, that adage rings very true. Writing is the twin sister of reading, a powerful way to integrate what you know with the information presented in a text as well as to find out what you really understand and what you don't. Writing is powerful because it requires a reader to manipulate information and ideas actively. Unfortunately, the significance of the link between reading and writing has only recently been adequately recognized, and only now is this powerful relationship beginning to be made full use of in the classroom.

Obviously, writing does not lie exclusively in the domain of postreading activities. Writing also has its place as both a prereading activity—a tool for motivating, for activating background knowledge, for relating a selection to students' lives—and as a during-reading activity—a device for guiding students' thought processes as they build meaning from a text. But writing is often particularly useful as a postreading activity. As a postreading activity, writing can serve all the purposes we listed at the beginning of the chapter—demonstrating understanding of the information and ideas presented in a text; applying, analyzing, synthesizing, evaluating, and elaborating text information and ideas; and connecting information and ideas in a logical way. Writing also provides opportunities for students to extend ideas, to explore new ways of thinking, doing, and seeing—to invent, evaluate, create, and ponder.

In discussing writing activities, we focus on two issues that go hand in hand—purpose and audience. Why are we encouraging students to write? What purpose does the writing serve? And for whom is the student writing—himself or herself, or someone else?

Breaking down writing purposes into two broad categories—writing to learn and writing to communicate with others—should help you identify the kinds of writing you can encourage students to do after they read a selection, as well as determine the appropriate audience for their writing. However, it is important to keep in mind that whether students are writing to learn, to explore, or to communicate, they are actively manipulating ideas and language. Thus, learning is always taking place.

Shown below are some writing activities appropriate for each of these purposes.

Writing Activities for Learning about Oneself or the World

Audience: Self

Informational Writing	*Creative Writing*
Personal journals	Stories
Diaries of daily events	Poems
Free writing	Freewriting
Learning logs	
Charts and diagrams	
Notes, summaries, time lines, and outlining	

Writing Activities for Communicating with Others

Audiences: Teachers, other students, authors, family members, perspective employers, and the greater community of readers

Informational Writing	*Creative Writing*
Letters	Poetry
Reports	Stories
Charts and diagrams	Plays
Dialogue journals	Creative non-fiction
Essays	Memoirs
	Biographies
	Essays

In the first of the two writing activities that follow, students are writing primarily for themselves; in the second, they are writing primarily for others.

Writing Sample Activity 1—Writing to Learn:
Compare/Contrast

In *Compare/Contrast*, after completing a Venn diagram students write three paragraphs to compare and contrast two topics.

Selection: The chapter "Members of Our Solar System" in *Science in Your World* (Hackett & Moyer, 1991). The last section of this chapter, "Other Members of Our Solar System," explains how comets and meteoroids are both members of our solar system. Comets, which come from the far outer edges of the solar system, have very large orbits and are composed of ice mixed with dust particles. Meteoroids are small pieces of metal or rock that are scattered in different orbits around the sun.

Students: Students of mixed abilities; three gifted students.

Reading Goal: To understand the concepts of comets and meteroids—what part they play in the solar system, the differences between them, and the similarities they share—in order to appreciate the intricacies and diversity of the universe as well as the laws that govern it.

Goal of Activity: To help students organize the textual information on comets and meteroids, showing similarities and differences to understand better what comets and meteoroids are and how they function as members of our solar system.

Rationale: Although they may have heard the terms, most students will probably not have a good understanding of exactly what comets and meteoroids are; in fact, they may well lump the two together. After having read the first part of the chapter, they will have learned about the planets, their differing orbits, and how the planets themselves share differences as well as similarities. Having students organize the textual information on comets and meteoroids by using a graphic aid such as a Venn diagram will aid them in understanding, remembering, and appreciating these two concepts. Completing a Venn diagram requires that students classify information to highlight differences and similarities. They then use the completed diagram to write three paragraphs—one describing the unique qualities of comets, one the unique qualities of meteroids, and one the qualities the two have in common.

Procedure: After students have finished reading the chapter on the solar system, briefly discuss some of the similarities and differences they found among the planets. Next, tell them that there is a good device—the Venn diagram—they can use for looking at the similarities and differences between things. Draw a sample Venn diagram such as that shown below on the board. Show students how they can use it in comparing and contrasting Venus and Earth, and have them refer to their texts as you complete the diagram together.

Next, explain that the Venn diagram is also useful in organizing their thoughts for writing an essay or writing to get a better understanding of a subject. Together, compose a three-paragraph composition on Venus and the Earth, using the information recorded on the Venn diagram. Tell students that the audience for this composition is themselves; they are writing to get a better understanding of the two planets, rather than to communicate this information to someone else. As they write, they should add anything that connects the information they have written in the diagram with something they already know. Figure 6-2 is an example of what the Venn diagram and these paragraphs might look like.

Figure 6-2   Venn Diagram Comparing and Contrasting Venus and Earth

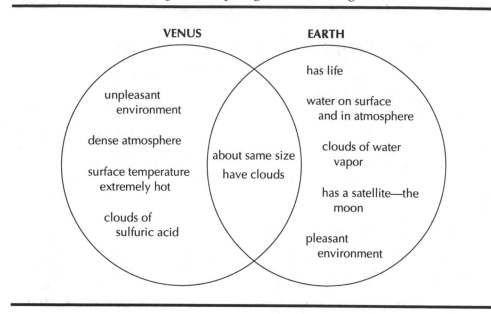

Venus is not a planet I'd want to live on. Its environment is very unpleasant. It's extremely hot and smelly because the atmosphere is thick with clouds of sulfuric acid. (I think I remember sulfur has the smell of rotten eggs. Yuk!)

In contrast to Venus, Earth has a great atmosphere. One reason is that it has water—water on the surface and water in the air (clouds). Also, Earth has life on it, probably because it has water and a temperature that's not too hot or cold for people and animals. Earth also has a satellite called the moon.

Venus has been called Earth's twin because they are nearly the same size. Other than that, I can't see too much the same about these two planets. Oh, I guess they both orbit the sun!

Use the Venn diagram to compare and contrast as many other planets as you feel appropriate, composing three-paragraph expositions that use the information from the diagram. When students sufficiently understand the activity, have them develop a Venn diagram for comets and meteroids and write three paragraphs using the information they have recorded on the diagram. Remind them that they themselves are the audience for the composition—the purpose of their writing is to better understand comets and meteoroids.

If this activity doesn't appear challenging enough for the three gifted students, have them do the same exercise but take the information from chapters 1, 2, 4, and 5 in the trade book *Meteors and Meteorites: Voyagers from Space* by Patricia Lauber.

Adapting the Activity: Venn diagrams are particularly useful for writing-to-learn with expository texts in which the author has presented material that can be compared and contrasted, but they can also be used with narratives. Students can use them to analyze differences and similarities between characters in the same story or to compare and contrast characters in different stories. For example, you might have students use a Venn diagram in writing about the two protagonists, Prince Brat and Jemmy, in Sid Fleishman's *The Whipping Boy.* The appropriate audience for this composition might be the teacher or classmates. Or students might use a Venn diagram in writing an essay comparing and contrasting Patricia MacLachlan's *Sarah, Plain and Tall* and *Prairie Songs* by Pam Conrad. The audience for this composition might be the authors of these two works. The students are attempting to communicate to the authors what they perceived as the similarities and differences in the two books. This will give students' writing a slightly different flavor compared to the writing they might do for themselves, their teacher, or their classmates.

Reflection: This activity, in which a Venn diagram is used to facilitate learning and writing, is only one of many graphic approaches that might be used in dealing with informational material. Instead of using a Venn diagram, students might record information in outline form using each of the members of the solar system as a subtitle and recording two or three important details about each member under the title. After they compose, students would then use their notes to write a paragraph on each topic. Or students might use a tree structure to show the hierarchical organization of a topic, producing a structure such as that below.

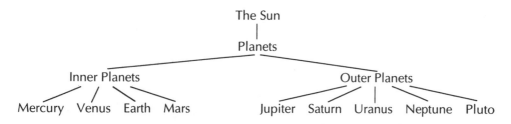

Then, they could use the tree to organize their writing.

One matter to consider as you plan what sorts of graphic aids you might suggest students use for organizing their writing is how many different kinds of graphics you want to present. On the one hand, different graphics accomplish somewhat different purposes, and students appreciate variety. On the other hand, it takes time for students to learn to use different graphics, and introducing too many of them may take too much time or even be confusing for some students.

Whatever sorts of graphic students use, the audiences can be the students themselves, students in other classes, parents, and any number of others. With any writing activity, students should be aware of its purpose as well as the audience for whom the writing is intended, and writing that is intended for an audience other than students themselves will usually require that students revise their initial drafts.

Writing Sample Activity 2—Creative Writing for an Audience: *What If?*

What If is a creative writing activity that extends the concepts in a selection by allowing students to explore alternate possibilities. Students must combine what they know and what they have learned about a topic to create a novel situation.

Selection: "Members of Our Solar System" in *Science in Your World* (Hackett & Moyer, 1991). This chapter discusses our solar system—the sun and the space objects around it. These include the nine planets and their moons, as well as the asteroids, comets, and meteoroids.

Students: Students of mixed abilities; three gifted students.

Reading Goal: To understand the characteristics of the various members of our solar system, the parts they play, and their differences and similarities in order to appreciate the intricacies and diversity of the universe as well as the laws that govern it.

Goal of the Activity: To encourage students to apply and extend concepts by describing a situation in which one of the characteristics or laws they have read about in a selection is changed and having students consider how that change would affect the other factors.

Rationale: Virtually all scientific advancements and discoveries have been achieved because someone was able to take what they knew and manipulate it in a way no one else had thought of. Students need to be encouraged to practice this kind of thinking with science material. Not only it is worthwhile and fun, but it is risk-free—there are no right answers. In this type of activity, students are not writing to learn what someone else already knows; they are writing to discover—a crucial component of creative thinking.

Procedure: Begin the activity by brainstorming with students, asking them to list facts about the solar system and scientific laws that they have learned from the chapter. Write their responses on the board. Some of them might include:

> The force of gravity keeps each planet in orbit around the sun.
>
> The tilt of the earth causes seasons.
>
> Planets travel around the sun.
>
> Venus contains dense clouds of sulfuric acid.
>
> There is no water on Venus.
>
> Earth has water.
>
> Earth has a moon.
>
> Mars has a thick atmosphere of carbon dioxide and a little water vapor.
>
> Oxygen is needed for life to exist.

Next, create What If questions for some of the facts and laws by changing those facts and laws. For example:

> What if the sun shrunk? What would happen to the planets?
>
> What if the sun grew? What would happen to the planets?
>
> What if the sun disappeared? What would happen to the planets?
>
> What if the earth weren't tilted? How would life in our city be different?
>
> What if Venus contained clouds of water vapor instead of sulfuric acid? What might be different about that planet.
>
> What if earth had no moon? What would be different about our life?
>
> What if Mars had oxygen instead of carbon dioxide?

Students can suggest their own What Ifs after you give them a few examples. After you have written a sufficient number of What If statements on the board, have students write their responses, either in their journals or on paper you provide. These responses can range from a phrase or two to a paragraph or more. Some students may be inspired by one prompt to write a whole story. They should be encouraged to follow whatever path these prompts suggest for them. The idea is to stretch the imagination, not crimp it.

Students might write What If responses just for themselves, to explore ideas just for the fun of seeing where it takes them, or they might also like to share their ideas with others. If the latter is the case, create an audience for this activity by telling students you will publish their responses in a What If book for their classroom science library. Therefore, as they write, they should keep their classmates in mind. Also, remind them that the latter type of writing—published writing—will require more than just one draft.

Students might also enjoy proposing additional What Ifs and exploring those ideas. Also, besides writing their own stories, gifted students might be posted at computers to serve as editors and publishers of What If stories other students compose.

Adapting the Activity: Having students write their responses to What If questions is readily adaptable to nearly any reading selection—expository texts, narratives, or poetry. After reading Virginia Hamilton's *The People Could Fly*, students might compose stories prompted by the question "What if you could fly?" After reading the poems of Patricia Hubbell in *A Grass Green Gallop*, a student might write a poem in response to "What if you had a horse?" The title of the poem might be "If I Had a Horse" or perhaps "Racing the Wind."

Reflection: *This example illustrates one possibility for getting students to think creatively or to extend their thinking about concepts found in informational texts. Obviously, there are as many more as there are creative teachers to dream them up. Narratives also abound in opportunities to inspire creative writing. Here are a few of them:*

- *Select a scene from a book and rewrite it to show what might happen if a character did something differently than was done in the book. For example, in the scene from the Katherine Paterson novel,* The Great Gilly Hopkins, *in which Gilly first meets William Ernest, students might develop the scene showing an assertive instead of passive William Ernest.*

- *Write an alternative ending to a story.*

- *Write a sequel to a story.*

- *Present the events of a book in newspaper format.*

- *Rewrite a contemporary story as a fairy tale. "Once upon a time there was a girl named Galadriel Hopkins, but most everyone called her Gilly."*

- *Write a scene from the perspective of another character. For example, in* The Great Gilly Hopkins, *any one of the scenes that include Gilly and William Ernest might be written from William Ernest's viewpoint instead of Gilly's.*

- *Write What If stories for folk tales by changing one aspect of the story. For example, in the Native American folk tale* Big Thunder Magic *by Craig Kee Strete, in which Great Chief visits the "City" taking his sheep Nanabee with him, students could change the character Nanabee to a different type of animal and write their own tales based on the original story line.*

Writing with the purpose of exploring ideas and possibilities not only nurtures students' writing abilities but nurtures their spirits as well. Students need time to give their imaginations free reign. As Neil Postman reminds us in The Disappearance of Childhood *(1982), this is particularly true for many students in today's world—students for whom the pressure to succeed, or poverty, or uncertainty of what will come tomorrow bring adulthood all too soon. Also, for students who struggle with the basics, it means a chance to do something whose success is measured only by the pleasure of pursuing an idea to see where it will take them.*

As we noted at the beginning of this section, the importance of the close link between reading and writing has only recently been recognized adequately. Here, we have only dealt with a few facets of that relationship. For further information on the reading-writing relationship, we suggest Reading/Writing Connections: Learning from Research *(Irwin & Doyle, 1992),* Reading and Writing Together *(Shanahan, 1990),* Making Connections: Language and Learning in the Classroom *(Hynds, 1994), and the chapter on writing in* Reading and Learning in Content Areas *(Ryder & Graves, 1994).*

Drama

Drama is a natural part of childhood. As soon as their language and social skills begin to develop, children play "house," "doctor," and "school" with their playmates. They enact dramas with their dolls, trucks, cars, or plastic figures of their favorite cartoon, movie, and TV characters. Not only are children participants in these playtime dramas, but they are also their creators. Through drama, the child is translating what he or she knows about the world into oral and body language.

Drama as a postreading activity encourages students to extend existing meanings and generate new ones. And it is fun, a highly motivating way to involve students in all of the cognitive tasks we listed at the beginning of the chapter—recalling, applying, analyzing, synthesizing, evaluating, and creating.

In postreading dramatic activities, students create settings, characters, dialog, action, and props by combining the meaning they have constructed with the text, the resources available to them, and their own ideas to produce a play—using their bodies and voices to communicate. This play might consist of a one-minute pantomime involving just one actor or a 50-minute production of *The Best Christmas Pageant Ever* involving the entire class, props, costumes, and lighting.

Dramatic activities can emerge from fiction, non-fiction, or poetry. Two fifth-graders might play the parts of Gilly and Miss Ellis, Gilly's caseworker, and dramatize the opening scene from Katherine Paterson's, *The Great Gilly Hopkins*; an entire class of second-graders might dramatize Indian tigers after reading or listening to Ted Lewin's informational picture book, *Tiger Trek*; and small groups of first- through third-grade students might gather to dramatize their favorite poems in Jack Prelutsky's *Tyrannosaurus Was a Beast*.

As students dramatize informally, they are involved in all sorts of decision making. What will I say? How will I say it? What actions and facial expressions will I use? What costumes or props will I need? Will I need to play more than one part? To illustrate that last question, let us say two first graders are dramatizing "The Kite" from Arnold Lobel's *Days With Frog and Toad*, which has two main characters, Frog and Toad, and a choir of minor characters, the Robins. One student might take the part of Frog and the other Toad, and both might assume the roles of the Robins. Problem solving, which requires students to use the resources available to them to devise their own unique interpretations of a selection, is part of the creative process.

Although an audience is sometimes appropriate, dramatizations don't require one. The audience may consist of only the students who are enacting the drama. After reading a chapter in a history or social studies text, students might pair up, choosing two historical figures to portray. After reading a chapter that discusses the sixties, for example, two fifth or sixth graders might decide to portray Martin Luther King, Jr. and Lyndon B. Johnson. First, they need to collect data on these individuals—policies, actions, attitudes, style of speech—and then select a topic or topics to discuss. What would Martin Luther King, Jr. and Lyndon B. Johnson talk to each other about? For the dramatization, students might carry on a conversation posing as these individuals. This dramatization could end here, or students might tape record it and later play it back for others as a "radio" show, or they might choose to perform it for other students or an even greater audience such as another class or parents. Drama doesn't need to, but certainly can, move beyond the school walls to places such as day care centers or nursing homes.

With dramatic activities, the teacher will play a variety of roles, again depending on the students, the selection, and the purpose of the activity. Occasionally, a teacher might need to assume the role of director/producer, but more often his or her job will be that of facilitator/encourager. In that capacity, he or she might step in to fill the role of the Troll in *Three Billy Goats Gruff*, read passages from *The Magic School Bus* series by Joanna Cole, help build a puppet stage or sew puppets, or show students how to make princess hats for Ruth Sanderson's version of *The Twelve Dancing Princesses*.

Drama has great potential for showing students that language can be transformed and that ideas can be seen, heard, and felt, as the next sample activity demonstrates.

Drama Sample Activity: *History Comes to Life*

In *History Comes to Life*, groups of students dramatize scenes from a biography.

Selection: *Harriet Tubman, Call To Freedom* by Judy Carlson. This biography chronicles the extraordinary life of Harriet Tubman, an African American woman of invincible spirit and determination who worked unceasingly to bring freedom and justice to African Americans. Harriet was born in Maryland in 1820 or 1821 and died in Auburn, New York, in 1913. For almost a century, Harriet fought for the ideals she believed in—human dignity, justice, and equality. Strong in body and spirit and empowered by an unshakable faith in God, Harriet led hundreds of slaves to freedom through the Underground Railroad, was an eloquent anti-slavery spokesperson, worked in the Union army as a nurse and a scout, established schools and homes for the poor, and supported the rights of Blacks and women to vote.

Students: Fifth and sixth graders of mixed abilities.

Reading Purpose: To learn more about the plight of African-Americans during the mid-1800s and to appreciate and be inspired by the courage, resourcefulness, and commitment of Harriet Tubman.

Goal of Activity: To provide students with an opportunity to practice their problem-solving and decision-making skills, to come to a better understanding of Harriet Tubman and the times and conditions in which she lived.

Rationale: To successfully dramatize a scene from the biography, students must combine their knowledge of what they know about dramatizing events and portraying characters generally with the specific information in the text. They need to make decisions about what events to portray, what characters to include, who will play these characters, what action will take place, what will be said, which props (if any) will be used, and a number of smaller matters. These are the sorts of cognitive tasks students are continually involved in both in and out of school. Providing a supportive setting in which children can succeed at these tasks is one way to increase their confidence and encourage risk tasking, certainly a desirable goal since children's willingness to take risks is crucial to their growth in skill and knowledge.

Procedure: After students have read the biography and you have spent some time discussing its main themes and issues, explain that they are going to form small groups and dramatize various events in the book. Have them suggest incidents from the biography that might work as dramatizations and write these on the chalkboard. Along with these incidents, list the actors required for each. Some of these incidents might include:

> Harriet being sent off at age six to work for the Cooks, getting the measles, and being brought home sick. Roles needed: Mr. and Mrs. Cook, Harriet, Harriet's mom.

> Harriet working for Miss Susan, trying to dust and take care of the baby, stealing the sugar cube, running away. Roles needed: Miss Susan, Miss Emily, Harriet.

> Harriet's family life—eating together, singing, talking, listening to Bible stories. Roles needed: Harriet, Old Rit, Ben, brothers and sisters.

> Harriet trying to help the slave escape and getting hit with the two-pound weight. Roles needed: Harriet, Slave, overseer, Old Rit, Ben.

> Harriet leading her brother James and two friends to freedom. Roles needed: Harriet, James, two friends, search party, Thomas Garrett.

As a class, discuss why these incidents would or wouldn't work as dramatizations. (*Interesting action to portray/too much action/not enough action; good speaking parts/not enough dialog/ too much dialog; reasonable number of characters in scene/ too many characters/not enough characters; workable setting or settings/ too many changes of scenes*)

Divide the class into groups of two to six students to work on a dramatization of their choice. Remind students that they will need to cooperate in assigning roles. Explain that for a successful dramatization they will need to be thoroughly familiar with the incident they are dramatizing and that each person will need to know what he or she is to say and do. They may want to write scripts which detail the dialog and summarize the action.

Be available as the groups are working to encourage creative thinking, praise cooperative behavior, and supply resources. Use one or two class periods for students to prepare the dramatizations and another to present them.

Adapting the Activity: This kind of activity in which students are recreating through drama events from a specific selection can be used with expository or narrative works that contain memorable characters and vivid, portrayable scenes—biographies, history texts, contemporary stories, and folk and fairy tales. Some of the scenes from *Fourth Grade Rats* by Jerry Spinelli might be fun for third or fourth graders to enact because they will be able to identify so well with the protagonist, Suds, and his need for peer approval, his desire to grow up and have some status, and his feelings of self doubt. Fourth to sixth graders might enjoy dramatizing scenes from the action-packed fantasy novel, *Amy's Eyes,* by Richard Kennedy, and first-graders might enjoy dramatizing *The Five Silly Fishermen* by Roberta Edwards.

Reflection: *Prerequisite to dramatizing scenes is spending some time discussing character and theme as well as pinpointing those events and scenes that are dramatizable. Also, students are bound to get frustrated if they don't know or can't do what is expected of them. Thus, giving them clear explanations of what it is they are to do and how they are to do it before they form their groups is imperative for success. Additionally, students need to know the purpose of these dramatizations. Are they to work out a scene that can be presented to other students, or are they simply doing it for the enjoyment and understanding it will bring to them?*

The chance of a successful experience can also be enhanced by putting students into heterogeneous groups. Dispersing your leaders, competent readers, creative thinkers, diplomats, and good followers among the groups can help ensure that groups achieve their goals. Each student should be aware of the unique contribution he or she is able to make to the group effort and that his or her contribution is both necessary and appreciated. Adam may not be the best reader, but he has a heck of a voice and can be a model of good voice projection for the rest of the group. Adam's gift should be recognized and encouraged. Kudos should not be handed exclusively to those who know the most or read the best. If throughout the year students are encouraged to discover what their particular talents are and given opportunities to hone and polish these talents, when it comes time for group work they will be ready to put these talents to work in achieving the group goal. Working toward achieving a common goal with their peers helps students realize that each person's contribution is important toward achieving that goal—in this case, putting together a dramatization that makes sense in terms of its faithful rendition to the text and students' expectations of what the drama should achieve.

Also, dramatizing scenes from historical pieces immerses students in a powerful context for understanding unique times and people. In putting themselves in the roles of historical characters, students can discover some common threads that weave through different ages, stories, and characters—humans' desire for respect, love, freedom, and justice. Hopefully, too, they will also discover the attributes that allow individuals to achieve these goals—courage, diligence, and concern for others—as well as identify those attributes that work against achieving them—greed, self-interest, ignorance, and hatred.

Artistic, Graphic, and Nonverbal Activities

In this category, we include the visual arts, music, and dance—each a specialized language that can be used in response to printed and spoken communication. In this section, too, we include response activities that involve the creation of media productions such as audio tapes, videos, slideshows; visual displays such as bulletin boards, artifacts, and specimens; and visual representations of information such as graphs, maps, and charts. Each of these varied forms of expression provides students with a special way to deepen and broaden their understanding of the ideas and information found in the texts they read.

To illustrate how the languages of art, music, and dance can be connected to written and spoken language, we present the following example. Suppose that your third-grade class has just finished a unit on animals. Over a four-week period, students have read numerous fiction and non-fiction trade books, and you have read *Dr. Doolittle* aloud to them as well. As a culminating activity, you read William Jay Smith's book of poems, *Birds and Beasts*. Next, you divide the class into three heterogeneous groups and assign each group one of the three non-verbal expressive languages—art, music, or dance. Each group then decides which animal it will portray in its appointed "language" and brainstorms about what materials and approach to take. For example, the art group might suggest water-color painting, collages, scratch boards, paper sculpture, clay modeling, papier-mâché, or wood sculpture. After students have brainstormed together and decided on their animal and some possibilities for visually depicting this animal, they work individually, in subgroups, or in pairs to create their animals using whatever medium they feel will best capture the essence of their animal.

The music group's goal is to create an instrumental piece to depict its animal. During their brainstorming session, students think about the musical resources available as well as the characteristics of their particular animal. They consider rhythm and percussion instruments and those that produce melody. Some of their suggestions might include drums, cymbals, sticks, sandpaper blocks, recorders, song flutes, xylophone, bells, piano, and keyboard. After they think about what animal they are going to depict and how they might depict this animal through music, they begin working in pairs or small groups to recreate their animal through music.

The dance group's goal is to depict its chosen animal through movement. During their brainstorming session, students offer suggestions about what body movements represent this animal. Their discussion involves both showing and telling, with these sorts of words describing the characteristics and movements of their chosen animal—*slow, steady, heavy, swinging, head moving, tail swishing,* and *clomp, clomp, clomp.* The members of the group might decide to work altogether to create one dance that represents their animal or they might choose to work in pairs or subgroups.

After their brainstorming sessions, students spend an hour or so over two or three days to come up with non-verbal expressions of their chosen animals. On the fourth day, they present their work; their animals come to life in a visual art, in music, and in dance; and other students guess the animals they are depicting.

A similar approach might be used for many other subjects and selections. A few possibilities for connecting art, music, and dance to reading are:

- After reading several books on Native American culture, read *The Dancing Teepees* by Virginia Driving Hawk Sneve and have students chose a tribe or nation to depict in art, music, and dance.
- After reading folk tales from many cultures, read the poem "Lord of the Dance: An African Retelling" by Veronique Tadjo and choose one culture to illustrate in art, music, and dance.
- After a unit on seasons, read Myra Cohn Livingston's *A Circle of Seasons* and have students choose one of the four seasons to illustrate in art, music, and dance.
- After a unit on feelings with middle grade students, read Cynthia Rylant's *Waiting to Waltz: A Childhood* and have students choose one of the emotions of growing up to depict in art, music, and dance.

Books, journals, and periodicals abound with suggestions for artistic and nonverbal activities that students can do in your classroom. Because it is impossible to even begin suggesting all the possibilities or to describe the ones that might work best for you—in your particular situation, with your particular students—we can only offer a sampling of ideas. Undoubtedly, you can think of many more immediately and will discover even more as time goes on.

On the next several pages, we have jotted down some of our ideas for implementing visual art, music, dance, and audio-visual presentations and displays. Think of these pages as formative. Use them to write down your own ideas as you read through the categories and examples. When you run across another idea some place else, you might want to jot it down here also. Following this potpourri of activities, we present a complete artistic and nonverbal activity.

Potpourri of Visual Arts Activities

Learning Activities

After reading about art or an artist:

> Invite a guest artist to demonstrate a technique a children's book illustrator uses
> See a film about an artist you have read about
> Visit an art museum or gallery
> Borrow paintings from the library

Creating Activities

Kinds of activities	**What to Make**
sculpting	masks
origami	murals
weaving	dioramas
painting	collages
drawing	mats
carving	quilts
etching	posters
macrame	baskets
	totem poles
What to Use	pottery
finger paint	puppets
water colors	costumes
chalk, crayons,	props
clay	scenery
wood	jewelry
paper	t-shirts
magazines	
objects from nature	
material scraps	
yarn, straw	

Potpourri of Musical Activities

Learning Activities

Learn

to sing or play a song — period songs after historical fiction

to play an instrument

about the instruments — go to hear an orchestra play, listen to recordings, invite a musician to class

about composers — listen to recording of their works, do research on a composer

about the kinds of music — contemporary, classical, jazz, rock, rap, country, gospel — go to a concert, listen to recordings

Creating Activities

Experiment

with rhythm and tempo

with percussion

with melody and harmony

with instruments, voices, and computer synthesizers

Create a song or poem about

horses (after reading *Misty of Chincoteague* by Marguerite Henry)

a famous person (after reading about Abe Lincoln or Michael Jordan)

a time in history (after reading about the expansion of the West)

a place (after reading about Japan)

a story character (after reading about Pippi Longstocking or Huckleberry Finn)

a feeling or mood (after reading poetry)

Create different kinds of songs about story characters—a jingle, a ballad, a funny song, a sad song, a happy song

Potpourri of Dance Activities

Learning Activities

See a dance

invite a person from an ethnic group to perform a dance

watch a film or video of a dance

go to a dance production—notice dance titles

invite a dancer to talk about "dance language"

Learn a dance

ethnic dances—Native American, Russian, Scottish, Polish, Hawaiian (invite a person from an ethnic group to teach a dance) kinds of dances—square dance, period American dances from the '20s, '30s, '40s, '50s, '60s, '70s, '80s, and '90s.

Creating Activities

Invent a dance to show:

a scene from a story

a poem

a character from a story

a culture you have read about

a subject you have read about—wind, turtles, exploration, dinosaurs, robots

an abstract idea from a story you have read about love, friendship, courage, personal growth

Potpourri of Audio-Visual Displays

Create

video tapes

audio tapes

filmstrips

bulletin boards

charts

maps

graphs

diagrams

models

displays

scrapbooks

photo albums

board games

posters

time lines

Artistic and Nonverbal Sample Activity: *Worth a Thousand Words*

In *Worth A Thousand Words,* students create a collage by cutting pictures from magazines that illustrate the concepts in *From Seed to Plant.*

Selection: *From Seed to Plant* by Gail Gibbons. *From Seed to Plant* is an outstanding informational book. The author does an exceptional job of conveying the concept of plant reproduction with simple, straightforward prose and colorful illustrations. Parts of a flower are described, as well as the processes of pollination, seed dispersal, and germination.

Students: Third graders of average ability; two ESL students.

Reading Goal: To learn how plants reproduce and to gain an appreciation for the creative processes at work in nature.

Goal of the Activity: To reinforce and expand upon the concepts presented in the text and to encourage creative thinking and responding.

Rationale: Making a collage that represents concepts found in a text encourages critical thinking, since it requires students to make decisions about what to include and what not to include based on what they have learned from reading the text. In selecting pictures for a plant reproduction collage, students must think about all the elements that go into producing new plants and flowers. Making a collage also gives students an opportunity to express themselves creatively, something they may not have the opportunity to do as often as we would like.

Procedure: After students have finished reading the book, write these words on the board: *seeds, flowers, pollen, stamen, pistil, stigma, animals, birds, fruit, pods, streams, ponds, rivers, rain, soil, buds.*

Taking a word at a time, have students briefly tell what part each of these plays in growing a new plant. After students have had a chance to think about the role of each, tell them they are going to make a collage that represents the "from seed to plant" idea that Gail Gibbons illustrates in her book. Explain that in creating their collages they will cut out pictures from magazines. In choosing which pictures they will include in their collage, they will need to decide if each picture represents a part in the "seed to plant" idea in Gail Gibbons' book. Tell them that doing this kind of thinking and decision making will help them understand better and appreciate how plants are produced. It will also give them a chance to think about how to use color, shape, and design to create something that is pleasing to look at.

If students haven't made collages before, show them an example (such as those in author/illustrator Eric Carle's picture books) and explain that a collage is made by pasting different items onto a piece of board or paper in a way that pleases the eye. Explain further that for their collages, they will be cutting pictures out of magazines that illustrate things that are involved in making a new plant. They might create collages that are abstract—don't represent an object in a direct way—or they might want to arrange their cut-outs in such a way that they represent something—some sort of flower or plant, or perhaps a scene depicting a landscape or garden. (If you have Eric Carle's books, you could show how he creates scenes and objects using collages.)

Next, hold up a few magazine illustrations and ask students to suggest what they might cut from these pictures for their collage. Cut these out and demonstrate how students might arrange them.

Supply students with ample magazines, scissors, paste, and sheets of construction paper or tagboard to paste their cut-outs on. After they have completed their collages, display them on a bulletin board. Keep a copy of Gail Gibbon's *From Seed to Plant* on display nearby also.

Adapting the Activity: Creating collages like this is an appropriate postreading activity for any selection that contains several concepts for which illustrations can be found. For example, after reading a chapter on medicines and drugs in a science text, sixth-grade students could make a collage by cutting out pictures in magazines as well as using real labels and parts of the packaging from these items. Students might, for instance, paste part of an Alka Seltzer package or the label from an aspirin box on a collage of common over-the-counter medicines. After reading *The Senses* by John Gaskin, third graders might make a collage representing each of the five senses. Magazines abound with pictures depicting various aspects of sensory experience. After reading Alice Provensen's *The Buck Stops Here: The Presidents of the United States,* in which the author illustrates the contributions of the presidents with a collage surrounding each, students might make a collage of artifacts and symbols that represent their own lives or perhaps someone whom they admire.

Reflection: Because we assumed that the third graders in this example had created col-lages before, very little was said about the techniques for creating an aesthetically pleasing composition. If students have had little instruction on what makes for a pleasing two-dimensional design—balance, color, and repetition, for example—then these ideas will need to be discussed. To help students develop an understanding of the difference be-tween designs that work and those that don't, you can show them examples and non-examples (shapes pasted haphazardly onto the paper, no repetition in shape or color, no unifying point of interest) of eye-pleasing designs. Providing students with plenty of expo-sure to the quality art that abounds in children's literature is one way to provide them with excellent models. (That is one good reason why picture books should be made accessible to students of all ages.) Another way is to display art work in your classroom. Reprints of well known works are, of course, available at a relatively low cost at most discount stores and also through loan programs at many libraries. Wall calendars and appointment calen-dars are another good source for art reprints. Around December, you might want to encourage students to check with their parents to see if they have any of these types of calendars and ask them to bring them to school in January. Display the calendar art around the room or create a bulletin board. Collecting old calendars is a wonderful way to build your own reprint library. These prints can be used as examples of good art, and their subject matter is often appropriate to use for other reading activities.

You may have noticed that we did not provide any special activities for the two ESL students in the class. This was deliberate. One advantage of nonverbal activities such as this one—and one reason for using them—is that students with varying proficiency in English can succeed equally well with them.

Application and Outreach Activities

Books open doors. They invite us to step out, to go beyond the text to see for ourselves, to act on our new found knowledge, and to apply it in a unique way. In this sense, all of the previously mentioned categories in one way or another reflect the idea of going beyond the text to explore other realms and other applications of information and ideas.

Activities that we are labeling specifically as Application and Outreach endeavors are those in which students take the ideas and information from a text and deliber-ately test, use, or explore them further. Students might read an article on how to make friends, but the information has little value unless they try out the author's ideas to see if they work. Students might read a story about making ice cream or an article describing several science experiments, but it's not quite as much fun as actually following the steps and eating the ice cream or doing the experiments in books like Sandra Markle's *Science Mini-Mysteries* to see if they actually work. The logical next step after reading about something is to try it out in the real world.

It is not just "how-to" books that invite real-world applications, however. A chapter on the environment in a science text might inspire students to do something themselves to better care for the Earth. Or, after finishing a novel in which the main character has a disability, a reader might change his or her attitude about persons with disabilities and begin to act differently toward them. Application activities invite and encourage many different kinds of personal and social action.

The fiction, non-fiction, and poetry that students read can open doors to the wider world. Mary Ann Hoberman's poem, "Cricket," might send them into summer fields to find out for themselves if a cricket's wing can really "sing a song" or to the science museum to explore the entomology exhibit to find out if "a cricket's ear is in its leg." Or, after reading Jane Yolen's *Owl Moon*, 7- and 8-year-olds might beg their parents or grandparents to take them "owling" in the night woods.

Outreach activities not only take children beyond the school walls to explore a topic or idea further or to discover more but also can inspire them to social action. After reading Chris Van Allsburg's *Just A Dream*, in which a child dreams of a future wasted due to poor management of the environment, students might decide to write letters to state and local representatives encouraging them to support environmental legislation or develop an environmental ad campaign for their school or neighborhood. Barbara Huff's *Greening the City Streets: The Story of Community Gardens* might inspire urban readers to plan and develop community gardens in their neighborhood. Or, after reading Mem Fox's touching picture book *Wilfrid Gordon McDonald Partridge*—in which a young boy discovers a unique way to help the forgetful Miss Nancy recapture her memories—students might be inspired to share the story with residents in a nursing home or try this memory-recapturing approach with an elderly relative or friend.

Students will not always make the connections necessary to transfer ideas from the text to the real world on their own. By providing activities that demonstrate this connection, you can drive home a critical aspect of the nature of text—we should not be the same after we have read it. We are a little more than we were before. Our new selves contain new information and ideas that we can now use. The following activity shows one way students might apply what they have discovered in a text by reaching out to others.

Application and Outreach Sample Activity:
Getting to Know You

In *Getting to Know You,* students think about ways to get to know senior citizens better and plan ways to achieve this.

Selection: *Anastasia Again!* by Lois Lowry. In *Anastasia Again!*, 12-year-old Anastasia Krupnik moves from her apartment in the city to the suburbs, taking with her some rather negative assumptions about the people who live there. Her next door neighbor, Gertrude Stein, turns out to be an eccentric old recluse who looks like a witch. However, as Anastasia gets to know Gertrude Stein, she discovers much to admire and like in this woman. On an outing to the library one day, Anastasia happens upon the Senior Citizens' Drop-in Center. She invites the people at the center to a party at her house with the idea of introducing Gertrude to some new friends. On the day of the party, two of Anastasia's old friends from the city arrive at Anastasia's house as does a potential new friend from her new neighborhood. Many a myth about the young, old, city dwellers, and suburbanites are dispelled at this delightful, if somewhat outlandish, gathering.

Students: Fifth graders of mixed abilities.

Reading Purpose: To understand and enjoy an engaging story.

Goal of the Activity: To help students see how ideas found in literature can be applied to the real world and to encourage understanding and appreciation of people who are a number of years older than they are.

Rationale: This novel is a wonderful springboard for activities that provide opportunities to dispel stereotypes and to build bridges of understanding, especially between generations. Anastasia's idea for the party comes very much out of her desire to get the reclusive Gertrude Stein involved with life and people again. Ideally, after reading this book and participating in this activity, students might come up with their own ideas of ways to reach out to others in addition to having some of their stereotypes dispelled.

Procedure: After students have read the story, talk about Anastasia's first impressions of Gertrude Stein. (*She looked like a witch and acted grouchy and unfriendly, although she was nice to Anastasia's, brother, Sam.*) Ask how Anastasia felt about Gertrude Stein after she got to know her. (*She thought she was very interesting, nice and funny. Anastasia learned that when Gertrude acted brusquely, it wasn't because she was mean, but because she was scared — scared of being rejected.*) You might want to talk about the idea of stereotypes and why people have them. Talk about the stereotypes Anastasia had and how some of her ideas about the suburbs and older people had changed by the end of the story.

Encourage students to talk about the older people in their own neighborhoods, places of worship, or families. Ask if they are friends with any of these people, then discuss what Anastasia did that helped her become friends with Gertrude Stein. Talk about some things students have done to get to know people who are much older than they are. Next, discuss what Anastasia wanted to do for Gertrude Stein after they became friends (*help her make new friends*).

Talk about what students might do as a group or as individuals to bring together seniors and young people. Record their suggestions on the chalkboard or a chart. (You may need to remind students that they will need their parents' permission do some things on their own, such as visiting or giving gifts.) If having a party—such as the one Anastasia had—for seniors is one of the students' suggestions, you may want to do this as a class activity. Students could invite seniors from their neighborhood, place of worship, family, or a nearby nursing home. Together, students can plan a time and a place for their party, refreshments, activities, and decorations.

Adapting the Activity: This type of activity can be used after reading any story in which the protagonist begins by having mistaken assumptions about a person or group of people and ends up changing his or her views after getting to know that person or group of people. Postreading discussion would first focus on what the protagonist did, or what things happened to the protagonist that made him or her think differently at the end of the story. The discussion could then move to what students might do in similar situations. However, parties and other outreach activities such as letters, gifts, and visits should come out of a sincere spontaneous desire by the students, not as a teacher assignment. Outreach activities that focus on a changed perspective or attitude might include having third or fourth graders invite a class of younger students (or older) to a "Getting to Know You" party after reading *Fourth Grade Rats* by Jerry Spinelli or inviting a guest from the Native American community come to talk about Native American rites and traditions to a class of second graders after they have read the mystical story *Bring Back the Deer* by Jeffrey Prusski.

Reflection: Outreach activities can certainly be preplanned, but often the best ones are generated from the students themselves as they respond to a selection. This is the ultimate goal of this kind of activity—to get students to make their own connections, to see how a text can build bridges to other ideas and other places.

Still and all, the central theme of this book is scaffolding, and many students will require scaffolding to move from passive to active modes of responding to what they read—to reaching outward as a result of the inward effect reading has had on them. Much of what today's students encounter—much of what they see on television or at the movies—seems likely to dull their sensitivity, to suggest that the pain and problems of the world belong to some distant others and are not their concern. Instilling in students the realization that the ideas suggested in what they read have implications for the world they live in and suggesting to students that they often can and should act on those ideas to improve their world will almost certainly require your carefully planned efforts.

Reteaching

One of the advantages of categorizing ideas is that it allows us to focus our thoughts, to structure and order them so that we can see relationships among ideas. Through this mental effort, logical patterns of organization will often emerge and with them a workable framework—a structure that will help us move ideas from the abstract to the concrete and suggest ways of implementing them in real life situations, in this case, the classroom. The disadvantage is that categorizing can sometimes lure us into thinking ideas can be pigeonholed. They cannot. When dealing with such a complex and organic process as teaching, we need to search for models that will help guide our thinking and suggest ways for effectively designing and implementing instruction in the classroom. But because teaching is so complex and organic, any kind of order or structure, any kind of model, can only serve as a guide, a beginning, a framework. Coming to this final category of postreading activities—reteaching—we are reminded of that truth.

In our ordering of activities, we have placed reteaching in the postreading category. However, as anyone who has spent even an hour in the classroom knows, reteaching is an ongoing process. Teachers, as the artists they are, are constantly assessing the efficacy of their instruction. "Are the students understanding what I'm saying and doing? Do I need to try another approach?" Teachers are continually using the feedback they receive from students to modify their approach *as they teach.* Sometimes, however, after the entire lesson has been completed, and even though the teacher has tried his or her best to ensure that all students succeeded, some still fall short of their goals. When this happens, reteaching is called for.

Reteaching is typically necessary when students, after reading a selection and engaging in various activities, have not reached their reading goals. If the goal was for them to recall the organs of the human body and understand their functions, and discussion, questioning, or writing activities indicate that students did not achieve this goal, reteaching is in order.

Reteaching will often focus on encouraging students to self-evaluate, to become metacognitive readers. After all, while the teacher is there to encourage and assist, it is the student who is ultimately responsible for his or her own learning. Activities that encourage students to ask questions for themselves can help nudge them in the direction of being responsible, active readers. Here are some of the questions students might be asked to consider after not understanding the information in a text about the organs of the body.

- Why didn't I understand what the author said about the way the heart functions? Were there too many words I didn't know? Was I reading too fast? What might I do to understand the information?
- Was I concentrating on what the author was saying or was my mind wandering? What might I do to help me concentrate?

Help students see the importance of asking these sorts of questions and suggest possible strategies for students to use:

- Adjust your reading speed to reflect difficulty of material.
- Write down key words or phrases.
- Draw a map to show the relationship among the ideas in the chapter.

Such assistance will foster the development of readers who know how to construct meaning from text—how to be co-partners with the author. Let students know that their job is just as important as the author's. Without their own effort, no communication takes place, no meaning is born, no idea comes to life. The words exist as mere marks on a page.

In addition to encouraging metacognitive thinking in students, reteaching activities might include your retracing the steps of a specific activity *with* students to see what went wrong and where. Perhaps students had difficulty completing a reading guide or answering postreading questions. In these cases, reteaching might include discussing with students the problems they had, and why they had them, and then reviewing the purposes and steps involved in completing the guide or answering the questions. During this review process, you might decide to alter the approach used in the original activity to reflect the new insights the discussion revealed or to create a totally different activity. Alternately, you might have students simply repeat the original activity with their new level of understanding. The purpose of these approaches—discussing the problem and then modifying the activity, creating a new activity, or repeating the original one—is to give students another opportunity to succeed.

Reteaching Sample Activity: *Play it Again, Sam*

In *Play it Again, Sam,* a previous activity is repeated with those students who didn't achieve the goals of the activity.

Selection: *Frozen Fire* by James Houston. *Frozen Fire* is the story of Matthew Morgan and his Eskimo friend Kayak, who battle to stay alive in the harsh Canadian wilderness close to the Arctic circle while attempting to rescue Matthew's father and a helicopter pilot who are lost.

Students: Sixth graders of mixed abilities.

Reading Goal: To understand and enjoy an exciting survival story.

Goal of the Original Activity: To help students understand how literature can be a medium for understanding the various ways people respond to similar situations and issues, and to provide **all** students with the opportunity to voice their opinions and reach their own conclusions.

Goal of Reteaching Activity: To make sure all students have the opportunity to successfully draw their own conclusions about ideas presented in the text.

Rationale: In the *Both Sides Now* postreading discussion, a handful of students had problems coming up with more than one or two reasons to support their responses to the question, "Should Matthew have taken the gold nuggets?" By repeating this activity in a supportive setting, students have the opportunity to review procedures or concepts not grasped in a previous lesson and to achieve success.

Procedure: On the chalkboard, overhead, or a handout, provide students with a copy of the original discussion web. Then, read aloud the section from the novel in which Matthew finds the gold nuggets. After each page or so, pause and let students think about the question "Should Matthew have taken the gold nuggets?" and have them suggest reasons why Matthew should have taken the nuggets and why he shouldn't have. Write these on the chart or have students record them.

For example, below is an excerpt from the text that might support the position that Matthew *shouldn't* have taken the nuggets and therefore belongs in the *NO* column.

Matthew pushed up the right sleeve of his parka shirt and sweater as far as he could and, lying on the ice, reached down into the water.

"Wahh! You're acting crazy," whispered Kayak. "You'll freeze your arm off, freeze yourself to death."

Then, write a word or phrase in the NO column that supports the position that Matther should not have taken the nuggets as shown below.

Reasons

freeze yourself to death   _____

_____

_____   **NO**   Should Matthew have taken   **YES**   _____

_____   the gold nuggets?   _____

_____   _____

_____   _____

Conclusions

Proceed similarly with the remaining pages, encouraging each student to participate in giving his or her responses. After you have finished reading aloud and students have provided several responses for each column, have each student write his or her own conclusion based on the chart you have constructed together. Then, have each student choose the reason that best supports his or her answer. Let students tell what reason they have chosen and why, and be sure to commend them for their efforts.

Adapting the Activity: *Play it Again Sam* can be used whenever students haven't achieved their reading goals and repeating that activity with assistance from you will help ensure a successful experience. For example, let us say some students had problems answering some of the questions in the *Yellow Brick Road* postreading activity. Meet with those students, find out which questions posed problems, read aloud parts of the story that might provide the answers, and lead students to discover the answers. Alternately, if some students had difficulty writing paragraphs using the Venn diagram in the *Compare/Contrast* activity, meet with them and review the procedures for gathering information on the diagram and those for using that information in their writing.

Reflection: *A reteaching activity of this sort in which you are primarily repeating the original procedure with students is helpful when they are likely to profit from additional exposure and practice of a particular activity. Sometimes, however, a reteaching activity will involve trying a whole new approach. In this case, you will toss out your original activity and return to your primary reading goal. For the folk tale,* Vasilisa the Beautiful, *the purpose was "To enjoy a traditional folk tale and to understand events in the order in which they occur in the story." Suppose that some students have read the story and tried to answer the story map questions you posed but just haven't been able to follow the story. As a reteaching activity, instead of your writing questions for the* Yellow Brick Road *as you did originally, perhaps students will be more successful writing their own questions. Perhaps the reason they couldn't get into the story was that your questions didn't make sense or appeal to them; they aren't the ones that were the most striking or important to them. Or let us say some of your students weren't quite ready to tackle writing three paragraphs using the Venn diagram in the* Compare/Contrast *activity. Return to the reading goal there—"To understand the concepts of comets and meteoroids, what part they play in the solar system, the differences they have and similarities they share . . . ." Restructure the activity so that instead of using writing to describe the similarities and differences between comets and meteoroids, students use another medium—art, for example. They could draw, paint pictures, or make models using the information in the diagram. Alternately, they might use oral language, or a dramatization of some sort. They could assume the role of an expert on comets and meteoroids on a talk show and record the information from the Venn diagram into a tape recorder. Again, there are any number of approaches that you might take with individual students to help them understand and appreciate the concepts of comets and meteoroids.*

• Postreading: A Final Word •

Many of the postreading activities described in this section have been traditionally thought of as enrichment activities. And indeed they are, for they do "enrich" the reader. But we need to be careful when we use this label that we are being *in*clusive and not *ex*clusive in selecting students who will be enriched. If we think of *all* students who read as *rich*—those who soar as well as those who flounder—then we need to be certain to provide activities that will enrich them all. Sometimes, those students who struggle with the basics, those who are lacking in traditional literacy skills, have been left out of these activities and thus have not been allowed the opportunities for the growth that enrichment activities can provide. We believe that all students deserve and will benefit from a variety of postreading activities and should be given opportunities to explore as many of them possible. Activities that students engage in after reading drive home the fact that reading has purpose—students find that they can actually *do* something with the ideas in books. They can make connections between what they know and what they discover in texts and apply that new knowledge so that their lives become more enjoyable, more productive, and more meaningful—enriched, if you will.

References

Alvermann, D.E. (1991). "The discussion web: A graphic aid for learning across the curriculum." *The Reading Teacher, 45,* 92–99. A complete description of this very useful graphic aid and the teaching procedures that accompany it.

Beck, I.L., & McKeown, M.G. (1981). Developing questions that promote comprehension: The story map." *Language Arts, 58,* 913–918. Discusses problematic approaches to selecting and sequencing questions and offers a valuable alternative.

Beck, I.L., & McKeown, M.G. (1988). Toward meaningful accounts in history texts for young learners. *Educational Researcher, 17* (6), 31–39. One of several descriptions of the authors' excellent research on what constitutes effective expository text.

Hynds, S. (1994). *Making connections: Language and learning in the classroom.* Norwood, MA: Christopher-Gordon. Provides many insights about interrelationships among the language arts.

Irwin, J.W., & Doyle, M.A. (Eds.). (1992). *Reading/Writing connections: Learning from research.* Newark, DE: International Reading Associations A variety of researched-based insights on the relationships between reading and writing.

McKeown, M.G., Beck, I.L., & Worthy, M.J. (1993). Grappling with text ideas: Questioning the author. *The Reading Teacher, 46,* 560–566. Describes a unique approach to enticing and leading children to read informational text actively and critically.

Monson, D.L. (1992). Realistic fiction and the real world. In B.E. Cullinan (Ed.), *Invitation to read: More children's literature in the reading program.* Newark, DE: International Reading Association. Succinct and practical discussion of the importance of linking literature to life and of ways of doing so.

Postman, N. (1982). *The disappearance of childhood.* New York: Delacorte. Thought-provoking discussion of the fate of childhood in the modern world.

Ryder, R.J., & Graves, M.F. (1994). *Reading and learning in content areas.* Columbus, OH: Merrill. This comprehensive text on content-area reading includes a straightforward and practical chapter on writing to learn.

Shanahan, T. (Ed.). (1990). *Reading and writing together: New perspectives for the classroom.* Norwood, MA: Christopher-Gordon. Diverse, scholarly perspectives on the reading/writing relationship.

Children's Books Cited

Carlson, J. (1989). *Harriet Tubman, call to freedom.* New York: Fawcett Columbine.

Cole, J. (1990). *The magic school bus: Lost in the solar system.* New York: Scholastic.

Conrad, P. (1985). *Prairie songs.* New York: Harper & Row.

Cooper, I. (1990). *The kids from Kennedy Middle School: Choosing sides.* New York: Morrow.

Edwards, R. (1989). *The five silly fishermen.* New York: Random House.

Fleischman, S. (1986). *The whipping boy.* New York: Greenwillow.

Fox, M. (1985). *Wilfrid Gordon McDonald Partridge.* New York: Kane/Miller.

Fritz, J. (1987). *Shh! we're writing the Constitution.* New York: Scholastic.

Gaskin, J. (1985). *The senses.* New York: Franklin Watts.

Gibbons, G. (1991). *From seed to plant*. New York: Holiday House.

Hackett, J.K,. & Moyer, R.H. (1991). *Science in your world*. New York: Macmillan/McGraw-Hill.

Hamilton, V. (1985). *The people could fly*. New York: Knopf.

Henry, M. (1947). *Misty of Chincoteague*. New York: Macmillan.

Hoberman, M.A. (1976). *Bugs*. New York: Viking.

Hong, L.T. (1991). *How the ox star fell from heaven*. Chicago: Albert Whitman.

Houston, J. (1977). *Frozen fire*. New York: Margaret K. McElderry.

Hubbel, P. (1990). *A green grass gallop*. New York: Atheneum.

Huff, B.A. (1990). *Greening the city streets: The story of community gardens*. New York: Clarion.

Kennedy, R. (1985). *Amy's eyes*. New York: Harper & Row.

Lauber, P.C. (1989). *Meteors and meteorites: Voyagers from outer space*. New York: Crowell.

Lewin, T. (1990). *Tiger trek*. New York: Macmillan.

Livingston, M.C. (1982). *A circle of seasons*. New York: Holiday House.

Lobel, A. (1979). *Days with frog and toad*. New York: Scholastic.

Lord, B.B. (1984). *In the year of the boar and Jackie Robinson*. New York: Harper & Row.

Lowry, L. (1981). *Anastasia again!* Boston: Houghton Mifflin.

MacLachlan, P. (1985). *Sarah, plain and tall*. New York: Harper & Row.

Markle, S. (1988). *Science mini-mysteries*. New York: Atheneum.

Parker, S. (1989). *Touch, taste, and smell*. New York: Franklin Watts.

Paterson, K. (1977). *The great Gilly Hopkins*. New York: Crowell.

Prelutsky, J. (1988). *Tyrannosaurus was a beast*. New York: Greenwillow.

Provensen, A. (1990). *The Buck Stops here: The presidents of the United States*. New York: Harper.

Prusski, J. (1988). *Bring back the deer*. San Diego: Harcourt Brace Jovanovich.

Rylant, C. (1984). *Waiting to waltz: A childhood*. New York: Bradbury.

Sanderson, R. (1990). *The twelve dancing princesses*. Boston: Little Brown.

Smith, W.J. (1990). *Birds and beasts*. New York: Godine.

Sneve, V.D.H. (1989). *Dancing teepees*. New York: Holiday House.

Spinelli, J. (1991). *Fourth grade rats*. New York: Scholastic.

Steptoe, J. (1987). *Mufaro's beautiful daughters*. New York: Lothrop, Lee & Shepard.

Steven, J. (1989). *Androcles and the lion*. New York: Holiday House.

Strete, C.K. (1990). *Big thunder magic*. New York: Greenwillow.

Tadjo, V. (1989). *Lord of the dance: An African retelling*. New York: Lippincott.

Van Allsburg, C. (1990). *Just a dream*. New York: Houghton Mifflin.

Whitney, T.P. (1970). *Vasilisa the beautiful*. New York: Macmillan.

Yep, L. (1991). *The star fisher*. New York: Penguin.

Yolen, J. (1987). *Owl moon*. New York: Philomel.

7

Comprehensive Scaffolded Reading Experiences

In the past three chapters, we have focused on individual pre-, during-, or postreading activities. In this chapter, we show how these activities are interrelated—linked, one to the other, in response to the students, the selection, and the overall purpose for reading—as shown in the basic model for SREs repeated below.

Figure 7-1

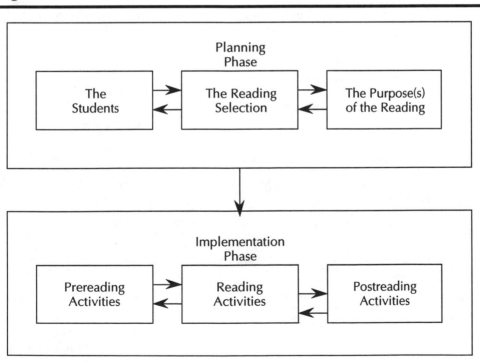

Suppose, for example, the selection your second graders are going to read is *Nate the Great* by Marjorie Sharmat. One SRE might look like this:

SCAFFOLDED READING EXPERIENCE

Students	Selection	Purpose
Second graders including three ESL students and one academically challenged student	*Something Queer at the Library* by Elizabeth Levy	To understand and enjoy a light-hearted mystery

Prereading Activities	During-reading Activities	Postreading Activities
• Motivating • Preteaching Vocabulary • Building Background Knowledge • Suggesting a Strategy	• Guided Reading • Oral Reading by Teacher • Silent Reading	• Discussion • Drama • Artistic Activity • Reteaching (This became part of the scaffolding when it became apparent students were having problems using the strategy suggested during prereading.)

Now here is how another SRE for the same selection might look with a different group of students:

Students	Selection	Purpose
First graders (above average and gifted)	*Something Queer at the Library* by Elizabeth Levy	To understand and enjoy an engaging story

Prereading Activities	During-reading Activities	Postreading Activities
• Building Background Knowledge (which combines motivation and purpose setting)	• Silent Reading	• Writing

And here is one for an entirely different selection, students, and purpose:

Students	Selection	Purpose
Fifth graders of mixed ability and five ESL students	Chapter on WWII Postwar Years	To understand and recall the most important topics and issues in the chapter

Prereading Activities	During-reading Activities	Postreading Activities
• Motivating	• Guided Reading	• Discussion
• Preteaching Concepts	• Oral Reading by Teacher	• Nonverbal Activity
• Activating Background Knowledge	• Oral Reading by Students	• Writing (modified for ESL)
• Suggesting a Strategy	• Modifying the Text (for ESL students only)	

You can see from these brief examples the effect the students, the reading purpose, and the selection have on the type and quantity of activities. Perhaps this is a good time to emphasize a point we have made throughout the book—the purpose of the SRE is not to fill up precious reading time with a lot of activities, no matter how engaging or purposeful in their own right they might be, but rather to provide a scaffold that helps students successfully build meaning with the texts that they read and do something with their newly gained knowledge and insights.

Prereading	During-reading	Postreading
Prepare for meaning	Build meaning	Respond to meaning

Some activities in the scaffold may be quite brief, taking only a few minutes, while others will take much longer. For example, a motivational activity might include no more than your saying, "I learned more about the Civil War by reading this article than from anything I've read before," whereas a concept-building activity that includes demonstrations of Newton's laws of motion may take 20 minutes or more. What you need to consider is the cost effectiveness of each activity: "How much scaffolding do students need to successfully build meaning and respond to this selection? How much help will they need to build meaning to enjoy a folktale? To write a mathematical sentence for a story problem? To recall and respond to the major events that led up to the Civil War?"

Another point to remember is that what is important to understand is the function or functions an activity serves, not what it's labeled. For instance, if you know from past experience that you really have to motivate your fourth graders before they read any kind of expository material, then in planning an SRE for an informational trade book on Japan you know you must include motivation. While creating a motivational activity, you discover that it is accomplishing several purposes simultaneously. It is relating the reading to the students' lives, activating their prior knowledge, and introducing vocabulary. You sought motivation and ended up with additional aids in the scaffold. This overlapping of functions will cause no problems. You know what your activity is accomplishing, and that should be enough—except for explaining the purpose of the activity to your students, which we recommend you do frequently.

Although your motivational activity may include activating prior knowledge and introducing vocabulary, you may still choose to build a sturdier prereading scaffold by including a separate preteaching vocabulary activity. Overlap between activities is to be expected.

The length of an entire SRE can range from minutes to days, depending again on your students, selection, and purpose. If the reading selection were a short picture book to be read by an average group of third graders for the purpose of understanding the theme, the SRE might be broken down this way:

Students	Selection	Purpose
Third graders reading at second-third grade level	Picture book: *Musical Max* by Robert Kraus	To enjoy the story and identify its theme

Prereading Activities	During-reading Activities	Postreading Activities
• Activating Background Knowledge, which includes preteaching the concept of theme (15 mins.) • Direction-Setting activity —identify story's theme (5 mins.)	• Silent Reading (10 mins.)	• Small group discussions on the story's theme (15 mins.) • Large group discussion on the story's theme (10 mins.)

A lot of activity time for 10 minutes of reading? Perhaps. But the next day your students will be independently reading self-selected books from your library table.

Although this SRE on *Musical Max* takes only about an hour, an SRE could also take several weeks. Let us suppose you are going to have your fifth-grade students read biographies of people they have been studying about in history. Here's an abbreviated version of what a 20-day SRE might look like:

Students	Selection	Purpose
Fifth graders of mixed abilities	Various biographies of historical figures of men and women who have influenced history	To understand and appreciate the lives of these influential men and women

WEEK 1:

Day 1

Prereading Activities	During-reading Activities	Postreading Activities
• A Motivating activity, which may include a visit from a person in the community who has written or been the subject of a biography (15 mins.)	• Oral Reading by Teacher or guest author (20 mins.)	• Discussion focusing on biographical writing, comparing and contrasting it with other genres (15 mins.)

Day 2

Prereading Activities	During-reading Activities	Postreading Activities
• Previewing and Building Text-Specific Knowledge: Give previews and information about biographies students will be selecting from. (20 mins.)	• Oral Reading by Teacher: Read excerpts from biographies. (20 mins.) • Silent Reading: Have students read selected biographies. (20 mins.)	• Discussion: Return to ideas raised in Day One's discussion and how they apply to biographies students will read. (15 mins.)

Day 3

Prereading Activities	During-reading Activities	Postreading Activities
• Prequestioning: Have students develop a set of questions they would like to have answered in biographies, along with a set of teacher-developed questions. (10 mins.) • Direction Setting: Focus students' attention on the questions they raised and the teacher-developed ones. (5 mins.)	• Silent Reading (30 mins.)	None

Day 4

Prereading Activities	During-reading Activities	Postreading Activities
• Direction Setting: Review previous day's questions. (10 mins.)	• Silent Reading (35 mins.)	None

Day 5

Prereading Activities	During-reading Activities	Postreading Activities
• Preteaching Concepts— semantic map for *perseverance* (10 mins.)	• Guided Reading: Students look for examples of perseverance in their biographies and flag these. • Silent Reading (20 mins.) • Oral Reading by Students: Students read passages that exemplify perseverance. (15 mins.)	• Discuss perseverance of historical figures using concrete examples. (10 mins.)

WEEK 2 (FURTHER ABBREVIATED):

Prereading Activities	During-reading Activities	Postreading Activities
• Suggesting a Strategy— surveying • Building Background Knowledge: Preview several more biographies.	• Use surveying strategy to select additional biographies to read. • Silent Reading • Oral Reading by Teacher	• Writing: Construct a Venn diagram to use in writing an essay comparing and contrasting two historical figures.

WEEKS 3 & 4 (STILL FURTHER ABBREVIATED):

Prereading Activities	During-reading Activities	Postreading Activities
• Preteaching Concepts— *commitment, vision* • Relating Reading to Students' Lives: Where are attributes of historical figures represented also in lives of students?	• Oral Reading by Teacher • Silent Reading • Guided Reading: examples of key concepts discussed • Modifying the Text: biographies on tapes	• Writing: biographies of someone the student knows • Artistic and Nonverbal: Compose songs; make a bulletin board or mural. • Drama: Dramatize events from biographies. • Outreach: Take dramas to senior citizens' center; visit history museum.

In the remainder of the chapter, we give samples of three complete Scaffolded Reading Experiences. In each sample, we include an overview of the entire SRE, a detailed day-by-day description of possible pre-, during-, and postreading activities, and a brief reflection on the entire SRE.

Guide to SREs for Chapter 7

SAMPLE 1: *SARAH, PLAIN AND TALL*

Students: Third graders of mixed abilities.

Selection: *Sarah, Plain and Tall* by Patricia MacLachlan.

Purpose: To understand an enjoy an award-winning piece of literature.

SAMPLE 2: *EARTHQUAKES*

Students: Fifth-grade students with low to average reading ability in an ethnically diverse classroom in California.

Selection: *Earthquakes* by Seymour Simon.

Purpose: To learn about earthquakes, what causes them and what effect they have.

SAMPLE 3: A STUDENT-GENERATED, THEME-BASED SRE ON "SELF-DISCOVERY AND PERSONAL TRIUMPH"

Students: Fourth graders reflecting a variety of abilities and ethnic backgrounds.

Selections: Self-selected books reflecting the theme "Self-discovery and Personal Triumph."

Purpose: To understand and enjoy good literature and to understand how people deal with and solve various kinds of issues, challenges, and problems.

SAMPLE 1: A COMPLETE SRE FOR *SARAH, PLAIN AND TALL*

Students: Third graders of mixed abilities.

Selection: *Sarah, Plain and Tall* by Patricia MacLachlan. Two frontier children, Anna and Caleb Witting, whose mother died the day after giving birth to Caleb, long for a mother. Their father advertises for a bride and receives a reply from a woman named Sarah, who lives in Maine. After communicating through several letters, Sarah agrees to come to live for a month in the Witting's prairie home. The children are captivated with Sarah and hope desperately that she will stay and marry their father. They do everything in their power to win Sarah's heart, worrying all the while that she will decide after the month's time to return to Maine. But Sarah comes to love the children and the prairie, and even their father, Jacob Witting, whom she marries, giving Anna and Caleb a new mother.

Reading Purpose: To understand and enjoy an award-winning piece of literature.

OVERVIEW

Students	Selection	Purpose
Third graders of mixed abilities	*Sarah, Plain and Tall* by Patricia MacLachlan	To understand and enjoy an award-winning piece of literature

Day 1

Prereading Activities	During-reading Activities	Postreading Activities
• Activating and Building Background Knowledge (15 mins.) • Preteaching Vocabulary (15 mins.) • Building Text Specific Knowledge—Previewing (5 mins.)	• Oral Reading by Teacher (10 mins.)	• Writing (15 mins.)

Day 2

Prereading Activities	During-reading Activities	Postreading Activities
• Questioning and Direction Setting (15 mins.)	• Silent Reading—chapters 2, 3, and 4 (30 mins.)	• Writing (15 mins.)

Day 3

Prereading Activities	During-reading Activities	Postreading Activities
• Questioning and Direction Setting (10 mins.)	• Silent Reading—chapters 5, 6, and 7 (30 mins.)*	• Writing (20 mins.)

Day 4

Prereading Activities	During-reading Activities	Postreading Activities
• Questioning and Direction Setting (10 mins.)	• Silent Reading—chapters 8 and 9 (20 mins.)*	• Writing (15 mins.)

Day 5

Prereading Activities	During-reading Activities	Postreading Activities
None	None	• Discussion and Dramatics (40 mins.)

Prereading For Day 1

ACTIVATING AND BUILDING BACKGROUND KNOWLEDGE: *Seeing Is Believing*

The *Seeing Is Believing* activity uses a filmstrip, slide presentation, or photographs to help students visualize the story's setting.

Goal of Activity: To enhance students' repertoire of visual images so they will more fully appreciate those they meet in this text.

Rationale: *Sarah, Plain and Tall* takes place on the American prairie at a time when neighbors were separated by miles and local transportation was limited to horses and wagons. Of course, there was no electricity or indoor plumbing, let alone any of the amenities of modern-day life. Students may have some understanding of the prairie and the life and conditions of people who lived on the frontier in the 1800s from movies and television, particularly the *Little House of the Prairie* series. Activating this knowledge and then showing slides or a filmstrip of this locale and era will help students appreciate the special situation faced by the characters in the story.

Procedure: Select a filmstrip, set of slides, or photographs that show various aspects of frontier life as well as those that depict the prairie landscape. Before showing these visuals to your students, tell them that they will be reading a story that takes place in a part of the country called the prairie. On a map of the United States, show them where the prairie lands are located. Ask them to think about movies and television shows that have settings on the prairie and that take place in the past. Encourage students to talk about what kind of life these people had. Discuss what the good things were about living on the prairie and what the hardships were. Explain that the story, *Sarah, Plain and Tall,* takes place on the prairie more than a hundred years ago. Ask students to speculate on what they might expect to see on the prairie in the time before electricity and automobiles. Write their responses on the board. Next, show the filmstrip, slides, or photographs. After the visual presentation, add to or revise students' list of speculations as seems appropriate.

---

*The text is approximately 8,700 words long. We have based reading times on students' reading about 100 per minute.

PRETEACHING VOCABULARY: *Rebus*

In this activity, selected words are presented as pictures in the context of a sentence or paragraph.

Goal of the Activity: To ensure that students can visualize the images described in the story.

Rationale: Verbal images abound in this novel. Some of your students will probably be able to conjure up fairly accurate mental pictures on their own, but others may need some extra help. Providing illustrations along with textual information will help students visualize the images the author has created.

Procedure: Select several words that require visualization and that are important to understanding and enjoying the story. We have chosen *prairie, pitchfork, bonnet, conch shell, sea, seals, wooly ragwort, Indian paintbrush, Maine,* and *dunes.* Locate pictures in magazines (or draw your own if you're artistic) that illustrate each of these words. Next, compose sentences to introduce them. Write these on the chalkboard or a large sheet of tagboard, and instead of writing the selected words, insert the illustrations. For example:

> When I look out on the (picture of *prairie*), I see grass for miles and miles and only a few trees here and there. My father uses a (picture of a *pitchfork*) to stack big piles of hay.
>
> Sometimes I wear a (picture of a *bonnet*) to keep the sun off my face.
>
> When Sarah came to our house on the (picture of *prairie*), she brought a (picture of a *conch shell*) from (illustration of U.S. map showing location of *Maine*). Sarah lives by the (picture of the *sea*) where she has seen many (picture of *seals*). One of the wildflowers that grows in Maine is called (picture of *wooly ragwort*), but we have (picture of *Indian paintbrush*) here on the (picture of *prairie*). When Sarah was small, one of her favorite things to do was to slide down the (picture of a sand *dunes*).

Also, somewhere on the side of the chalkboard or tagboard, print out the words that are pictured.

Explain that the sentences and pictures on the chalkboard introduce some of the words that are used in *Sarah, Plain and Tall.* Read the list of words aloud as you point to each; then ask students to read the first sentence silently and decide which of the words listed on the chalkboard describes the picture in the sentence. For example, for the picture of the prairie, students should select the word *prairie.* Proceed similarly through the remaining sentences. After all the words have been matched with their illustrations, review the words by having students read them out loud.

BUILDING TEXT SPECIFIC KNOWLEDGE: *Stepping Into the Story*

In *Stepping Into the Story,* students are given a preview that includes the setting and characters in the opening scene.

Goal of the Activity: To pull students out of their immediate world and into the world of the story.

Rationale: Since this story takes place some time in the 1800s and students are fairly rooted in the here and now, presenting concrete details from the beginning of the novel will help readers visualize (and smell and hear as well) the setting and the characters, and this will help pull them into the story. It will be easier for students to build meaning with the text if they have something concrete to build with.

Procedure: Prior to creating a preview, read through the first chapter of the story, focusing especially on those sensual details that describe the characters and the setting. Select those elements you feel will help your students develop a good mental picture of the first scene in the story. Next, either write out or outline a preview that will draw your students into the story. Prior to reading the story, give students your preview. Here is a preview we have created to introduce *Sarah, Plain and Tall.*

> Close your eyes for a minute and imagine yourself going way back in time. You find yourself in the kitchen of a little log house on the prairie. It is late afternoon and there is a fire burning in the fireplace. Two dogs are lying on the warm hearthstones, the stones on the floor around the fireplace. The room feels cozy and warm, and you smell the aroma of stew cooking.
>
> A young girl about 8 years old is kneading bread dough on a marble slab on the kitchen table. The girl's name is Anna. Close by is her little brother, Caleb, who sits in a chair near the fire. The two children are in the house alone. Their father is out working in the fields, and they have no mother. She died the day after Caleb was born. The story begins with Caleb asking Anna lots of questions, questions Anna has heard many times before.

Reading For Day 1

READING TO STUDENTS

Read the first chapter from the novel aloud to students. The story begins with these words, "Did Mama sing every day?" asked Caleb. "Every-single-day?"

Postreading For Day 1

WRITING: *Dear Diary*

In this *Dear Diary* activity, students write diary entries from the point of view of one of the supporting characters in the story.

Goal of the Activity: To involve students in the narrative more fully by encouraging them to look at the story events from various characters' points of view and to use their writing skills to communicate their ideas to others.

Rationale: Even though the story is told by Anna, each of the characters plays a unique and important role. Having students look at the events of the story through one of the minor character's eyes will help expand their vision and understanding of this novel. Also, assuming the role of a story character requires the reader to do some critical and creative thinking in order to understand the part the character plays in the story.

Preparation: Write diary entries from the point of view of two or three of the minor characters in the first chapter. Later, you will model composing diary entries on the board as part of showing students how to write them.

Procedure: After you have finished reading the first chapter aloud, have students identify the characters introduced in it (*Anna, Caleb, Papa [Jacob Witting], and Lottie and Nick [the dogs]*). Write the word *narrator* on the board. Tell students that a narrator is the person who tells the story, the person through whose eyes we see the story events unfold. Ask students who the narrator is in *Sarah, Plain and Tall* (*Anna*). Also, ask how they know that Anna is the one telling the story (*The pronoun "I" is used.*).

Next, talk about one of the other characters in the story, Caleb, for example. Ask if students think Caleb might see the things that happened in the first chapter a little bit differently than Anna does. Say something similar to "Now, pretend that you are Caleb and are going to write something in your diary, something about what happened in the chapter. What would you write? Let's try it and see." Compose a sample diary entry on the chalkboard. For example:

> Dear Diary,
>
> There are so many things I don't know about my mother. I ask my sister, but she gets tired of answering my same old questions. Funny, but I don't get tired of asking them. I want to know so many things and one of them is why my Papa doesn't sing anymore. I think it's because we don't have a Mama. But guess what? Papa sent a letter to a lady in Maine, and she sent one back. I told Papa to write back and ask if she sings!
>
> > Your friend,
> > Caleb

Compose another letter or two from one or two of the other characters. For example:

> Dear Diary,
>
> Sometimes it makes me sad to see Anna having to do so much work. She bakes bread, makes stew and watches Caleb, things a grown woman should be doing. I wish she had more time to play and have fun. But maybe that will happen yet. I put an advertisement in the newspaper for a wife and received a reply from a Miss Elisabeth Wheaton, who lives in Maine. I think the children are pleased.
>
> > Jacob Witting

Tell students that the next day they will each get a copy of *Sarah, Plain and Tall* to read plus a diary. They will use the diary to write one entry for each of the nine chapters in the novel. You will also be writing entries in your diary. (Writing these will help you focus on any difficulties your students might encounter in the task and, of course, provide a good model for students.) Explain that after they have finished reading the story and writing their diary entries, each of them will get together with a classmate and talk about their diary entries. At the end of the week, they will each get a chance to share some of the entries they found most interesting.

Prereading For Day 2

QUESTIONING AND DIRECTION SETTING: *Who, What, and How?*

In *Who, What, and How,* questioning is used to review the characters and events in the first chapter.

Goal of the Activity: To help students recall the characters and events in the first chapter, to review the diary entries, to explain how students might go about choosing their minor characters and what they might include in a diary entry, and to set a purpose for reading.

Rationale: Since a day has passed since the students have thought about the story, they may need to be drawn into it again. This activity serves to activate prior knowledge by questioning the students about previously read or discussed material. Also, students may need additional instruction on how to choose their minor characters and write their diary entries. This activity helps clarify the task.

Preparation: Prior to the class, write an entry in your diary for chapters 2, 3, and 4. Also, write the following on the board:

> Read chapters 2, 3, and 4 in Sarah, Plain and Tall. After you finish reading each chapter, pick one of the characters from it. Look at what happened in the chapter through that character's eyes, and write an entry in your diary pretending you are that character.

Procedure: Before distributing the diaries, review the characters in the novel by asking students to name them and tell something about each. Next, explain that today they will read chapters 2, 3, and 4 and write a diary entry for each chapter from the point of view of one of the minor characters in the chapter. Explain that in this activity any character but Anna can be considered a minor character.

Review the characters from Chapter 1 and the sample diary entries. Ask students to think about what is alike and what is different about each diary entry. (*Alike: Each begins with "Dear Diary;" each talks about the things that happened in the first chapter; each ends with a signature. Different: Each sees the events of the first chapter differently; each includes different details; each signs his or her name differently.*)

Remind students that after they finish each chapter, they are to record their entry for that chapter in their diaries. Before students begin reading, briefly discuss what had just happened at the close of the first chapter. (*Mr. Witting received a letter from Sarah Wheaton from Maine.*) Read the last paragraph of the chapter aloud, then ask students to read further to find out if Caleb's gets an answer to his question, "Does she sing?"

Reading For Day 2

SILENT READING

Have the students read chapters 2, 3, and 4 silently.

Postreading For Day 2

WRITING: *Dear Diary*

Dear Diary (con't.) At this point, students write their own diary entries from the point of view of one of the supporting characters.

Procedure: Have students write a diary entry for each of the three chapters. Be available to offer guidance and encouragement while students are working on this activity. If students are having problems choosing a character, you might want to list some possibilities on the chalkboard.

Chapter 2: Caleb and Papa (Jacob Witting)

Chapter 3: Caleb, Papa, Sarah, Jack (the horse), Nick (the dog), and Seal (Sarah's cat)

Chapter 4: Caleb, Papa, Sarah, Seal (cat), and Lottie and Nick (the dogs)

Prereading For Day 3

QUESTIONING AND DIRECTION SETTING: *Who, What, and How?*

Here, you use questioning to review the characters and the events in chapters 2–4. You might also want to review the diary entries from Chapter 1 for the students who still need help in writing their diary entries.

Goal of Activity: These are the same as those for Day 2—to help students recall the characters and events in the first chapter, to review the diary entries, to explain how they might go about choosing their minor characters and what they might include in a diary entry, and to set a purpose for reading.

Rationale: Again, because a day has passed since the students have thought about the story, they might need to be drawn into it again.

Preparation: Prior to the lesson, write entries in your diary for chapters 5, 6, and 7. Also, write this prompt on the board:

Read chapters 5, 6, and 7 in *Sarah, Plain and Tall*. After you finish reading each chapter, again pick one of the characters from it and write a diary entry through that character's eyes.

Procedure: Before students begin reading, ask them to name the minor characters found in chapters 2–4. (*Chapter 2: Caleb and Papa ; Chapter 3: Caleb, Papa, Sarah, Jack (the horse), Nick (the dog), and Seal; Chapter 4: Caleb, Papa, Seal, Lottie and Nick.* Ask for student volunteers to read their diary entries aloud. You may want to choose one of the more interesting entries to record on the chalkboard and encourage students to talk about what makes it an appealing entry. Remind students that again today after they finish each chapter they are to record their entry for that chapter in their diaries.

Also, before the students begin reading, briefly discuss what had just happened at the close of the fourth chapter. (*Sarah told the children she wanted to see the sheep, that she had never touched one.*) Read the last page or so of the chapter aloud, then ask students to read to find out what Sarah thinks of the sheep. Ask them to think about how her reaction shows how she feels about living on the farm.

Reading For Day 3

SILENT READING

Have the students read chapters 5,6, and 7 silently.

Postreading For Day 3

WRITING: *Dear Diary* (same as previous days).

Goal for Activity and **Rationale:** Same as previous days.

Procedure: Have students write diary entries for chapters 5, 6, and 7. Again, you might want to list some possibilities on the chalkboard.

> Chapter 5: Caleb, Papa, Sarah, Nick and Lottie, and some sheep.

> Chapter 6: Caleb, Papa, Sarah, Jack, Old Bess (horse), Nick, Lou (lamb), Mattie (lamb), and cows

> Chapter 7: Caleb, Papa, Sarah, Matthew (neighbor), Maggie (neighbor), Old Bess, Jack, Rose, Violet, Seal, Nick, Lottie, and chickens

Prereading For Day 4

QUESTIONING AND DIRECTION SETTING

Who, What and How. Use the same procedure here you used on previous days.

Rationale: Again, this activity serves to activate prior knowledge by questioning the students about previously read or discussed material and also provides clarification of the task. Of course, if students appear to be ready to read without prereading assistance, you can simply indicate that they are again to write diary entries and let them begin reading.

Preparation: Prior to the lesson, write these instructions on the board:

> Read chapters 8 and 9 in Sarah, Plain and Tall. After you finish reading each chapter, again pick one of the characters from it and write a diary entry through that character's eyes.

Procedure: Once again, if it seems appropriate, before students begin reading ask them to name the minor characters found in previous chapters. (*Chapter 5: Caleb, Papa , Sarah, the sheep, Nick and Lottie, and the sheep; Chapter 6: Caleb, Papa, Sarah, Jack, Old Bess, Nick, Lou*

*and Mattie (lambs), and cows; Chapter 7: Caleb, Papa, Sarah, Matthew, Maggie, Old Bess,
Jack, Rose, Violet, Seal, Nick, Lottie, and chickens)*

As before, you may want to ask a few students to read from their diaries. If students still need
some help with their diary entries, you might again write one entry on the board and talk about
what makes it appealing reading. Also, before students begin their silent reading, briefly discuss
what had just happened at the close of Chapter 7. (*The neighbors—Maggie, Matthew, Rose and
Violet—go home; Sarah names the chickens; Papa brings Sarah the first roses of summer.*) Read
the last page or so of the chapter aloud, and then tell students that in the next chapter Sarah has
an argument with Papa. Ask them to speculate on what the argument is about. Then, tell them
to read to find out what the argument is about and whether Sarah ends up staying with the
Wittings or going back to Maine.

Reading For Day 4

SILENT READING

Have students read chapters 8 and 9 silently.

Postreading For Day 4

WRITING: *Dear Diary*

Goal for Activity and **Rationale:** Same as previous days.

Procedure: Have students write diary entries for chapters 8 and 9. As always, be available to
offer guidance and encouragement while they are writing.

Postreading For Day 5 (a continuation of that on Day 4)

DISCUSSION: *One on One*

In *One on One,* students meet in pairs and take turns reading their diary entries to one another
and responding to each other's writing.

Goal of the Activity: To provide a real audience for students' writing and to give students an
opportunity to give and receive feedback on the effectiveness of their communication.

Rationale: Reading their own written material aloud to another student provides students with
both an audience for their writing and a forum for sharing their ideas. It also gives them an
opportunity to discover where they have been successful in their communication as well as
what they might need to do to communicate more effectively in the future.

Procedure: Explain to students that they will meet with a partner and take turns reading their
diary entries.

Call on a volunteer to bring his or her diary to you. Tell the class that you are going to use the volunteer to help model what students are to do when they meet with their partners.

Sit down at a table with the volunteer. (You may want to have students gather around the table.) Tell them that you and "Mitch" are going to take turns reading your diary entries for a few of the chapters in *Sarah, Plain and Tall.* After reading each entry, you will talk about one thing that made the entry interesting and understandable and *one* thing that might have made the entry more interesting and understandable. Before discussing some examples, read an entry from your journal.

> Dear Diary,
>
> Being a dog is great. Today the house was so nice and warm and Anna baked bread and made stew. During dinner Caleb dropped some stew on the floor. It was delicious. The family seemed happy tonight. Papa brought out a piece of paper and read from it. Everyone was quiet afterwards, but I think it was good news. I saw Anna put her arm around Caleb.
>
> Nick

Ask Mitch to name something about your entry that made it interesting or understandable. (*"You told about the things that a dog might have seen or heard."*) Next, let several other students offer one comment. (*"You used the pronoun 'I',"* *"You began the entry with, 'Dear Diary' and ended it with Nick's name;"* *"You included interesting details such as the stew falling on the floor and Anna putting her arm around Caleb;"* *"By the words you chose, you helped me see what happened through Nick's eyes. A dog would be concerned about food, comfort, and the family's mood and well-being."*) Next, let Mitch say what you might do to make the entry more interesting or understandable. (*Leave out some of the details that don't have much to do with what happened in the story such as "Being a dog is great."*) Also, give students a chance to point out other possibilities for improvement. (*Give more specific details. Tell about the sounds Nick heard, what he might have felt.*)

After this, have Mitch choose one of his diary entries to read.

> Dear Diary,
>
> I am so excited. Sarah is coming. She is coming on a train. Soon!
>
> Caleb

Give one positive comment about Mitch's entry. (*"You told about the most important thing that happened in the chapter from Caleb's point of view."*) Comment on how Mitch might have made the entry more interesting or understandable. (*"You might have included a few more details such as what Caleb did with Sarah's letters and what he said to Anna and Papa."*)

Read as many other entries as you feel are appropriate. Don't belabor the comments. The main purpose of this activity is to give students the opportunity to share their written ideas and to feel successful in doing so. It is not to correct grammar, spelling, or punctuation.

Before students meet with their partners, ask if there are any questions, and remind them that the main purpose of the activity is to read and enjoy each other's diary entries. The comments are just to help them make their writing more interesting and understandable. They should be supportive of each other and not overly critical. After they have finished reading all the entries, they are to choose their partner's entry that they found to be the most appealing and be ready to read it to the class.

Give students about 15 minutes to meet with their partners. Then, call on students to read the diary entries of their partner that they liked best. Encourage them to explain why they chose these entries as their favorites.

As a concluding activity, you might want to bring students together for a few minutes to share their overall responses to the story and then show the video of *Sarah, Plain and Tall*, produced by Hallmark Hall of Fame. After seeing the video, you might discuss the similarities and differences between the book and the video. Other postreading activities might include having students:

- form groups and dramatize their favorite scenes
- write a sequel to the novel or an alternate ending
- compose an instrumental piece to depict a favorite scene or one of the characters
- turn the story into a 100-word or so picture book

Adapting the Activity: A similar SRE might be build around Pam Conrad's novel *Prairie Songs*, Laura Ingalls Wilder's *Little House* series, the *Betsy-Tacy* books by Maud Hart Lovelace, or *Caddie Woodlawn* by Carol Ryrie Brink.

Reflection: The purposes of these five days of activities have been to help students successfully read and enjoy Sarah, Plain and Tall, *to understand and respond to the text, and to come away from the experience with a few new insights about themselves and the world as portrayed though literature. The SRE began with three prereading activities. First, students' background knowledge about the novel's setting was activated and supplemented by using a filmstrip and slides. Next, vocabulary was introduced by using illustrations to represent some of the words students will encounter in the story. Finally, students were provided with text-specific knowledge through a preview of the opening scene of the novel designed to help draw them into the story's setting and introduce the characters. The reading portion of the activities began with reading the first chapter aloud to students. For the next three days, students read subsequent chapters silently. The students participated in a similar postreading activity all five days. For this activity, Dear Diary, students wrote diary entries from the point of view of one of the minor characters in each of the chapters. This activity was designed to engage students more fully in the story as well as to give them an opportunity to interact with the text and express themselves in writing. Each day, students were prepared for that day's reading and postreading tasks by the teacher's reviewing characters and events in the chapters and providing instruction and clarification of the* Dear Diary *activity. On the last day, students shared their diary entries with another student, and, optionally, watched a video of the novel.*

SAMPLE 2: A COMPLETE SRE FOR *EARTHQUAKES*

This SRE uses the K-W-L procedure recommended by Donna Ogle (1986). K-W-L includes pre- , during-, and postreading activities in which students actively consider what they Know, what they Want to know, and what they Learn.

Students: Fifth-grade students with low to average reading ability in an ethnically diverse classroom in California; 5 ESL students.

Selection: *Earthquakes* by Seymour Simon. This informational book gives a dramatic photographic account of the causes and effects of earthquakes around the globe.

Reading Purpose: To learn about earthquakes, what causes them, what effects they have on people and property, and what might be done to prepare for them.

OVERVIEW

Students	Selection	Purpose
Fifth graders of average to low ability and five ESL students	*Earthquakes* by Seymour Simon	To learn more about earthquakes

Day 1

Prereading Activities	During-reading Activities	Postreading Activities
• Motivating and Relating Reading to Students' Lives (10 mins.) • Activating Background Knowledge (10 mins.) • Direction Setting (5 mins.)	• Guided Reading • Reading to Students (10 mins.)	• Discussion • Questioning

Day 2

Prereading Activities	During-reading Activities	Postreading Activities
• Focusing Attention—Pre-questioning and Direction-setting	• Modifying the Text • Guided Reading (30mins.)	• Discussion • Application and Outreach using jigsaw groups

Prereading For Day 1

MOTIVATING AND RELATING READING TO STUDENTS' LIVES: *What's Your Story?*

In this activity, an event relating to the topic of the text is described and then students relate their own similar experiences.

Goal of the Activity: To pique students' interest in a topic and activate their background knowledge.

Rationale: Describing an event in a way that requires students to infer or guess what is happening can be an effective way to stimulate interest and introduce a topic at the same time. Having students then discuss their own experiences requires that they access relevant knowledge, which will help them build meaning with the text.

Procedure: Begin by describing a scenario similar to the following. "Imagine yourself in this situation. You are asleep in bed. Suddenly, the bed begins to move back and forth. Half awake, you say to your brother or sister in the bed next to yours, 'Stop shaking the bed.' " Ask students to explain what is going on. Tell them that this was an experience you had with earthquakes, and encourage them to talk about their own experiences with earthquakes.

ACTIVATING BACKGROUND KNOWLEDGE: *What I Know*

In this activity, students brainstorm to find out what they know about a topic and then generate categories of information that are likely to be found in the text they will read.

Goal of the Activity: To have students activate their prior knowledge about a topic and consider what information on that topic might be included in a specific text.

Rationale: These California students are likely to have some knowledge of earthquakes. Activating this knowledge before reading can help establish a framework to aid them in building meaning with text.

Procedure: On the chalkboard, write the title *Earthquakes*. Underneath that title and to the left, write the heading *What I Know*. Ask students to give some of the facts they know about earthquakes. Jot their responses under the heading *What I Know*.

EARTHQUAKES

What I Know

Can cause damage

Are unpredictable

Are scary

Happen in California

Not all are the same

Shake the earth

Don't happen at night

Are getting worse

As you will notice, not all of the students' responses are accurate. During this brainstorming session, you might ask students various questions such as, "How did you learn that?" or "How could you prove that?" Later, during the postreading discussion, you can clear up any remaining misconceptions.

After students have given a variety of responses, show them the cover illustration on the book, *Earthquakes*. Ask them to think about the kind of information that might be included in the book, and write their suggestions on the board to the left of their initial responses. Some of their suggestions might include how earthquakes happen, where they happen, what we can do about them, how much damage they do, why they happen, and descriptions of some of the worst quakes.

FOCUSING ATTENTION—PREQUESTIONING AND DIRECTION-SETTING: *What I Would Like to Know*

In this activity, students consider what they would like to know about a topic that might be discussed in a specific text.

Goal of the Activity: To turn students' interest in earthquakes into a desire to read about them.

Rationale: Having students think about what they would like to know about a topic sets up a purpose for reading. If students have questions in mind, they will be looking for answers to those questions as they read, and meaning-building will be facilitated.

Procedure: Explain that informational books such as *Earthquakes* are written to give us information that we might need or want. Ask students to think about what they would like to know about earthquakes—things they don't already know or aren't quite sure of. Write their responses on the board in a column to the right of the *What I Know* column.

EARTHQUAKES

What I Would Like to Know

What causes earthquakes

How earthquakes are measured

What places have earthquakes

What was the worst earthquake

Where most earthquakes are

What we can do about earthquakes

Reading For Day 1

GUIDED READING: *What I Find Out*

In this activity, students write down answers to the questions they posed prior to reading, and then they consider which of their questions still need answering.

Goal of the Activity: To have students transform questions into answers and thoughts into writing.

Rationale: Having students search for answers to their questions requires active meaning-building on their part. Transforming that meaning into writing requires and promotes even deeper understanding. Having students go a step further and check what questions still need answering lets them know that the information an author chooses to include is limited and that they may need to check other sources to get their answers.

Procedure: On the chalkboard to the right of the previous two headings, write **What I Found Out**. Explain to students that this will be the last part of the K-W-L procedure—a procedure they can use when they read informational books and articles. They have already completed the first two steps—thinking about and writing down what they know about earthquakes and what they would like to know. The last step is to record the information they discover.

Direct students' attention to the information they wanted to know. Explain that, as they read, they will look for the answers to these questions.

READING TO STUDENTS: *The Appetizer*

In this activity, you read the first few pages of the book aloud to students.

Goal of the Activity: To interest students further in the topic of the book and motivate them to read it on their own.

Rationale: Reading the beginning of a text aloud helps ease students into the material. A good enthusiastic rendition can also be an enticement for students to read on their own. In addition, this shared experience allows you to complete the third step of the K-W-L procedure as a group and provide clarification of the task before students read and record answers on their own.

Procedure: Ask students to listen carefully as you read the first five pages of the book aloud. They should be thinking about the questions they had listed on the board and deciding whether or not they are answered in these pages.

Postreading For Day 1

DISCUSSION: *Questions Answered?*

In this activity, students decide which questions were answered in the text.

Goal of the Activity: To have students realize that, although a specific text may answer some of their questions, it may not answer all of them and they will need to seek other sources to answer some questions.

Rationale: To become critical thinkers and readers, students need to realize that while our questions about a topic might be answered in a text, they also might not be. Authors have to be selective in what they include. What we may wish to know may not be in a particular text, and therefore we may need to consult others.

Procedure: After you have read the first few pages aloud, draw students' attention to the questions asked in the prereading activity.

EARTHQUAKES

What I Would Like to Know	*What I Found Out*
What causes earthquakes	
How earthquakes are measured	
What places have earthquakes	
What was the worst earthquake	
Where most earthquakes are	
What we can do about earthquakes	

Begin by asking students, "Was the first question, *What causes earthquakes?*, answered in the first five pages of the book?" If students answer "yes," ask them to tell you what the answer is and write that answer in the column **What I Found Out**. Proceed in a similar manner with each of the questions. If questions aren't answered, tell students that these questions still might be answered in the remainder of the text or that they may not be answered in this particular text at all and they will need to consult other sources for the answers.

Prereading For Day 2

FOCUSING ATTENTION—PREQUESTIONING AND DIRECTION-SETTING: *K-W-L*

In the K-W-L procedure, students record what they know about a topic, what they would like to know, and what they learned from reading a text. This prereading activity prepares students to use the K-W-L procedure independently.

Goal of the Activity: To help students learn to independently access their knowledge on a topic, think about what more they would like to learn about that topic, and record what they learn from their reading.

Rationale: Having students access appropriate knowledge before reading a text, pose their own questions, and write down the answers to those questions can help them better understand and remember text material.

Procedure: Hand out the *What I KNOW—What I WANT to Know—What I LEARNED Chart shown below.*

What I KNOW	What I WANT to Know	What I LEARNED

When students have their charts, review the three types of information they will record. First, they will think about and record what they **know** about earthquakes in the first column, then they will write down what they **want** to know in the second column. As they read the book, they will write the answers to their questions or what they **learned** in the third column. Remind students about what they did as a group the day before and explain that today they will have the opportunity to focus on their *own* knowledge and interest in earthquakes as they read.

Remind students that not all of their questions, of course, will be answered in the text. This might be a good opportunity to talk about locating other resources for finding answers if this particular text doesn't provide them.

Tell students that, when they finish, they will get a chance to share what they learned about earthquakes.

Reading For Day 2

MODIFYING THE TEXT: *Tape It.*

In this activity, an audio tape recording is made available for students to listen to as they follow along in the text.

Goal of the Activity: To make the concepts in the text accessible to readers who might have difficulty reading the text on their own.

Rationale: Although this text is richly illustrated and not particularly dense, some students, particularly those ESL students who are still in the process of mastering English, may have difficulty with it. Having an audio tape available will help make the concepts accessible for those students whose oral skills are more developed than their reading skills.

Procedure: Make a recording of the book on an audio tape, or have an older or particularly competent student do it. Make as many copies as necessary.

✓ **GUIDED READING:** *What I Learned*

Students read the text silently (or while listening to a tape), guided by the questions they have written on their K-W-L chart, and write any answers to their questions as they find them in the text as well as other information they would like to record.

Goal of the Activity: To actively engage students with the text and to encourage and facilitate meaning-building.

Rationale: Having students search for answers to their questions requires active meaning-building on their part. Transforming that meaning into writing requires and promotes even deeper understanding of the information and ideas in the text.

Procedure: Have students read the entire book silently, recording what they learn about earthquakes as they read. Students who are following along in the text while listening to a taped version also write what they learn on their K-W-L charts.

Postreading For Day 2

DISCUSSION I: *What Did You Learn?*

Here, students meet in small heterogeneous groups to discuss what they learned from the text.

Goal of the Activity: To give students the opportunity to express their ideas to an audience and hear other students' ideas as well.

Rationale: Expressing themselves in an informal small group setting gives students the opportunity to clarify their thoughts and also gain new information and insights from their classmates.

Procedure: After students have finished reading the text and have completed their K-W-L charts, have them meet in groups of three to six. Appoint a facilitator and a recorder for each group. In the groups, students take turns telling what their questions were, which ones were answered, and what the answers were. The facilitator's job is to make sure everyone gets a chance to speak, and the recorder keeps an account of the questions that were *not* answered in the text.

DISCUSSION II: *Research It.*

The recorders from each small group discussion session report to the class what questions are still left to be answered, and then each group takes a question to research.

Goal of the Activity: To have students work in small groups to check multiple sources in order to find answers to a question.

Rationale: As previously mentioned, students need to realize that finding the information they want sometimes requires searching in one or more additional sources. Working in heterogeneous groups to locate these sources and answers requires that group members support one another in their efforts. Learning to work cooperatively is a skill that is necessary not only in school but in many aspects of life.

Procedure: After the groups have met to discuss what they learned in *Earthquakes,* have the recorders report to the entire class what questions their group members still have. Write these questions on the chalkboard. Have each group choose one question to research. Each group is then responsible for finding the answer to their question and reporting their findings to the entire class.

This may also be a good time to compare the statements students listed in the *What I Know* activity with what they actually did learn from the text. For example, one student had said,

"They are getting worse." Ask students if the idea that earthquakes are getting worse was validated by the text. If the consensus is "no," the student who offered this initial comment may concur or perhaps decide to pursue independent research to try to confirm his or her statement.

We are assuming that this class is familiar with library research techniques; therefore, students need only be reminded at this time on how to proceed. This may require a brief discussion to activate their prior knowledge and a brief review of guidelines they might follow.

APPLICATION AND OUTREACH

Students form Jigsaw groups (a description of these groups can be found in Chapter 8), select a topic that emerged from their readings, and make posters that will be displayed in the school cafeteria, library, or other public places.

Goal of the Activity: To help reinforce the concepts students learned in their reading and to provide the opportunity for students to apply their knowledge in a practical, helpful way.

Rationale: Having groups of students work together to create posters designed to communicate information they learned from reading about earthquakes can provide students with practice in working cooperatively; recalling, analyzing and summarizing information; and thinking creatively about how to present information in a clear, concise, yet eye-catching way. It also demonstrates that information garnered from reading can be shared with others and can be important and useful.

Procedure: After students have met in their discussion groups, bring the entire class together again. Discuss some of the major points of interest in their reading about earthquakes, and ask students to think about what information might be of interest to other students in the school. Have students offer their suggestions and write these on the board. Some of their suggestions might include:

How earthquakes are measured

What you should do to prepare for an earthquake

What you should do when an earthquake happens

How earthquakes happen

Where earthquakes happen

Assign (or let each group choose) one of the topics to make a poster of. If sample posters are available, show these to students or clip appropriate advertisements from magazines and discuss what makes these informative and eye catching.

Each group will then meet to decide what information, graphics, and illustrations will go on their poster. Next, they will use the resources available to them to produce a poster that will communicate information on their topic in the most interesting way possible. Finally, they will publically display their poster.

Adapting the Activity: The K-W-L activity can be used any time students' purpose for reading is to learn information. Students might use this procedure while reading content-area textbooks, magazine articles, or any number of informational trade books. For example, students might use a K-W-L chart to help them learn more about Benjamin Franklin while reading *The Many Lives of Benjamin Franklin* by Mary Pope Osborne, to learn more about ancient civilizations while reading books in *The Ancient World* series published by Silver Burdett, or to learn about the Revolutionary War while reading *The War for Independence: The Story of the American Revolution* by Albert Marrin.

Reflection: We believe that the K-W-L procedure is an extremely useful technique for dealing with informational material. The three phases of the procedure—brainstorming, purpose setting through asking questions, and finding answers to those questions—virtually guarantee that students will be actively involved in their learning. The procedure provides a scaffold that helps support students' own interests and inquiries. Also, as Ogle (1986) points out, K-W-L "helps students keep control of their own inquiry, extending the pursuit of knowledge beyond just the one article. The teacher is making clear that learning shouldn't be framed around just what an author chooses to include, but that it involves the identification of the learner's questions and the search for authors or articles dealing with those questions."

In concluding our remarks on K-W-L, we wish to make three additional comments on the method. First, K-W-L can be used as both a teacher-directed activity and an independent learning activity, a strategy. If students are going to fully internalize the strategy so that they both can and do use it independently long after you have introduced it, they are likely to need a good deal more instruction than presented here. As we have previously noted, we describe such strategy instruction in detail in Graves, Watts, and Graves (1994).

Second, as an addition to the original K-W-L, Eileen Carr and Donna Ogle (1987) have described an enriched form of K-W-L, which they term "K-W-L Plus." The enriched form supplements the original components of K-W-L by adding mapping and summarizing. If K-W-L is a technique that you want to know more about, we suggest you investigate both forms of the procedure.

Finally, one of our reviewers, Dr. Mary Jolfy, a reading resource instructor in the Dade County, Florida Public Schools, suggested another excellent modification to K-W-L. Here is her suggestion.

> *When presenting the procedure on the board, students should also have their own copy in front of them. They should complete this graphic organizer, noting board information and their own interests simultaneously. The language activities of thinking, speaking, listening, and writing together reinforce the goal and procedure of K-W-L-. Also, tell the students their K-W-L chart can serve as a study guide. To review, they simply fold over the* Learned *column and see if they can answer the questions posed in* What I Want to Know. *They can check their answers by uncovering the* Learned *section and refering back to specific sections of the text if necessary.*

SAMPLE 3: A STUDENT-GENERATED, THEME-BASED SRE ON "SELF-DISCOVERY AND PERSONAL TRIMPH"

This is quite a different type of SRE from the two previous ones and requires some explanation. The SRE described here is built around a theme that arises from a student-generated need, concern, or interest. For example, suppose students find a dead bird on the playground, or perhaps a student's grandparent, parent, sibling, friend, or pet dies. Here is an opportunity to have students read selections on the theme of death or coping with loss. Or perhaps Jenny, April, and Chloe have a horrible argument on the playground and continue it in the classroom; or Jeff, Shaun, and Blake enter the classroom grinning, with their arms draped over one another.

The joys and pains of friendships are perennial springboards for theme-based reading in the classroom. Another opportunity might arise when a student is moving to another state and the theme of change becomes immediately relevant. Or perhaps a student achieves some personal goal or success, such as writing a story for the first time for the school newspaper, or building a birdhouse, or overcoming a fear such as speaking in front of the class; these are occasions to celebrate and explore more deeply by reading books on the theme of self-discovery and personal triumph. Having students read about people who experience situations similar to theirs is an excellent way to expose them to the idea of literature as a vehicle to express and explore our common humanity.

In the following example, we show how a theme-based, student-generated SRE might be developed.

Scenario: Chad, one of the lower achieving students in your fourth-grade class, appears one day with an elaborately constructed model to share. You learn that the model is a space vehicle Chad calls the "Crater Cruiser." He has designed and put together the model on his own. On further inquiry, you learn the project was fraught with design and construction problems that Chad had to solve over the course of many days.

Students: Fourth graders reflecting a variety of abilities and ethnic backgrounds.

Selections: A few texts that illustrate problem solving.

Mrs. Armitage on Wheels by Quentin Blake. An engaging picture book that illustrates in a comical way how inventions are precipitated by need.

Sixth-Grade Sleepover by Eve Bunting. Book-loving Janey must overcome her secret "problem"—her fear of the dark—for a coed sleepover in the school cafeteria.

Cracker Jackson by Betsy Byars. Cracker takes responsibility for helping a babysitter who is victim of physical abuse.

Stone Soup by John Warren Stewig. A young girl figures out a way to get stingy people to share. (Picture book.)

The Fourth Question: A Chinese Tale by Rosalind C. Wang. Yee-Lee figures out a way to solve his family's poverty as well as the dilemmas of many others. (Picture book.)

The True Confessions of Charlotte Doyle by Avi. A prim 13-year-old school girl turns seasoned sailor in this historical novel of adventure and intrigue.

Camper of the Week by Amy Schwartz. Rosie solves her dilemma of living up to her "camper of the week" status and still having fun with her friends. (Picture book)

Hatchet by Gary Paulsen. Through his courage and ingenuity, 13-year-old Brian is able to survive for 54 days in the Canadian wilderness.

Journey by Patricia MacLachlan. With the help of his grandfather and some torn photographs, Journey learns about forgiveness and acceptance.

Amazing Grace by Mary Hoffman. Illus. by Caroline Binch. Plucky Grace overcomes obstacles and earns the role of Peter Pan in the school play. (Picture book)

Two Short and One Long by Nina Ring Aamundsen. Three friends—two Norwegians and one Afghani boy—deal with the problems of friendship.

. . . and Now Miguel by Joseph Krumgold. Set in the Sangre de Christo mountains of New Mexico, a young boy learns the joys and struggles of being a sheepherder.

Flight by Robert Burleigh. Illus. by Mike Wimmer. The tale of the determined Charles Lindberg's exciting solo flight across the Atlantic Ocean. (Picture book)

Yossi Asks the Angels for Help by Miriam Chaiken. Yossi looks to angels for help in buying Hanukkah gifts after he loses his gift money.

How Sweetly Sings the Donkey by Vera Cleaver. Determined and resourceful teen Lily Snow works to improve her family's life.

The Sky is Falling by Barbara Corcoran. Set during the Depression, Annah learns about growing up by accepting change.

Reading Purpose: To read a text or number of texts for the pleasure of seeing how they can help us understand how people deal with and solve various kinds of issues, challenges, and problems.

OVERVIEW

Students	Selection	Purpose
• Fourth graders of mixed abilities	*Crow Boy* by Taro Yashima and a variety of selections reflecting the theme of self-discovery and personal triumph	Enjoyment and new insights

Day 1

Prereading Activities	During-reading Activities	Postreading Activities
• Motivating (10 mins.) • Relating Reading to Students' Lives (10 mins.)	• Reading to Students (20 mins.)	• Discussion (10 mins.)

Day 2

Prereading Activities	During-reading Activities	Postreading Activities
• Direction Setting (10 mins.) • Building Text-Specific Knowledge (15 mins.)	• Silent and Oral Reading (? mins.*) • Modifying the Text—tape recordings available	• Writing—graffiti board and journal entries (? mins.*) • Artistic Activity (? mins.*)

Day 3 - to End of Unit

Prereading Activities	During-reading Activities	Postreading Activities
• Individualized	• Individualized	• Discussion—small group (20 mins.) • Dramatics, Artistic and Nonverbal Activities (music, dance) (? mins.*) • Writing (? mins.*)

* Time will vary with individual students.

Prereading For Day 1

MOTIVATING: *Let's Talk About You! Self-discovery and Personal Triumph*

In this activity, students talk about the challenges they have faced and the problems they've encountered and how they dealt with these.

Goal of the Activity: To encourage students to think about problems and challenges and what can be done about them.

Rationale: Because youngsters at this age are still quite egocentric, they almost always enjoy thinking and talking about themselves. Getting them to ponder and discuss their own life experiences is the first step in leading them to make connections between themselves and the characters in literature.

Procedure: Encourage Chad to elaborate on what he was hoping to accomplish with his "Crater Cruiser" invention, what problems he ran into, and how he solved them. Also, try to get him to talk about how he felt about himself and his project at various points along the way. What were some of the problems he encountered? What made him keep going? How did he feel when things went wrong? What did he do to correct things that went wrong? Did he learn anything new about himself? Steer the discussion to include the rest of the class and their experiences. Encourage students to talk about something that was hard for them to do but that they accomplished. Elicit the problem-solving strategies they used and feelings they had.

RELATING READING TO STUDENTS' LIVES: *They Did It!*

In this activity, students discuss stories they have read in which the characters triumphed in difficult situations.

Goal of the Activity: To move students' thinking from themselves to story characters and to help them make the connection between real life and literature.

Rationale: Students need to know that they are not alone in what they think, feel, and experience—people everywhere, in other times and other places, no matter what sex, religion, or ethnic background, have similar needs, emotions, and thoughts, and similar ways of dealing with difficult situations. These common characteristics are expressed through literature.

Procedure: Ask students to think about stories they have read in which the characters faced a situation they thought was difficult or impossible but were able to triumph.

Explain that there have been many stories written over the years that show the kind of situation in which a character has a problem to solve or goal to achieve. Ask students to think about why this is so. (Because it is a situation that most people face many times in their lives. Life, it seems, is always presenting us with challenges—problems to solve, goals we want to achieve.) Ask students to name stories in which the main characters were able to solve a problem or achieve a special goal. Did the characters learn anything about themselves while they were working so hard or when they achieved (or didn't achieve) their goal? List characters on the board with the challenges they faced.

Ask students if they like these kinds of stories, and if so why. Keep the discussion lively and brief. If students show interest in the topic, continue the activity into the next day or two by bringing in books that illustrate the theme of self-discovery and personal triumph.

Reading For Day 1

READING TO STUDENTS: *Shared Experience*

In this activity, a selection is read aloud to students that exemplifies the topic or theme you want them to consider.

Selection: *Crow Boy* by Taro Yashima. This story tells of a young Japanese student named Chibi, who through the help of his teacher is able to discover his unique gifts and after years of ridicule and misunderstanding by his classmates earns their admiration and respect.

Goal of the Activity: To give students the opportunity to hear noteworthy literature and to provide all students with a common literary experience.

Rationale: Since each student will be reading different texts for this SRE, providing one shared experience establishes a common source of background information on which future discussions might be based. It also gives students the opportunity to hear quality literature read aloud and is a way to focus their attention on the theme of personal triumph and self-discovery.

Procedure: Tell students that *Crow Boy* by Taro Yashima is one of your favorite stories and one that you think exemplifies the idea of personal triumph and self-discovery. Explain that the story takes place in a village in Japan, and ask them to listen carefully to see if they think that triumph and discovery are illustrated in the story. Read *Crow Boy* aloud.

Postreading For Day 1

DISCUSSION AND QUESTIONING: *Do You Agree?*

In this activity, the teacher suggests a story's theme and students discuss whether or not they agree.

Selection: *Crow Boy* by Taro Yashima.

Goal of the Activity: To encourage students to think about themes and how themes are portrayed through the words and actions of the story characters.

Rationale: Getting students to consider what a story says to them can help them appreciate their role as readers and understand how the elements of character and theme are intertwined.

Procedure: After reading the story, discuss whether or not it exemplifies the theme self-discovery and personal triumph by asking these kinds of questions and letting students give their answers:

> Did Crow Boy have a problem or problems? What was that problem or problems?
>
> What did Crow Boy do about the problems he faced? Did he solve his problems? How? In what way?
>
> Was Crow Boy different at the end of the story from what he was at the beginning? If so, in what ways was he different?
>
> Did anyone else in the story change? Who? In what ways did they change and why?
>
> What did Crow Boy discover about himself? In what way did he triumph?

Prereading For Day 2

DIRECTION SETTING: *Graffiti Board: Self-discovery and Personal Triumph*

In *Graffiti Board,* students write their personal responses to texts on a large sheet of butcher paper.

Goal of the Activity: To encourage students to think about and respond to what they read and to communicate those responses to others.

Rationale: Students need to know that what they think has value. An activity like this can give them confidence in their ability to consider ideas and respond to them. It also provides an opportunity to learn how others respond to literature and become aware of common issues and themes.

Procedure: Prior to beginning the SRE, tack up a large sheet of butcher paper on one section of a wall. At the top of the sheet in bold letters write "Self-discovery and Personal Triumph." Nearby, provide several colored felt tip pens for students to write their "graffiti." Display the books you have selected for students on a table or chalkboard ledge.

Begin your prereading discussion by reminding students of Chad's and Crow Boy's special accomplishments and your previous discussions about solving problems and achieving goals. Indicate the books on display and explain that each of them in one way or another expresses the theme of self-discovery and personal triumph. Write that phrase on the chalkboard and discuss what it means, drawing on the previous day's discussion and using Chad's "Crater Cruiser" and Crow Boy as examples. (How did Chad triumph? What did he learn about himself? How did Crow Boy triumph? What did he learn?)

After the discussion, draw students' attention to the butcher paper on the wall. Tell them this is a "graffiti board" and ask them to speculate on what it might be for. Call on someone to read the heading and hold up the colored pens. Explain that the graffiti board has something to do with the books they will be reading and the theme "Self-discovery and Personal Triumph."

Next, explain that graffiti are sayings written on walls in public places. The graffiti they will write on the wall will be about the stories they read and their themes. Tell them about a book you have recently read, *The Impressionist* by Joan King, explaining that the book is about the famous impressionist painter, Mary Cassatt, and that Mary began painting at a time when few women did. To achieve her goal of becoming a painter, she had many obstacles to overcome— first convincing her very obstinate and domineering father to send her to art school and then proving her competence to the world in an area dominated by men.

Tell students that while you were reading the story, you had many thoughts that you wanted to share with someone else, but no one else was around. If you had a graffiti board nearby, you might have written on it. That's what gave you the idea of a graffiti board in class. On the chalkboard, model the activity by writing down the kinds of thoughts you might want to express on the graffiti board.

> *The Impressionist by Joan King. I can't believe how persevering Mary Cassatt was, how determined she was to become a painter even though there were very few women painters at the time. Nothing came easy for her yet she persisted. Her small successes and her intense love for art must have kept her going. She learned she did have what it takes to be an artist among men. Mrs. G.*

Explain that they can use the graffiti board to write anything they choose, but ideally it will relate to the theme of self-discovery and personal triumph. Students should write the title of the book they're responding to, the author, their graffiti, and their name. Copy your graffiti onto the graffiti board to serve as your contribution as well as a sample for students. Ask students to suggest any graffiti they might write for *Crow Boy*, and let volunteers write that graffiti.

BUILDING TEXT SPECIFIC KNOWLEDGE: *The Coming Attraction*

In *The Coming Attraction,* a preview of a selection is provided in which some of the most salient and interesting details of the selection are revealed. Previews of this sort have been described by Graves, Prenn, and Cooke (1985).

Goal of the Activity: To pique students' interest in various selections and give them information on what the books contain.

Rationale: Using previews to introduce books can help students decide which books to select. These brief sketches can also serve as enticements to read and as schemata builders.

Procedure: Give a thumbnail description of each of the books—something about the character, setting, and plot. Explain that each book in a different way reflects the theme of self-discovery—each one describes a character (or characters) who solves a problem or achieves a goal. Let students peruse and select a book to read.

Reading For Day 2

SILENT AND ORAL READING: *To Each His Own*

In this activity, students have the option to read their chosen selections in a variety of ways—alone silently, orally with partners or in small groups, or silently while listening to a tape recording of the story.

Goal of the Activity: To provide students with the opportunity to read books that interest them and that they can handle successfully.

Rationale: Providing students with a variety of texts and a variety of ways to build meaning with the texts gives them many supports for an enjoyable and worthwhile reading experience.

Procedure: Tell students they may read their books alone or with a partner and that a few of the books are available on tape, so that is also an option. You may want to make some specific recommendations to individual students—books that will have some special meaning for that student and is at his or her reading level—to ensure a successful experience. For instance, in a class of fourth graders you might enthusiastically suggest *Amazing Grace* to Amanda, a rather shy student with adequate but not superior reading skills, and *Journey* to Stephen, a good reader who lives in a foster home, and *Flight* to Michael, who is a average reader and is always drawing airplanes. You might recommend that two friends, Josh and B. J., read *Two Short and One Long* together. You might also suggest that superior readers Emily, Monika, and Summer read *The True Confessions of Charlotte Doyle* and have a three-way discussion after each chapter, reading aloud some of their favorite scenes. And you might let Natalie, a struggling reader, know that you have made a tape of *Camper of the Week,* which she is welcome to listen to as she follows along in the text.

Before they begin reading, remind students that their purposes for reading the story are first to just enjoy it and second to see how stories reveal ways in which people from different times and places are similar in important ways. They also might want to think about what the main character hopes to achieve or what problem the character must solve. While they read, they are free to write on the graffiti board, and journal writing is always an option. After they finish reading, they will have a chance to talk about their ideas in small discussion groups.

The time it takes students to read will vary tremendously. You will want to provide adequate time for the novel readers and encourage the picture book and short chapter book readers to choose additional books to read or to respond to the stories by drawing pictures or writing responses on the graffiti board or in their journals. Tell students approximately the amount of class time they will have (three days, two weeks, or whatever you decide is appropriate) to read books dealing with self-discovery and personal triumph. Also, at this time or some time during the SRE, you will want to prepare students for their self-selected postreading activities (see the *Express Yourself!* postreading activities on pages 183–184).

Postreading for Day 2

WRITING AND ARTISTIC AND NON-VERBAL ACTIVITIES: *Now* You *Respond*

After students finish reading one of their selected texts, they respond to it by writing in their journals, writing on the graffiti board, or creating illustrations that communicate some aspect of self-discovery and personal triumph as illustrated in the story.

Goal of the Activity: To provide students with the opportunity to respond to the theme of a text in a personal way.

Rationale: In order to respond, students will need to have understood what they read, reflect on it, synthesize events and ideas, and decide how these events and ideas relate to the idea of self-discovery and personal triumph. This kind of reflective thinking and responding gives students an opportunity to grow in their ability to ponder, analyze, and draw thoughtful conclusions about the meaning of text.

Procedure: Explain to students that after they finish reading a story, they can write or create with a drawing, painting, collage etc., something that communicates the theme of self-discovery and personal triumph in that particular story. They can write or draw on the graffiti board or in their journals or both. Explain that they will have a chance to share their ideas in small group discussions.

Postreading Culminating Activities
Day 3 to End of Unit

DISCUSSION: *Let's Talk About Story Characters: Self-discovery and Personal Triumph*

In this activity, students gather in small groups to discuss the theme of self-discovery and personal triumph as expressed through the characters in the books they have read.

Goal of the Activity: To give students the opportunity to think about the issues of character and theme, to discuss what they have discovered through literature, and to listen to the responses of their classmates.

Rationale: Discussion provides an excellent forum for students to express, clarify, and expand their thinking. Hearing others' ideas can also give them new insights and perspectives. Additionally, discussing the problems story characters grapple with and how they resolve these issues can help students realize that problems have various faces, are common to everyone, and can be solved in many different ways.

Procedure: After students have finished reading their selections, have them meet in groups of three to six to discuss the problems their characters faced, what they did about these problems, whether or not they triumphed in the end, and what these characters learned about themselves. If you think your students need extra support in focusing their discussion, you might provide the discussion leaders with questions similar to the ones you created for the story *Crow Boy.*

> Did the main character have a problem or problems? What was that problem or problems?

> What did the main character do about the problems he or she faced? Did he or she solve his or her problems? How? In what way?

> Was the main character different at the end of the story from what he or she was at the beginning? If so, in what ways was he or she different?

> Did anyone else in the story change? Who? In what ways did they change and why?

> What did the main character discover about himself or herself? In what way did he or she triumph?

After the discussion, students might like to write their responses on the graffiti board. Also, after the small groups have had an opportunity to meet, you might want to conduct a whole-class discussion, in which students can share the discoveries they made about their story characters with the whole class.

DRAMA; ARTISTIC, GRAPHIC, AND NONVERBAL ACTIVITIES; and WRITING: *Express Yourself!*

In this activity, students select the way or ways they would like to respond to a story.

Goal of the Activity: To give students the opportunity to express themselves in a way that best suits them and the story.

Rationale: Providing students with a number of options for expression can increase their chances for creating a response or application that is meaningful to them.

Procedure: Sometime during the SRE, encourage students to think about how they might like to respond to the story or stories they are reading. Would they like to dramatize a scene with a partner or partners or to dress like the main character and do a pantomime or monologue?

Would they like to take a novel they have read and turn it into a picture book, diorama, or mural? Would they like to make a poster to advertise the book? Would a sculpture or collage be the best way to express their character or characters?

Would they like to create a dance that would show how the character developed from the beginning of the story to the end? Or a dance that expressed the mood of the story?

Would an instrumental piece or a jingle or ballad express their main character? Could they compose a score to accompany the reading or dramatize one of the scenes from the story?

Perhaps they would like to write something in response to their story—a letter to the author or main character, an ending that would be more satisfying to them, a sequel to show what happens to the character after the end of the story that takes the character to a totally different setting.

Ideally, the activities should allow for as much freedom to explore as possible, with the only restriction being that students base their responses on the characters and themes of their stories.

Adapting the SRE: Instead of, or in addition to, focusing on works of fiction, you might have students read expository selections that express the idea of solving a problem and that also provide the resources and the steps taken (or that might be taken) to solve it.

Kids' Computer Capers: Investigations for Beginners by Sandra Markle. History and workings of computers and computer programming.

Robotics by Stuart and Donna Paltorwitz. How robots work and ways in which they are useful.

How to Think Like a Scientist by Stephen P. Kramer. Clear presentation on using the scientific method to answer several of life's everyday questions.

Science Mini-Mysteries by Sandra Markle. Twenty-nine short mysteries to be solved with science experiments.

Before the Wright Brothers by Don Berliner. Chronicles the history of flight beginning in 400 BC.

Totem Pole by Diane Hoyt-Goldsmith. Photos and text show techniques for creating a totem pole, traditional designs, and their meanings.

Greening of City Streets: The Story of Community Gardens by Barbara Huff. Photo essay shows how Manhattan families and individuals develop and maintain urban garden plots.

Round Buildings, Square Buildings, & Buildings That Wiggle Like a Fish by Phillip M. Isaacson. Photographs and lyrical text describe elements that go into architectural planning and building.

Model Buildings and How to Make Them by Harvey Weiss. Clearly written text on model buildings.

Thinking Big by Susan Kuklin. Describes through photographs how an 8-year-old girl copes with problems of being a dwarf.

The Furry News: How to Make a Newspaper by Loreen Leedy. Light-hearted picture book illustrating through the character Big Bear how to start a newspaper.

Explorers and Mapmakers by Peter Ryan. Traces world exploration and the need for maps.

The President Builds a House by Tom Shachtman. Describes Jimmy Carter's work with Habitat for Humanity.

Women Pioneers in Science by Louis Harber. Biographical sketches of inspiring women in science.

Reflection: *What we have suggested here is only one of many possible variations that may have arisen for a student-generated, theme-based scaffold. As you can imagine, an SRE of this sort involves a large portion of the unknown and unpredictable, since the activities will* *develop out of students' needs and interests as they emerge minute by minute, day by day. While there is a good deal of effort and skill involved in orchestrating such an organic process, there are also great rewards—making discoveries along with your students and seeing them find in literature some new and special connections with their own lives and some insights that will stay with them long after they leave your classroom.*

• Comprehensive SREs: A Final Word •

The major purpose of this chapter has been to demonstrate how to combine pre-, during-, and postreading activities to create effective SREs to use in guiding your students toward full literacy. We sincerely hope we have accomplished that purpose. As we reread this chapter and think about what we want to particularly emphasize, three points come clearly to mind. First, a central principle of SREs is that pre-, during-, and postreading activities are each integral components that must work in concert if they are to maximize students' success. Each component affects and is affected by each other component. Second, SREs can take a huge variety of forms— forms appropriate for narratives, for exposition, for easy texts, and for challenging texts. Some SREs are quite lengthy, others extremely brief. Space has allowed us to present only three examples of complete SREs; we hope these three examples have suggested the diversity and richness possible. Finally, we again point out that constructing effective SREs is not a matter of surrounding students' reading with as many activities as possible. Use only enough scaffolding to ensure students' success, and frequently allow and encourage students to read selections that are so well within their capabilities that they require no scaffolding.

References

Carr, E., & Ogle, D. (1987). K-W-L plus: A strategy for comprehension and summarization. *Journal of Reading, 30*, 626–631. Presents an augmented version of K-W-L that includes mapping and summarizing.

Graves, M.F. , Prenn, M.C., & Cooke, C.L. (1985). The coming attraction: Previewing short stories to increase comprehension. *Journal of Reading, 28*, 549–598. A clear description of how to write previews and a summary of much of the research on previewing.

Graves, M.F., Watts, S., & Graves, B.B. (1994). *Essentials of classroom teaching: Elementary reading methods*. Needham Heights, MA: Allyn and Bacon. This concise text contains a thorough discussion of how to teach comprehension strategies as well as information on how to implement most of the other components of a comprehensive elementary reading program.

Ogle, D. (1986). K-W-L: A teaching model that develops active reading of expository text. *The Reading Teacher, 39*, 564–570. Initial description of the K-W-L procedure.

Children's Books Cited

Aamundson, N.R. (1990). *Two short and one long* . Boston: Houghton-Mifflin.

Avi. (1990). *The true confessions of Charlotte Doyle*. New York: Orchard.

Berliner, D. (1990). *Before the Wright brothers*. Minneapolis: Lerner.

Blake, Q. (1988). *Mrs. Armitage on wheels.* New York: Knopf.

Brink, C.R. (1973). *Caddie Woodlawn.* New York: Macmillan.

Bunting, E. (1986). *Sixth-grade sleepover.* New York: Lippincott.

Burleigh, R. (1991). *Flight.* New York: Philomel.

Byars, B. (1985). *Cracker Jackson.* New York: Viking Kestrel.

Chaiken, M. (1985). *Yossi asks the angels for help.* New York: Harper & Row.

Cleaver, V. (1985). *How sweetly sings the donkey.* New York: Lippincott.

Conrad, P. (1985). *Prairie songs.* New York: Harper.

Corcoran, B. (1988). *The sky is falling.* New York: Atheneum.

Harber, L., (1979). *Women pioneers in science.* San Diego: Harcourt Brace Jovanovich.

Hoffman, M. (1991). *Amazing Grace.* New York: Dial.

Hoyt-Goldsmith, D. (1990). *Totem pole.* New York: Holiday House.

Huff, B.A. (1990). *Greening of city streets: The story of community gardens.* Boston: Clarion.

Isaacson, P.M. (1988). *Round buildings, square buildings, & buildings that wiggle like a fish.* New York: Knopf.

King, J. (1983). *The impressionist.* New York: Beaufort.

Kramer, S.P. (1987). *How to think like a scientist.* New York: Crowell.

Kraus, R. (1990). *Musical Max.* New York: Simon and Schuster.

Krumgold, J. (1953). *And now Miguel.* New York: Crowell.

Kuklin, S. (1986). *Thinking big.* New York: Lothrop, Lee & Shepard.

Leedy, L. (1990). *The furry news: How to make a newspaper.* New York: Holiday House.

Levy, E. (1977). *Something queer at the library.* New York: Delacorte.

Lovelace, M.H. (1979). *Betsy-Tacy.* New York: Harper & Row.

MacLachlan, P. (1991). *Journey.* New York: Delacorte.

MacLachlan, P. (1985). *Sarah, plain and tall.* New York: Harper & Row.

Markle, S. (1983). *Kids' computer capers: Investigations for beginners.* New York: Lothrop, Lee & Shepard.

Markle, S. (1988). *Science mini-mysteries.* New York: Atheneum.

Marrin, A. (1988). *The War for independence: The story of the American Revolution.* New York: Atheneum.

Osborne, M.P. (1990). *The many lives of Benjamin Franklin.* New York: Dial.

Paltorwitz, S., & Paltorwitz, D. (1983). *Robotics.* New York: Jem Books.

Paulsen, G. (1987). *Hatchet.* New York: Bradbury.

Ryan, P. (1990). *Explorers and mapmakers.* New York: Lodestar.

Schwartz, A. (1990). *Camper of the week.* New York: Orchard.

Shachtman, T. (1989). *The president builds a house.* New York: Simon and Schuster.

Sharmat, M. (1972). *Nate the great.* New York: Dell.

Silver Burdett. (1990). *The ancient world.* Westwood, NJ: Silver Burdett.

Simon, S. (1991). *Earthquakes.* New York: Morrow.

Stewig, J.W. (1991). *Stone soup.* New York: Holiday House.

Wang, R.C. (1991). *The fourth question: A Chinese tale .* New York: Holiday House.

Weiss, H. (1979). *Model buildings and how to make them.* New York: Crowell.

Wilder, L.I. (1971). *Little house on the prairie.* New York: Harper & Row.

Yashima, T. (1964). *Crow boy.* New York: Macmillan.

8

Incorporating Scaffolded Reading Experiences in Your Classroom

In preparation for writing this chapter, the last in this book, we have done two things. First, we have met with a number of elementary and middle-school teachers and asked them what they see as the principal decisions that need to be made, what challenges they face in beginning to use SREs in their classroom, and how we can assist teachers in making those decisions and meeting those challenges. Second, we have repeatedly read and pondered over the preceding chapters and asked ourselves if there are additional topics that merit discussion.

As a result of these activities, we have focused on three issues, each of which is considered in a separate section. In the first section, we discuss some of the principal decisions you face as you move to implement SREs in your classroom. In the second section, we have added three topics—adjusting postreading tasks, involving students in constructing SREs, and preparing students for cooperative learning. Finally, in the last section, we consider the place of SREs in a comprehensive reading program and again stress that SREs are only one component of a comprehensive program.

Decisions and Challenges in Implementing SREs

Here, we consider the frequency of SREs, how much scaffolding to provide, how often to differentiate activities for different students, and the importance of providing a balance between challenging and easier reading material.

The Frequency of SREs

In Chapter 2, we emphasized that SREs definitely do not constitute a complete reading program, and at the end of this chapter we discuss some other important components of a comprehensive reading program. However, we have not yet directly addressed the question of how frequently SREs might be used in your classroom. Of course, the answer to this question varies for different students, different teachers, different goals, different times of the year, and different grade levels—to name just a few of the myriad of factors affecting what does and should go on in any classroom. Nevertheless, we can suggest some considerations and guidelines to use as you consider the matter.

To begin, we believe that SREs provide some of your best opportunities for extending students' zones of proximal development by scaffolding their efforts—helping them succeed in their reading, and giving them some common experiences to talk about, write about, and know that they share. In this sense, SREs have an intrinsic value that would lead us to use them quite frequently for their own sake—for the stretching, success, and shared experiences they can provide. To take advantage of these benefits, we would generally include at least one SRE as a part of reading instruction most school weeks, particularly in the lower grades.

From another perspective, SREs are useful for the extrinsic reason that they facilitate students' reading and learning in various content areas. Because students need to do a good deal of reading in social studies, science, health, and the like—and because some of this reading is challenging—SREs are often called for in content reading. Although SREs used in content areas will sometimes be quite brief, most school weeks will call for several of them.

Finally, the question of how the frequency of SREs should differ at different grade levels is worth considering. Two somewhat opposing lines of reasoning come into play. On the one hand, students obviously need to become increasingly independent and self-sufficient as they move toward adulthood. This, of course, argues for SREs becoming less frequent over time. On the other hand, remember that one purpose of SREs is to stretch students, enabling them to read material that would be too challenging without the assistance of an SRE. Certainly, we do not want to stretch students any less in later grades than in earlier ones.

The situation, then, appears to be this: Over time, students get increasingly competent. Over that same time, however, the materials students read and the tasks they complete with those materials become increasingly challenging. Thus, there continues to be a place for SREs throughout the middle grades and beyond. In fact, in our judgment, giving reading assignments without any scaffolding—the proverbial "Read chapters 4 and 5 and come to class on Tuesday prepared to discuss them"—is generally inappropriate, even in graduate school. Consequently, although SREs will often be shorter with older students than with younger ones, they continue to be appropriate.

How Much Scaffolding to Provide

We have already alluded to the matter of how much scaffolding to provide, but the topic is worth addressing directly. Our main point is that it is not a case of the more the better. The general rule is to provide enough scaffolding for students to be confident and successful in their reading but not so much that they are not sufficiently challenged, feel that they are being spoon fed, or become bored. In general, then, the suggestion is to provide enough but not too much. Further reinforcing the notion that you do not want to do more scaffolding than is needed is the fact that constructing scaffolds takes some of your valuable time, time that is always at a premium.

How Often to Differentiate Activities

Two sorts of differentiation are worth considering. On the one hand, you will some-times want to differentiate SREs based on students' interests. For example, students can read different books while pursuing a common topic or theme. Thus, in explor-ing the themes of death and grieving, some students might read Marion Dane Bauer's *On My Honor;* others, Katherine Paterson's *Bridge to Terabithia;* and still others, Candy Dawson Boyd's *Breadsticks and Blessing Places.* Similarly, some students may choose to respond to a reading selection in writing; others, with some sort of art work; others, with an oral presentation; and still others, by going to the library to pursue the topic further. The constraints on differentiation of this type are your time, ingenuity, and ability to orchestrate diverse activities. Additionally, you need to keep in mind that the more different activities students are involved in, the less time you have to assist them with each activity. At the extreme, if 30 students are each involved in a different activity, you can give each of them less than two minutes of your time each hour. Thus, there are a number of practical limits on differentiating on the basis of student interest. However, if these limits are kept in mind, differentiation based on interest is very often desirable.

Another sort of differentiation to consider is differentiation based on students' ability or skill. Here, the same limits that influence differentiation based on interest apply. That is, constraints include your time, ingenuity, ability to orchestrate diverse activities, and ability to assist students when many activities are going on at once. Beyond these considerations, however, is the matter of the effect that being repeat-edly placed in a lower group has on students. Our experiences, common sense, research (Allington, 1983; Juel, 1990), and a good deal of recent writing (Anderson, Hiebert, Scott, & Wilkinson, 1985; Flood, Lapp, Flood, & Nagel, 1992) testify to the fact that being repeatedly placed in a low group leads students to achieve less. Given these facts, differentiation based on ability and skill should be infrequent.

However, these are not the only facts to consider. There is also the fact that success begets success and failure begets failure. Thus, the suggestion that differen-tiation based on skill or ability should be infrequent because of the psychological damage it does must be tempered by the realization that differentiation can make the difference between success and failure. From time to time, it will be important to differentiate instruction to ensure success, but that differentiation should be no more frequent than is necessary.

Providing a Balance of Challenging and Easy Reading

Consideration of differentiating SREs leads directly to the matter of providing a balance of challenging and easy reading. Every student needs and deserves opportu-nities to read easy material that can be understood and enjoyed without effort and challenging material that he or she needs to grapple with (Anderson et al., 1985; Beck, McKeown, McCaslin, & Burkes, 1979). Reading easy material fosters automatic-ity, builds confidence, creates interest in reading, and provides students with practice in a task they will face frequently in their everyday lives. Reading challenging mate-rial builds students' knowledge bases, their vocabularies, and their critical thinking skills; it provides students with practice in a task they will face frequently in school and college, in their work outside of school, and in becoming knowledgeable and responsible members of a democratic society. Reading challenging materials also builds students' confidence in their ability to deal with difficult reading selections—if you ensure that they are successful with the challenging material.

The point that needs to be stressed here is that each student—more able, more skilled, and more knowledgeable students, as well as less able, less skilled, and less knowledgeable students—needs both challenging and easy reading. This condition cannot be met by providing only material that is of average difficulty for the average student. Assuming classrooms are made up of students with varying skills, knowledge, and abilities—and this description fits most classrooms—routinely providing only material of average difficulty ensures that some students will repeatedly receive material that is difficult for them, others will repeatedly receive material that is of average difficulty for them, and still others will repeatedly receive material that is easy for them. Such a situation is inappropriate for all students. Because the reading tasks we face in the world outside of school vary and because the benefits of reading vary with the difficulty of the reading tasks, all students need frequent opportunities to read materials that vary in the challenges and opportunities they present.

Three Additional Matters to Consider

In reviewing this book, talking to teachers, and thinking about our experiences in designing SREs, we found three topics that deserve more emphasis than they have had thus far and that seem particularly worth taking up here, now that you are familiar with SREs. These are **Adjusting Postreading Tasks to Ensure Success**, **Preparing Students for Cooperative Learning**, and **Involving Students in Constructing SREs**.

Adjusting Postreading Tasks to Ensure Success

In constructing and using SREs ourselves and in talking to teachers who have done so, we have found that sometimes—even after considering the students, the text, and the learning task and after constructing a scaffold of prereading, during-reading, and postreading tasks—some students are still not likely to have a successful reading experience unless something more is done. In such cases, the most feasible remedy is to simplify postreading tasks. Having been faced with this situation from time to time, we have identified five general ways of simplifying them. These are shown below.

Approaches to Simplifying Postreading Tasks

Asking students to do less rather than more

Requiring recognition rather than recall

Requiring assembly rather than creation

Cuing students to the place where answers can be found

Preceding production tasks with explicit instruction

Almost certainly the most straightforward approach to simplifying postreading tasks is to ask students to do less rather than more. We realize this sounds a bit flippant, but we are quite serious. Everything else being equal, tasks in which students answer fewer questions, construct less involved models, or write shorter pieces are distinctly easier. For example, after students read *The Island of the Blue Dolphins* by Scott O'Dell, you might ask them to identify *two* instances of courage and explain why these were courageous rather than having them deal with *four* instances.

Requiring recognition rather than recall is another straightforward approach to simplifying postreading tasks. Any time you allow students to return to the text to find answers or present them with alternatives from which to choose rather than requiring them to construct answers, their task is simplified. In the case of *The Island of the Blue Dolphins* described above, for example, letting students return to the text to find instances of courage is likely to make the task markedly easier.

Requiring assembly rather than creation is quite similar to requiring recognition rather than recall. For example, some students might find it difficult to construct a time line of major events after reading a history chapter on the origins of the Revolutionary War. However, these students would be greatly aided if you gave them a list of those events and a list of dates out of order and asked them to reorder the events and dates to construct a time line.

Cuing students to the places where answers can be found is an easily implemented approach and a particularly powerful one to use when students are dealing with lengthy and challenging selections. This approach was first suggested by Harold Herber (1970) for use with secondary students, but we believe it is equally applicable with elementary and middle-school students. Depending on the difficulty students face, you can cue them to the chapter, page, or even paragraph in which the information needed to answer a question is found. For example, suppose some of your third-grade students have had a difficult time reading *Manatee on Location* by Kathy Darling, yet you want them to remember some of the ways in which manatees have become endangered. Giving them the pages on which the factors that have adversely affected the manatees are discussed when you ask them to review these factors will increase the likelihood that they will successfully complete the review.

Our final suggestion here is to precede challenging production tasks with explicit instruction. If you are going to ask students to summarize information, synthesize information, make inferences, and complete other activities that require them to construct new information, you may need to explicitly teach them how to do these tasks before asking them to complete them. Of course, some students will already have been taught the needed procedures. However, even when students have been taught a procedure, it will sometimes be a good idea to review it. For example, if students' task is to compare and contrast two boys growing up during the Revolutionary War—perhaps Johnny in *Johnny Tremain* by Esther Forbes with Tim in *My Brother Sam Is Dead* by James Lincoln Collier and Christopher Collier—you might review the notion of a comparison and contrast essay, suggest some of the characteristics on which they might compare and contrast these two particular characters, and suggest some order for their essay, perhaps that of first listing the ways in which the two were the same and then listing the way in which the two differed.

At this point, you may be thinking that we have suggested a great deal of simplification and that what we are recommending amounts to spoon feeding and thus robs students of the opportunity to grapple with difficult tasks. We want to stress that this is not our message. We are not recommending that postreading tasks always be simplified, and we are certainly not recommending that some students routinely be given simplified postreading tasks. On the contrary, the simplifications suggested here are fix-up strategies to be used sparingly and only in cases in which students might otherwise fail. The essence of the SRE approach is to choose selections wisely and involve students in prereading and during-reading activities that will enable them to succeed with the postreading activities they engage in. Occasionally, however, even with everything you have done to accomplish this, you will look at some students and some postreading activities and say to yourself, "Some of these kids aren't going to be able to do this." This is the point at which simplifying postreading tasks becomes both appropriate and advisable.

Preparing Students for Cooperative Learning

Cooperative learning is another approach to maximizing the likelihood of success. As David and Roger Johnson (Johnson, Johnson, & Holubec, 1990), two of the principal architects of cooperative learning, have repeatedly said, "None of us is as smart as all of us." Groups of students working together have the potential to achieve well beyond the achievement of an individual working alone. Moreover, as the Johnsons and others convincingly argue, working in cooperative groups can produce multiple benefits. Cooperative learning can improve students' achievement, their effort to succeed, their critical thinking, their attitudes toward the subjects studied, their psychological adjustment, and their self-esteem. Cooperative learning can also foster students' interpersonal skills, improve their ability to work with others, and build interrelations among diverse racial, ethnic, and social groups. Because of their great potential, we have suggested group activities throughout the book. Although the groups we have suggested have not been formal cooperative groups—a concept we define below—many of them could be. Additionally, any sort of group is likely to work better if students are prepared to work in groups, and the sort of preparation students need for cooperative learning groups will help them achieve more in all sorts of groups. For these reasons, here we define *cooperative learning*, describe three of the most frequently used types of cooperative learning, and consider the skills students need to work cooperatively in groups.

What is cooperative learning?   Johnson et al. (1990) define cooperative learning as "the instructional use of small groups so that students work together to maximize their own and each other's learning" (p. 4). Robert Slavin (1987), another leading advocate of cooperative learning, defines it as "instructional methods in which students of all performance levels work together toward a group goal" (p. 8). It is important to realize that not every situation in which students work together is an effective cooperative learning situation. As Johnson et al. point out, effective cooperative groups have five characteristics.

Effective cooperative groups are positively interdependent. In positively interdependent groups, students are dependent on each other. Each student must accomplish the assigned task, and each student must ensure that other students in his or her group also accomplish it.

Effective cooperative groups include face-to-face promotive interaction. That is, in effective cooperative groups, students engage in face-to-face interchanges in which they prompt, assist, support, encourage, praise, and challenge each other as all work toward completing the common task.

In effective cooperative groups, each student is individually accountable for his or her work. It is not enough for students to be accountable for some shared product. Each individual is evaluated, and the results of the evaluation are reported to the individual and to the other members of the group.

In effective cooperative groups, students are given specific training in interpersonal and small group skills. Simply putting students together and telling them to cooperate is not sufficient. Students need specific preparation in getting to know and trust each other, accurately communicating with each other, accepting and supporting each other and each others' contributions, and resolving conflicts when they occur.

Finally, for cooperative groups to be most effective, students need to spend some of their time discussing how they functioned as a group, how effective they were in achieving the goals they worked on, and how effectively they worked together in achieving those goals. Effective groups reflect back on their work and consider what they did that worked, what they did that did not work, and what they can do to improve their work as a group in the future.

Three types of cooperative learning.   Three of the most frequently used types of cooperative learning are **Formal Cooperative Learning Groups, Student Teams-Achievement Divisions**, and **Jigsaw**. Formal Cooperative Groups (Johnson et al., 1990) are heterogeneous groups of three or four students, typically students differing in ability, ethnicity, social class, and gender. These groups incorporate the five defining characteristics of cooperative learning we just described, and they generally involve students working together for several class sessions. Tasks for such groups include problem solving and decision making, reviewing homework, answering questions or completing postreading activities, writing and editing assignments, and making class presentations. This sort of cooperative learning is particularly effective in fostering creativity, promoting problem solving, and building critical thinking skills.

Student Teams-Achievement Divisions (STAD) is a stylized approach in which groups of four students differing in ability, ethnicity, social class, and gender work together (Slavin, 1987). In STAD groups, the teacher initially presents the lesson, students in the group work together to ensure that each student in the group masters the material, and students are quizzed individually and receive points based on the extent to which each exceeds his or her previous performance. Individual scores are recorded and then totaled to form a team score, and students are rewarded for both their individual score and their team score. STAD groups generally work on a project for three to five class periods. The procedure is most appropriate for learning well-defined objectives with single right answers. This makes it particularly well suited for learning vocabulary, learning the main points of a selection, and learning central concepts in subject matter areas. Thus, while Formal Cooperative Learning is more appropriate for higher level tasks, STAD is more appropriate for basic learning tasks.

Jigsaw (Aronson, Blaney, Stephan, Sikes, & Snapp, 1978) is another stylized approach, but it is quite different from STAD. In the Jigsaw approach, a class of 30 or so students work in five heterogeneous groups of six or so students on material that the teacher has broken into subsections. To begin, each student in a group learns one part of the material being studied. For example, in studying a particular country, one student in each group might investigate its origins, another in each group its people, another its geography, and so on. After studying his or her subpart individually, the member of each group who has studied a particular subpart of the topic gets together with the four members from other teams who have studied the same subpart. The five students in each of these groups discuss their subtopic and become experts in it, and these experts then return to their own groups and teach their classmates about their speciality. Finally, students take individual exams on all of the material. Jigsaw can only be used in situations in which a subject can be broken into subparts, but many subjects lend themselves to such an approach.

Skills needed to work cooperatively.   Johnson et al. divide the sorts of skills needed to work cooperatively into three categories—**Forming Skills**, **Functioning Skills**, and **Formulating Skills**. Forming skills are prerequisites to effective group functioning. They include such basics as moving into groups without bothering others, staying with the group, talking in quiet voices, and encouraging everyone in the group to participate. Functioning skills are the specific skills that students use as they participate in group work. These include giving directions, expressing support and acceptance of others' ideas, asking for help or clarification when needed, and paraphrasing others' responses as a means of checking understanding. Finally, formulating skills are the skills needed to perform the roles that group members often assume. Some of the roles that cooperative group members perform are those of the summarizer, who summarizes the group's leaning; the elaborator, who elicits further information and explanation from group members; and the checker, who prompts group members to make the reasoning behind their thinking explicit.

This has been a very brief treatment of cooperative learning. For those of you who are not familiar with the approach, we hope it will serve as a prereading activity and that you will go on to read and learn more about cooperative learning. Of the books cited, Johnson et al.'s *Circles of Learning* is probably the most informative and a book we would consider required reading for teachers who want to develop effective cooperative groups. Slavin's *Cooperative Learning: Student Teams* and Aronson et al.'s *The Jigsaw Classroom* also contain many useful ideas and some approaches not included in Johnson et al.'s book. Additionally, Johnson, Johnson, and Holubec's *Structuring Cooperative Learning: Lesson Plans for Teachers* includes excellent and detailed lesson plans illustrating cooperative activities.

Involving Students in Constructing SREs

One of the central themes of current thinking about instruction and learning, and a theme that we have repeatedly emphasized throughout this book, is that to really learn something students need to be actively involved in their learning. One approach to getting students actively involved in their learning is the one we just discussed, cooperative learning. Another approach is cross-age tutoring, involving older students in the instruction of younger students. Our experience as teachers, a substantial body of research (Cohen, Kulik, & Kulik, 1982; Graves & Duin, 1991; Heath & Mangiola, 1991; Juel, 1991), and common sense suggest that cross-age tutoring is extremely effective. We very much agree with the sentiments expressed by Wilbert McKeachie (McKeachie, Pintrich, Lin, Smith, & Shafma, 1990), who has spent more than 40 years studying instruction, in this statement: "The best answer to the question, 'What is the most effective method of teaching?' is that it depends on the goal, the student, the content, and the teacher. But the next best answer is, 'Students teaching other students.' There is a wealth of evidence that peer teaching is extremely effective for a wide range of goals, content, and students of different levels and personalities" (p. 81).

One way in which older students can assist in teaching younger students—and in doing so become actively involved in their learning—is by preparing SRE materials for younger students. Consider what the student who is going to prepare a preview, a set of discussion questions, or a map of a short story needs to do in order to construct first rate materials. He or she needs to read the story, understand it, pick out what is important, pick out what is likely to be of interest to the younger students, decide what sort of language to use in addressing the younger students, and then prepare materials that will be interesting, informative, attractive, and engaging for the younger students. In other words, he or she needs to understand and appreciate the selection fully, to use his or her creative and problem solving skills to create material, and to use his or her linguistic skills to communicate with a genuine audience.

It is hard to imagine a task that presents more opportunities for learning, for doing something useful, and for feeling a sense of accomplishment. Moreover, the possibilities are certainly not limited to previewing, mapping, or writing discussion questions. Many prereading, during-reading, and postreading activities require some sorts of materials; with your help, older students are quite capable of constructing those materials. Selecting and teaching vocabulary and concepts, identifying the organization of a selection, recording parts of a selection on tape, developing a writing activity, and many other Scaffolded Reading activities are within older students' range. Finally, not only will students learn more from creating SRE activities, but having students participate in constructing SRE materials will also free up your time to work with students individually, prepare other interesting and enriching activities, or perhaps even take an evening off once in a while.

In general, we agree with the adage that if something seems too good to be true it probably is. However, we feel compelled to believe that students assisting teachers in constructing SRE activities is absolutely a win-win situation.

The Place of SREs in a Comprehensive Reading Program

In Chapter 2, we specifically pointed out that a Scaffolded Reading Experience is not a complete plan for a reading program. Here, as we approach the end of this book, we want to amplify on that point, saying a bit more about what we believe a comprehensive reading program should include. Our beliefs are essentially what they were at the beginning of this book, but they have certainly been enriched and broadened by writing this book and, with Susan Watts, a book that does describe a comprehensive reading program—*Essentials of Classroom Teaching: Elementary Reading Methods* (Graves, Watts, & Graves, 1994).

In the remainder of this chapter, we take a paragraph to describe each of 10 components that together constitute a program we believe would serve students well. For those who want more information on these components, we suggest our *Essentials of Classroom Teaching: Elementary Reading Methods*. Additionally, at the end of most paragraphs, we suggest one or two key readings that we highly recommend.

Building Positive Perceptions and Attitudes about Reading

We list building positive perceptions and attitudes about reading first because unless children learn to love reading and the enjoyment and knowledge it can give them, no amount of expertise in reading can be considered adequate. As Linda Fielding and her colleagues (Fielding, Wilson, & Anderson, 1986) point out in introducing their study of children's reading of trade books, in many cases "the problem is not that students cannot read, but that on most days they do not choose to do so." This is a real pity. Not surprisingly, Fielding and her colleagues found that "among all the ways that children can spend their leisure time, average minutes per day reading books was the best and most consistent predictor of standardized comprehension test performance, size of vocabulary, and gains in reading achievement." We must do everything possible to encourage children to love and value reading because only by loving and valuing reading—and therefore choosing to read frequently—will children reach their full potential as readers.

Providing Experiences to Foster Children's Emergent Literacy

Although *Scaffolding Reading Experiences* does not deal with the very beginnings of reading instruction, a comprehensive reading program must do so. For most students, kindergarten and first grade are the appropriate times for engaging in a host of relatively informal experiences that recognize children's emerging literacy skills, foster their further development, and begin teaching some of the formalisms they will use as they begin reading instruction proper. Among the key elements necessary to foster children's budding literacy are providing a nurturing environment that establishes reading as an engaging, successful, and meaningful activity; reading aloud interesting and enjoyable books that facilitate students' following along; giving students numerous opportunities to read simple and meaningful materials such as labeled objects, notes from the teacher, and classroom rules and procedures; providing plenty of opportunities for students to read brief texts, frequently predictable books; providing numerous opportunities for students to write (often using primitive characters and invented spelling in doing so) along with opportunities to read their writing; developing a basic sight vocabulary; and fostering phonemic awareness. Leslie Morrow's *Literacy development in the early years* (1993) and Jim Trelease's *New Read-Aloud Handbook* (1989) provide a wealth of information on fostering children's emergent literacy.

Instruction in Word Identification Strategies

As they read, children often encounter words they do not immediately recognize, and at least some of the time they need to apply strategies to identify these words. One word identification strategy they need to learn is phonic analysis, which includes using letter-sound correspondences, decoding by analogy, and blending sounds to form words. Another word identification strategy they need to learn is structural analysis, which includes using roots, prefixes, and suffixes in arriving at the pronunciation and meaning of words. As we have noted several times, students need to respond automatically to most words they encounter, and thus they will not be constantly using their word identification strategies, but they do need to have the strategies available when needed. Dolores Durkin's *Teaching Them to Read* (1993) provides a detailed description of word identification strategies and procedures for teaching them, and Stephen Stahl's "Saying the 'P' Word" (1992) presents a balanced view of phonics.

Systematic Vocabulary Instruction

Most children enter school with very small reading vocabularies—perhaps numbering only a few dozen words. Each year, however, the average student's reading vocabulary grows by something like 3,000 to 4,000 words (White, Slater, & Graves, 1990), and by the sixth grade the average student is likely to have a vocabulary of approximately 20,000 words that he or she can both read and understand (Nagy & Herman, 1987). Clearly, students need help with this monumental learning task. Such help should include direct teaching of individual words—primarily the important words and concepts in materials students are reading—and instruction in learning words on their own—using context, using words parts, using the dictionary and thesaurus, and the like. Such help should also include instruction that fosters word consciousness, a keen interest in words, and curiosity about words and their meanings. Graves' "The Elementary Vocabulary Curriculum: What Should It Be?" (1992) lays out much of such a curriculum, and Richard Anderson and William Nagy's "The Vocabulary Conundrum" (1993) presents a powerful argument for the importance of word consciousness.

Instruction that Fosters Comprehension of Specific Selections

This, of course, is the part of a comprehensive reading program that this book does cover. The Scaffolded Reading Experience is our approach to fostering comprehension of specific selections.

Instruction in Reading Strategies

In addition to receiving the assistance with individual selections SREs provide, students need to become adept at independently using reading comprehension strategies. As David Pearson and his colleagues (Pearson, Roehler, Dole, & Duffy, 1992) note, reading comprehension strategies are "conscious and flexible plans that readers apply and adapt to a variety of texts and tasks." They are deliberate processes that readers use to understand and remember what they read. Among the strategies that Pearson and his colleagues have identified as particularly important are using prior knowledge, asking and answering questions, determining what is important, summarizing, making inferences, dealing with graphic information, imaging, and monitoring comprehension. One approach to teaching these strategies, the approach we tend to favor, is to systematically provide focused, explicit instruction in each of them (Graves, Watts, & Graves, 1994). Another approach, one advocated by Michael Pressley and his colleagues (Pressley, El-Dinary, Gaskins, Schuder, Bergman, Almasi, & Brown, 1992), is to embed instruction in these strategies within the normal reading activities students undertake from day to day. Whichever approach is used, what is vital is that the strategies are taught and learned.

Integration of Instruction in Problem Solving, Critical Thinking, and Creative Thinking

Too often, we believe, schools concentrate on one sort of learning at the expense of others. Usually, the charge is that there is too much attention to factual information and too little attention to higher level thinking, and this may well be the case. However, the point we wish to make by including instruction in problem solving, critical thinking, and creative thinking as one part of a comprehensive reading program is that various sorts of learning—and thinking, and doing, and feeling—are important to a students' becoming independent, competent, productive, caring, fulfilled, and happy members of our adult society. Robert Marzano (1992) does an excellent job of explaining how different sorts of instruction, different sorts of literacy experiences, and a variety of other experiences are necessary if students are to become competent problem solvers, critical thinkers, and creative thinkers, as well as students with positive attitudes about themselves, positive attitudes about learning, and positive habits of using their abilities fruitfully.

Integration of Reading, Writing, Speaking, and Listening

We have addressed directly the matter of the close relationship between reading and writing, the fact that instruction in reading and writing ought frequently to be coupled, and the fact that instruction and practice in one of these modalities reinforces learning in the other. Here, we simply add that this close and reciprocal relationship holds among all four language modalities. Experiences in reading, writing, speaking, and listening go hand in hand, reinforce each other, occur together in the world outside of school, and ought to be integrated frequently in the classroom as well. We have attempted to take advantage of these interrelationships and highlight them in the sample SRE activities we have presented. Both Judith Irwin and Mary Anne Doyle's *Reading/Writing Connections* (1992) and Timothy Shanahan's *Reading and Writing Together* (1990) describe theory, research, and practice on the matter.

Literature Circles and Independent Reading

When using Scaffolded Reading Experiences, teachers can work with the whole class or relatively large groups of students to ensure understanding and success on the part of all students. SREs can also be used with small groups, and their use with such groups is frequently appropriate. Obviously, we believe that such experiences play a crucial part in students' developing literacy. So too, however, do literature circles—small groups of students who read, discuss, and respond to reading selections without large amounts of teacher assistance—and independent reading. Students will profit from the varied experiences and opportunities provided by reading together as part of Scaffolded Reading Experiences, reading in self-directed small groups, and reading by themselves. Bernice Cullinan's *Invitations to Read* (1992), Karen Wood and Anita Moss's *Exploring Literature in the Classroom* (1992), and Charles Temple and Patrick Collins' *Stories and Readers* (1992) contain a myriad of useful ideas on independent reading and related topics.

An Assessment Program

Assessment is a vital part of the reading program and an endeavor that extends well beyond the program itself and provides information for a variety of stakeholders in students' developing literacy. Students depend on assessment to know what they have learned and what they still need to achieve. Teachers depend on assessment as a gauge of the effectiveness of their teaching and an indicator of where and how they can further students' learning. Administrators depend on assessment to gauge the effectiveness or their schools and districts. Parents depend on assessment to know how their children are progressing in school. And public officials and the general public depend on assessment to reveal the success or failure of schools and to determine their further support for schools. Increasingly, schools are depending on the use of performance assessment, informal assessments, portfolios, and the like; and this is certainly a positive trend. However, as Roger Farr (1992) points out, given the diverse audiences for assessment, a variety of types of assessment have their place, and a truly comprehensive reading program will employ a carefully selected range of assessment procedures. Farr's article "Putting It All Together: Solving the Reading Assessment Puzzle," Scott Paris and his colleagues' "A Framework for Authentic Literacy Assessment" (Paris, Calfee, Filby, Hiebert, Pearson, Valencia, & Wolf, 1992), and Susan Glazer and Carol Brown's *Portfolios and Beyond* (1993) provide a range of current thinking on assessment.

Concluding Comments

In this final chapter, we have attempted to provide practical advice and some closure to this book by discussing some of the principal decisions you will need to make in implementing SREs. We have also described ways of adjusting postreading tasks, involving students in constructing SREs, and preparing students for cooperative learning; and we have discussed the place of SREs in the context of a comprehensive reading program. Our conclusion here will be brief.

Becoming literate has grown increasingly important to every individual in our society over each decade of this century. Today, as we near the twenty-first century, literacy is more important than ever. Effective communication throughout our society and with other societies is, quite simply, a requisite of survival. At the same time, the challenge of attaining literacy—which we believe includes both the ability to communicate with others and the will to do so, the ability to make our ideas known to others and the ability and desire to understand others' ideas—has never been greater.

The diversity of cultures, languages, and values in today's interdependent world makes it so. SREs can, of course, play only a small role in meeting this challenge, but we believe that they can play a significant role. By considering your students, the selections they are reading, and the outcomes that you and they seek and then constructing SREs specifically designed to allow those students to use those texts to achieve those outcomes, you will make those experiences successful ones—experiences that build students' sense of accomplishment, their competence, and their ability to communicate.

References

Allington, R.L. (1983). The reading instruction provided readers of differing abilities. *The Elementary School Journal, 83,* 548–559. Forcefully documents the fact that students in lower ability groups often receive different instruction than those in higher ability groups.

Anderson, R.C., Hiebert, E.H., Scott, J.A., & Wilkinson, I.A.G. (1985). *Becoming a nation of readers: The report of the Commission on Reading.* Washington, D.C.: The National Institute of Education. Concise and very readable summary of much that we know about reading and reading instruction.

Anderson, R.C., & Nagy, B. (1993). The vocabulary conundrum. Champaign: University of Illinois, Center for the Study of Reading. A powerful argument for the importance of fostering students' word consciousness.

Aronson, E., Blaney, N., Stephan, C., Sikes, J., & Snapp, M. (1978). *The jigsaw classroom.* Newbury Park, CA: Sage. A detailed look at Aronson's pioneering approach to cooperative learning.

Beck, I.L., McKeown, M.G., McCaslin, E.S., & Burkes, A.M. (1979). *Instructional dimensions that may affect reading comprehension: Examples from two commercial reading programs.* Pittsburgh: University of Pittsburgh, Learning Research and Development Center. An in-depth and insightful critique of factors affecting students' learning to comprehend from basal readers.

Cohen, P.A., Kulik, J.A., & Kulik, C.C. (1982). Educational outcomes of tutoring: A meta-analysis of findings. *American Educational Research Journal, 19,* 237–248. A comprehensive and sophisticated analysis of the findings on tutoring.

Cullinan, B.E. (Ed.). (1992). *Invitation to read: More children's literature in the reading program.* Newark, DE: International Reading Association. Suggests many ways of incorporating children's literature in the reading program.

Durkin, D. (1993). *Teaching them to read* (6th ed.). Boston: Allyn and Bacon. This widely used methods text provides a detailed description of word recognition strategies and procedures for teaching them.

Farr, R. (1992). Putting it all together: Solving the reading assessment puzzle. *The Reading Teacher, 46,* 26–37. Looks at the assessment needs of students, teachers, administrators, and the public, and proposes a multifaceted approach that meets the needs of various audiences.

Fielding, L.G., Wilson, P.T., Anderson, R.C. (1986). A new focus on free reading: The role of trade books in reading instruction. In T.E. Raphael (Ed.), *The contexts of school-based literacy.* New York: Random House. A forceful plea for using trade books.

Flood, J., Lapp, D., Flood, S., & Nagel, G. (1992). Am I allowed to group? Using flexible patterns for effective instruction. *The Reading Teacher, 45,* 608–616. A brief review of the research on ability grouping and a discussion of alternatives.

Glazer, S.M., & Brown, C.S. (1993). *Portfolios and beyond: Collaborative assessment in reading and writing*. Norwood, MA: Christopher-Gordon. Describes assessment procedures consistent with a holistic approach to reading and writing instruction.

Graves, M.F. (1992). The elementary vocabulary curriculum: What should it be? In M.J. Dreher & W.H. Slater (Eds.), *Elementary school literacy: Critical issues* (pp. 101–131). Norwood, MA: Christopher-Gordon. A discussion of the various elements that constitute a comprehensive vocabulary program.

Graves, M.F., & Duin, A.H. (1991). *Tutoring via telecommunications*. Minneapolis, MN: University of Minnesota, Center for the Interdisciplinary Study of Writing. Description of a project in which college students tutor high school students in writing using computers and telecommunications.

Graves, M.F., Watts, S.M., & Graves, B.B. (1994). *Essentials of classroom teaching: Elementary reading methods*. Needham Heights, MA: Allyn and Bacon. Our best effort at a concise text on how to design and run a comprehensive elementary reading program.

Heath, S.B., & Mangiola, L. (1991). *Children of promise: Literate activity in linguistically and culturally diverse classrooms*. Washington, DC: National Education Association. Describes four tutoring programs designed to improve the literacy learning of *all* children.

Herber, H.L. (1970). *Teaching reading in content areas*. Englewood Cliffs, NJ: Prentice-Hall. One of the first content-area reading texts and still a source of many useful ideas.

Irwin, J.W., & Doyle, M.A. (Eds.). (1992). *Reading/writing connections: Learning from research*. Newark, DE: International Reading Association. A variety of researched-based insights on the relationships between reading and writing.

Johnson, D.W., Johnson, R.T., & Holubec, E.J. (1990). *Circles of learning: Cooperation in the classroom* (3rd ed.). Edina, MN: Interaction Book Company. A superbly informative and readable book on cooperative learning.

Johnson, D.W, Johnson, R.T., & Holubec, E.J. (Eds.). (1987). *Structuring cooperative learning: Lesson plans for teachers*. Edina, MN: Interaction Book Company. Several dozen detailed lesson plans illustrating applications of cooperative learning.

Juel, C. (1991). Cross-age tutoring between student athletes and at-risk children. *The Reading Teacher, 45,* 178–186. Describes a unique and highly successful program in which college athletes tutor elementary-age children.

Juel, C. (1990). Effects of reading group assignment on reading development in first and second grade. *Journal of Reading Behavior, 22,* 223–254. Points out the large and enduring effects of grouping.

Marzano, R.J, (1992). *A different kind of classroom: Teaching with dimensions of learning*. Washington, DC: Association for Supervision and Curriculum Development. Thought-provoking description of a theory- and researched-based, comprehensive instructional program designed to promote five types of cognitive and affective learning.

McKeachie, W.J. Pintrich, P., Lin, Y., Smith, D.A., & Shafma, R. (1990). *Teaching and learning in the college classroom* (2nd Ed.). Ann Arbor: University of Michigan, National Center for Research to Improve Postsecondary Teaching and Learning. Comprehensive review of the research on college teaching.

Morrow, L.M. (1993). *Literacy development in the early years* (2nd ed.). Boston: Allyn and Bacon. A rich, sophisticated, and balanced approach to helping children enter the world of reading and writing by someone who has taught at the preschool, kindergarten, and primary grade level as well as the university level.

Nagy, W.E., & Herman, P.A. (1987). Breadth and depth of vocabulary knowledge: Implications for acquisition and instruction. In M. G. McKeown & M.E. Curtis (Eds.), *The nature of vocabulary acquisition*. Hillsdale, NJ: Erlbaum. Provides an accurate estimate of vocabulary size and growth..

Paris, S.G., Calfee, R.C., Filby, N., Hiebert, E.H., Pearson, P.D., Valencia, S., & Wolf, K.P.

(1992). A framework for authentic literacy assessment. *The Reading Teacher, 46,* 88–98. A framework developed from the collaborative efforts of these leading assessment experts.

Pearson, P.D., Roehler, L.R., Dole, J.A., & Duffy, G.G. (1992). Developing expertise in reading comprehension. In S.J. Samuels & A.E. Farstrup (Eds.), *What research has to say about reading instruction* (2nd ed., pp. 145–199). Newark, DE: International Reading Association. Presents a contemporary view of reading comprehension instruction, with particular emphasis on teaching comprehension strategies.

Pressley, M., El-Dinary, P.B, Gaskins, I., Schuder, T., Bergman, J.L., Almasi, J., & Brown, R. (1992). Beyond direct instruction: Transactional instruction of reading comprehension strategies. *The Elementary School Journal, 92,* 513–555. Report of an approach that embeds strategy instruction in the ongoing classroom program.

Shanahan, T. (Ed.). (1990). *Reading and writing together: New perspectives for the classroom.* Norwood, MA: Christopher-Gordon. Diverse, scholarly perspectives on the reading/writing relationship.

Slavin, R.E. (1987). *Cooperative learning: Student teams* (2nd ed.). Washington, DC: National Education Association. A brief introduction to several types of cooperative learning Slavin works with.

Stahl, S.A. (1992). Saying the "p" word: Nine guidelines for exemplary phonics instruction. *The Reading Teacher, 45,* 618–625. Well-reasoned guidelines for a phonics program that does not overwhelm other aspects of the reading program.

Temple, C., & Collins, P. (Eds.) (1992). *Stories and readers: New perspectives on literature in the elementary classroom.* Norwood, MA: Christopher-Gordon. Diverse views and suggestions on literature in elementary schools.

Trelease, J. (1989). *The new read-aloud handbook.* NY: Penguin. Presents books to read aloud, hints for reading aloud, and ideas for exciting children about reading.

White, T.G., Graves, M.F., & Slater, W.H. (1990). Growth of reading vocabulary in diverse elementary schools: Decoding and word meaning. *Journal of Educational Psychology, 82,* 281–290. Details on the size of first- through fourth-grade students' vocabularies.

Wood, K.D., with Moss, A. (1992). *Exploring literature in the classroom: Content and methods.* Norwood, MA: Christopher-Gordon. Reading educators and children's literature educators look at the use of literature in the classroom.

Children's Books Cited

Bauer, M.D. (1986). *On my honor.* Boston: Clarion.

Boyd, C.D. (1985). *Breadsticks and blessing places.* New York: Macmillan

Collier, J.L., & Collier, C. (1974). *My brother Sam Is dead.* New York: Four Winds.

Darling, K., Ill. with photos by T. Darling. *Manatee on location.* New York: Lothrop, Lee & Shepherd.

Forbes, E. (1971). *Johnny Tremain.* New York: Dell.

O'Dell, S. (1960). *The island of the blue dolphins.* Boston: Houghton-Mifflin.

Paterson, K. (1977). *Bridge to Terabithia.* New York: Crowell.

A

Text Difficulty and Accessibility

One of the factors taken into account in planning a Scaffolded Reading Experience is, of course, the text itself. You need to assess the difficulty of the texts you consider using, as well as the likelihood that students will be motivated to read them. Up until a few years ago, text difficulty was typically assessed with readability formulas, mathematical equations that take into account vocabulary difficulty and sentence complexity and assign a grade level to a text. In recent years, however, readability formulas have been severely criticized. In 1984, for example, Bernice Cullinan, then president of IRA, and Sheila Fitzgerald, then president of NCTE, issued a joint statement decrying the use of readability formulas as the sole criterion used in measuring text difficulty and matching students with texts. "If readability formulae are used at all," Cullinan and Fitzgerald wrote, "they MUST be used in conjunction with procedures that look at all the parts of a text which affect comprehension" (1984–85).

In the years that have passed since Cullinan and Fitzgerald issued their statement, textbooks and text difficulty have been the topic of a substantial body of research and writing (Britton & Black, 1985; Chambliss & Calfee, in press; Muth, 1989; Sawyer, 1991), and arguments and evidence against readability formulas have continued to accrue. The majority of this work has supported Cullinan and Fitzgerald's position that the information provided by readability formulas needs to be supplanted, or at least supplemented. Several authors have discussed factors to consider in assessing the difficulty of texts. The best known and probably most useful articles on the topic are those of Thomas Anderson and Bonnie Armbruster (1984) and of Isabel Beck and Margaret McKeown and their colleagues (Beck & McKeown, 1989; Beck, McKeown, & Gromoll, 1989; McKeown, Beck, Sinatra, & Loxterman, 1992).

The suggestions made here draw heavily on this work as well as on our experiences as English and reading teachers and on other work that suggests characteristics of material that children can and will read. Our intent is to provide you with a reasonably comprehensive yet manageable set of factors to consider in selecting reading materials. What we do is describe and discuss a set of factors for you to consider carefully, along with, of course, considering the students who will be reading the selection, your purposes and their purposes in reading it, and the assistance you will give them in dealing with it.

In all, we consider 10 factors, divided into two groups. In the first group are six factors that are fairly easily defined, fairly easily identified, and largely inherent in the text itself. Of course, since reading is an interactive process that involves both the reader and the text, no text factors are fully independent of the reader. In the second group are four factors that are less easily defined, less easily identified, and very definitely involve both the reader and the text. All 10 factors are shown in the following table.

Factors Influencing Text Difficulty

Vocabulary

Sentence Structure

Length

Elaboration

Coherence and Unity

Text Structure

Familiarity of Content and Background Knowledge Required

Audience Appropriateness

Quality and Verve of the Writing

Interestingness

As our title—Text Difficulty and Accessibility—suggests, these factors reflect both the ease or difficulty a reader may have in comprehending a text and how interesting and accessible the material will be for young readers. Of course, the more interesting and accessible the material is, the better the chance that students will pursue it, understand it, learn from it, and enjoy it.

Factors Largely Inherent in the Text Itself

The six factors considered here are **Vocabulary**, **Sentence Structure**, **Length**, **Elaboration**, **Coherence and Unity**, and **Text Structure**. The first two, vocabulary and sentence structure, are ones you are probably familiar with because they are the two factors considered in readability formulas. However, we want to stress that, while these two factors deserve consideration, they should not be relied on too heavily or to the exclusion of a number of other factors. In fact, as Richard Anderson and Alice Davison (1988) have pointed out, features of text other than vocabulary and sentence structure "almost certainly make a much greater difference to comprehension" than these two features.

Vocabulary

We list vocabulary as the first matter to consider because it is one of the most easily identifiable characteristics suggesting text difficulty. A substantial body of research testifies to the fact that texts containing a lot of difficult words are likely to be difficult.

However, this does not mean that texts can necessarily be simplified by replacing difficult words with easier ones. It appears that vocabulary is an excellent predictor of difficulty because vocabulary reflects difficulty; a difficult or unfamiliar topic frequently needs to be conveyed using the difficult and unfamiliar vocabulary that is inherent to the topic (Anderson & Freebody, 1981). Because of this, simply replacing difficult words with easier ones may not do much to simplify a text; in fact, it can even make a text more difficult.

Moreover, in considering vocabulary, you need to consider more than just difficulty; simpler is not necessarily better. The words used in a selection need to be appropriate to the selection and to convey the intended meaning precisely. If, for example, the intended meaning is *petrified*, the simpler substitutes *afraid* or *scared* do not convey the same meaning. These latter terms do not describe a fear so great that the person becomes immobilized and cannot react. This is another reason that replacing less frequent words with more frequent ones often fails to simplify a text; the words used to replace those originally used frequently do not mean quite the same thing and do not fit the context quite as well.

Finally, we want to stress that a few difficult words are unlikely to pose serious barriers to comprehension. In fact, research has shown that it takes a substantial proportion of difficult words—perhaps as much as one in three content words—to affect students' comprehension (Freebody & Anderson, 1983). Additionally, if students read only texts in which all the words are familiar, they will be denied a major opportunity for enlarging their vocabularies. Wide reading in texts that include varied and novel words is, in fact, the main route to vocabulary growth.

Sentence Structure

Sentence structure, another text characteristic that is fairly easy to assess and the other factor considered in readability formulas, is a second factor that reflects difficulty. Very long, very complex, and certainly very convoluted sentences make texts more difficult to read. However, sentence structure does not have nearly as strong an effect as vocabulary (Coleman, 1971). Moreover, the sentences in a text need to be complex enough to clearly convey the meaning of the text (Pearson, 1974-1975). If the intended meaning is something like "Ted failed to win the award because neither his test scores nor his grades were high enough," breaking that sentence up into something like "Ted failed to win the award. His test scores were not high enough. His grades were not high enough." is not going to result in more comprehensible text. Texts that lack logical connectives require students to infer relationships that could have been stated explicitly, and inferring relationships may cause problems for some students.

On the other hand, some sentences are clearly difficult. Here is one from "Shooting an Elephant" by George Orwell. "Its mahout, the only person who could manage it when it was in that state, had set out in pursuit, but had taken the wrong direction and was now twelve hour's journey away, and in the morning the elephant had suddenly reappeared in the town." Materials that contain a very large percentage of complex sentences are likely to present difficulties for younger and less able readers.

At the same time, texts that employ artificially short sentences, the sort sometimes written for beginning or remedial readers, do not have the sound of real language. Here is a paragraph from a high interest—easy reading book. To our ears at least, it sounds unnatural; and we suspect the author used this series of short sentences to keep the readability score down.

> Payton's training paid off. He rushed for 1,421 yards in 1983. He caught passes for 607 yards. That was the most passes (53) of any Bear. He passed for 95 yards. He gained a total of more than 2,000 yards for the second time in his career. His yardage was thirty-six percent of the Bear's total yardage. He was almost a one man team. (Leder, 1986)

Many readers, even remedial ones, would do better with a more natural sounding text, and at least one study (Green & Olsen, 1988) has shown that even less able readers comprehend original texts just as well as simplified ones and actually prefer original texts to simplified ones.

Length

An obvious but sometimes overlooked factor influencing the difficulty of a selection, and the likelihood that a less avid reader will make a real stab at finishing it, is its length. Particularly for students who do not read fluently, length alone can be a very formidable obstacle (Grobe, 1970). Additionally, research has shown that in some cases shorter texts—summaries or much reduced versions of complete texts—can actually produce better comprehension and memory than longer ones (Carroll, 1990; Reder, 1982). If the intent of a reading assignment is to have students retain key information, short summaries specifically designed to convey that key information may well be more effective than longer, less focused selections. Fortunately, how much material and what parts of the material we ask students to read is usually directly under our control as teachers.

However, as we discuss in the next section, shorter is not always better. In making a point, giving verbal illustrations and examples is often useful. And, of course, giving illustrations and examples increases the length of a piece.

Elaboration

Texts can be written so that they present concepts without much explanation, or so that they present concepts along with a good deal of explanatory material, examples, analogies, and linkages of various sorts.

Elaboration refers to a certain sort of explanatory material. Elaborative information is information that explains the reasons behind the bare bones information presented. Elaboration makes information more meaningful and understandable, and information that is more understandable is more memorable. The concept is an important one and worth some examples. Here are two examples, one from a psychological experiment on elaboration (Bransford & Johnson, 1972) and one from an elementary social studies text.

In the experiment, some students were given unelaborated statements such as "The tall man bought the crackers," "The bald man read the newspaper," and "The funny man liked the ring." Other students were given elaborated statements such as "The tall man purchased the crackers that had been lying on the top shelf," "The bald man read the newspaper in order to look for a hat sale," and "The funny man liked the ring that squirted water." Both groups were then given questions such as "Who bought the crackers?" "Who read the newspaper?" and "Who liked the ring?" Students who read the unelaborated statements could answer almost no questions, while those who read the elaborated text could answer nearly all of them.

The passage from a social studies textbook concerned Native American houses. It consisted of statements such as "The Indians of the Northwest Coast lived in slant-roofed houses made of cedar planks," "Some California Indian tribes lived in simple, earth-covered or brush shelters," and "The Plains Indians lived mainly in tepees." But the textbook contained nothing to explain these facts and make them something other than arbitrary pieces of information. For example, it said nothing about the relationships between the types of houses and the climates of the areas, the types of building materials available in the areas, or the lifestyles of the various groups. Unelaborated information is difficult to remember and not very interesting.

The idea that elaborations facilitate comprehension and recall makes good sense, and the facilitative effects of elaborated text have been empirically documented (Bransford & Johnson, 1972; Reder, Charney, & Morgan, 1986). However, as we noted above, shorter texts sometimes produce better comprehension and memory than longer ones. The matter of just when elaborations help and when they hinder is not yet resolved. It appears to be the case, though, that shorter texts may be more effective if the goal is simply to remember material, while elaborated texts may be more effective if one needs to understand material thoroughly—for example, to write about what he or she has read or apply it in some real world context such as operating computer software (Charney & Reder, 1988).

Coherence and Unity

Coherence refers to the integration of material, to how each topic and subtopic is defined and to how well the parts relate to each other (Anderson & Armbruster, 1984; Beck & McKeown, 1989). With young and inexperienced readers and with material that is unfamiliar to students, it is particularly important that authors be explicit about how each piece of information fits with the other information in the text and about how each piece of information helps explain the event or idea the text presents. Coherence is another text factor that can be adversely affected by undue attention to readability requirements. Rigid adherence to readability requirements often results in the deletion of connectives and clauses that explain how the parts of a topic fit together, and the deletion of such material is likely to make a text less coherent.

Unity refers to oneness of purpose. Good texts are directed toward particular topics, particular points, particular themes, and particular concepts. After reading a selection, the reader should be able to summarize the content of the text and explain its purpose fairly succinctly because the text has not dealt with a myriad of topics. Texts that wander, or those that contain pockets of irrelevant material, are difficult to read, to summarize, and to remember.

Beck and McKeown (1989) give a number of specific examples of elementary texts in which coherence and unity have been obscured. Here are three of them. In one fourth-grade text, an 800-word expository selection on subways is introduced with a 100-word anecdote in which the reader is asked to imagine that he or she is at home alone and needs to get someplace quickly: "It is Saturday morning. You are alone in the house when the phone rings. A friend of yours needs help." In this case, the reader may well be riveted, but unfortunately he or she is likely to be riveted on the wrong topic. The reader is focused on an adventure, while the text is intended to provide information about subways. In another fourth-grade text, a 950-word selection about volcanoes, a description of the volcano Mt. Fuji is interrupted with a 60-word digression about Mt. Fuji as a summer resort. It may be interesting to know that Mt. Fuji is a popular vacation spot, but the digression does nothing to further the reader's knowledge about volcanoes, the topic the passage is intended to present. As a third example, Beck and McKeown cite a 900-word, third-grade selection on the brain that attempts to describe diverse functions such as "neural impulse, memory and dreaming in addition to the brain's physical appearance." Such an attempt at presenting a huge and diverse body of information in so few words, Beck and McKeown note, "absolutely prohibits both supportive elaboration . . . and development of logical connections necessary for coherent presentation."

Text Structure

Text structure refers to the organization of a text. The majority of texts students encounter in school can be categorized as belonging to one of two broad categories, narratives or exposition, and these two types of texts are organized very differently (Drum, 1984). Typical narratives reflect the temporal order of real life events in which motives, actions, results, and reactions occur in sequence, and episodes in the main character's life are integrated by goals and subgoals. Time thus provides a natural structure for remembering episodic information. The majority of children's books are narratives, most of the materials parents read to children are narratives, and most of the selections in primary grade basal readers are narratives. Although there are certainly easier and more difficult narratives and ones that do not follow the prototypical structure, children generally do fairly well with narratives.

Exposition is another matter. Expository texts, even well written expository texts, can have a variety of organizations, and different authors have created different lists of the organizational patterns of expository writing. Anderson and Armbruster (1984), for example, list description, temporal sequences, explanation, compare/contrast, definition/examples, and problem/solution as typical organizational patterns. Calfee and Chambliss (1988), on the other hand, identify description and sequence as the two major rhetorical patterns and then further divide each of these categories. In addition to these rhetorical patterns, Calfee and Chambliss identify several functional devices—introductions, transitions, and conclusions—that serve to link the various parts of a text. Unfortunately, in surveying social studies texts, Calfee and Chambliss found that authors frequently employed weak rhetorical patterns such as lists or simply presented material without any apparent pattern. Additionally, the texts employed few effective functional devices to aid the reader. What is needed are expository texts that are clearly organized and that make that organization apparent to the reader (Chambliss & Calfee, in press), and it appears that many of the expository texts used in schools fail to meet these criteria.

Moreover, since there is no single prototypic structure for exposition, previous reading of exposition does not provide the clues to the structure of upcoming expositions that previous reading of narratives provides to the structure of upcoming narratives. Additionally, very little children's literature is exposition, parents read little if any expository material to preschoolers, and primary grade basal readers and even some intermediate grade basals contain little exposition. For these reasons, many students find expository text difficult.

Factors Involving the Reader and the Text

The factors considered here are **Familiarity of Content and Background Knowledge Required**, **Audience Appropriateness**, the **Verve and Quality of the Writing**, and **Interestingness**. As we have already noted, each of these factors definitely involves both the reader and the text; for example, one reader may find the content of a particular text quite familiar while another might find it largely unfamiliar. Additionally, it needs to be recognized that assessing texts along these dimensions is very much a subjective task.

Familiarity of Content and Background Knowledge Required

As we already noted, vocabulary is probably the excellent predictor of difficulty that it is because it is an index of how familiar students are with the content of the material. Reading a selection on a topic for which we have little familiarity is difficult. Reading a selection on a topic that is totally unfamiliar to us is simply impossible (Adams & Bruce, 1982). It is for this reason that the language experience approach in which children dictate their own stories and then read them offers some real advantages when used with children just beginning to read. The content of the stories that a child dictates are totally familiar to the child.

Of course, children read a great deal besides experience stories, but much of this material contains familiar content. A descriptive piece about a zoo will contain a good deal of content familiar to students who have visited zoos. Similarly, a narrative set in a suburban community and focusing on the adventures and misadventures of a Cub Scout will contain a lot of material familiar to a Cub Scout from the suburbs. However, the same narrative may contain much less material familiar to a young Chicano living in the Los Angeles barrio. Still, even when placed in unfamiliar settings, narratives are likely to contain familiar themes. Most children are raised by parents, a parent, or a parent substitute. Situations that arise between adults and children, between authority figures and youngsters, occur everywhere. Children have peers with whom they play, fight, and engage in a host of other pleasant and unpleasant human interactions. They go to school, shop at the store, and sleep at night. These commonalities result in a good deal of familiar content in most short stories and novels.

Not only must the reader have some familiarity with the contents of a selection, but he or she must also have the background knowledge assumed by the author (Adams & Bruce, 1982; Anderson, 1984). In some cases, the general knowledge that one picks up from day-to-day living is sufficient. This, as we just noted, is true of many short stories and novels. In other cases, much more specific knowledge is required to understand the text. This is particularly the case in technical and scientific areas; many of us could deal with a calculus text about as well with the cover closed as with it opened. However, many humanities and social science texts also require extensive background knowledge for comprehension and thus pose problems for some students.

An example from a television serial, an example in which the content is not difficult but for which those of you not familiar with the serial will lack relevant background knowledge, will perhaps illustrate the point. The serial is "Dr. Who," a fantasy series that was popular with many preteens and teens a few years ago.

Imagine that you are watching the beginning of the show and see a barren, desert-like scene, obviously hot and evidentially devoid of life. Suddenly, a red British phone booth appears in the desert. The camera zooms in to what should be the inside of the phone booth, but what you see is the cabin of some sort of a space ship, and it is much larger than the inside of a phone booth. In the cabin are a tall, lanky man wearing a long coat and a wool muffler reaching nearly to the floor and a young woman in contemporary clothes. The camera zooms out and you are again looking at the British phone booth in the desert, yet out of it walk the tall man and the young woman. The man then turns to the woman and says in a very solemn voice, "As the fourth Doctor, the Tardis is of course my responsibility." The woman nods, showing her full under-standing of the fourth Doctor's evidently poignant message.

What are the uninitiated to think? What is a phone booth doing in the middle of the desert? Is the large cabin supposed to be inside that little phone booth? Why does the man wear a long coat and an even longer muffler in the middle of a desert? In what sense is he the *fourth* Doctor? Is there a third Doctor? A fifth? What is a Tardis?

The answers to these questions and a host of others are readily available to Dr. Who fans but totally unavailable to those who know nothing of the show; and while in this case one could acquire the background knowledge rather readily, in many cases there are a myriad of facts, concepts, and relationships that a reader must know in order to approach a particular text.

Audience Appropriateness

Obviously, the topic of a selection and the sophistication with which the topic is treated need to be appropriate for the students reading the selection (Spiro & Taylor, 1987). Consider, for example, two human interest pieces, both out of periodicals and written for adults but both readily interpretable by fifth or sixth graders. The first is by William Geist, a columnist for the *New York Times*. It is titled "The Friends of Trees," and it begins like this.

> Marianne Holden could not restrain herself any longer. She whipped out her trusty-12 inch folding saw and attacked a Japanese pagoda tree.
> "It feels sooo good," she said, standing on her tiptoes while she removed a limb the tree did not need. A wise guy walking by yelled "Timberrrr!" when the little branch dropped to the ground.

The sketch goes on to describe a group of New Yorkers who help the city in caring for boulevard trees. It is well written, and we like it because it shows people doing something positive and caring, behaving in a way we don't often think of as typical of New Yorkers, perhaps in a way we don't often think of typical of these times. But how appropriate is it for fifth or sixth graders. Will they appreciate it, relate to it, be interested in it? We are not sure, but it seems likely that many students will not find it engaging.

Now consider another human interest piece. This one is by Charles Kuralt, the CBS journalist. It is titled "The Butterfly Mystery," and it begins like this:

> Monarch butterflies spend the winter in Pacific Grove, California. In early spring, the monarchs migrate north. This fact is part of a mystery that suggests all kinds of troubling questions.
>
> In the first place, the monarchs are confused by radio, television, and radar waves. And they are destroyed by fertilizer, insect sprays, and air pollution. So how do they survive at all?
>
> In the second place, after they leave Pacific Grove, they fly as far as 2,000 miles into Canada. They fly through storms and across mountains and deserts, even though they are as fragile as feathers. How do they do it?

The sketch goes on to describe some of the other mysteries of the butterflies' annual visit to Pacific Grove, never really explaining them but describing some of the folktales about the monarchs' visits and all in all presenting the visits as a rather magical and wonderful annual event. It too is well written, and we like it because we find the phenomenon an interesting one. But is it appropriate for fifth and sixth graders? Will they appreciate it, relate to it, and be interested in it? It seems likely that they will. It seems likely that of the two pieces, both about the same length, both about the same difficulty, and both well written, "The Butterfly Mystery" will be more appropriate for many fifth and sixth graders.

Quality and Verve of the Writing

In addition to the factors that have been presented thus far, one must consider the quality of the writing, the flair of the writing, the particular blend of topic, organization, and style that makes one piece of writing intriguing and memorable and another piece mundane.

Certainly, the texts we ask students to read should be lucid. But clarity is only one criterion for good prose. Joseph Williams, author of a short text titled *Style: Ten Lessons in Clarity and Grace,* addresses the topic in this way:

> Let us assume that you can now write clear [and] cohesive . . . prose. That in itself would constitute a style of such singular distinction that most of us would be more than satisfied to achieve so much. But even though we might prefer bald clarity to the complexity of [much] . . . prose, the unrelenting simplicity of the plain style can finally become very flat and dry indeed, eventually arid. Its plainness invests prose with the blandness of unsalted meat and potatoes—honest fare to be sure, but hardly memorable and certainly without zest. Sometimes a touch of class, a flash of elegance can make the difference between forgettable Spartan plainness and a well-turned phrase that fixes itself in the mind of the reader.

Exposing young readers to the power and beauty of the language ought to be one of our aims in selecting and recommending texts.

Interestingness

We left this factor for last because it is the most subjective factor and the factor most dependent on the reader. A poorly written piece on dogs is likely to be of great interest to a child who loves dogs while a very well written article on the topic will not capture the interest of a child who doesn't care much about animals. Moreover, the results of studies of interesting material on children's comprehension are mixed. Some studies have shown positive effects of interesting material (Anderson, Shirey, Wilson, & Fielding, 1987; Asher, 1980). Others have failed to show such effects and have even found that interesting anecdotes in textbooks can sometimes focus children's attention away from more important parts of a selection (Duffy et al., 1989; Garner, in press; Graves, Prenn, Earle, Thompson, Johnson, & Slater; 1991). Garner has aptly labeled these interesting but tangential topics that detract from comprehension "seductive details." Like the Sirens of Greek mythology, they lure unsuspecting readers from their true course with their arresting call. Recall, for example, the adventure narrative that begins the fourth-grade expository selection on subways, a passage we mentioned in the section on coherence and unity. The narrative is very likely to capture students' interest, but their attention will be focused on solving the problem of helping a friend and not on the information about subways.

In general, it appears that texts with interesting material that is an integral part of their makeup are likely to facilitate comprehension while texts in which the interesting material is an add-on are likely to impede comprehension. The implications for teaching are threefold. First, although there is a great deal written about what interests children, the best way to find out about what interests your particular students is to spend a lot of time with them, sharing your interests and seeking to learn about and share theirs. Second, excellent annotated bibliographies and other discussions of children's books abound. Many of them are listed in Appendix B, and we encourage you to make use of the sources listed. We encourage you even more to spend some time reading children's books and periodicals. Finally, be particularly aware of seductive details in expository writing for children. Try to choose writing that makes the subject matter itself interesting rather than writing that relies on irrelevant asides to gain its readers' interest, and alert students to the presence of irrelevant details in some texts—their learning to deal with such material is part of their becoming genuinely metacognitive readers.

Concluding Comments

In all, we have listed 10 factors likely to influence text difficulty. Six of them—vocabulary, sentence structure, length, elaboration, coherence and unity, and text structure—are largely inherent in the text itself. Four factors—familiarity of content and background knowledge required, audience appropriateness, the quality and verve of the writing, and interestingness—definitely involve both the reader and the text.

This set of factors is not a checklist in the sense that you can simply check off each factor as present or absent and then tally the check marks to arrive at a score.

Instead, it is a set of factors to consider carefully, to ponder as you try to decide whether or not a particular text ought to be used with a particular student or group of students.

We also want to point out that the factors are not presented in order of their importance. In fact, the first factor considered—vocabulary—is very seldom the most important factor to consider, and the second factor—sentence structure—is virtually never the most important one.

We should further note that a factor may be critically important with one text or situation but not very important with another. As one example, consider length. Length may be critically important in considering an expository selection that requires a great deal of background knowledge, that is not very interesting, and that is going to be used as a required reading for students who are not particularly good readers. Conversely, length may be unimportant in considering an interesting narrative selection that you plan to recommend as recreational reading for an adept reader.

As another example, consider style and verve. Style and verve are likely to be extremely important when considering a lengthy social science selection to be given to less than avid readers as a required assignment. On the other hand, style and verve are not very important considerations in choosing documentation for some computer software that a student really wants to learn to use. In fact, straightforward and unadorned prose may well be preferable for the software documentation.

We should also note that with some texts you will probably consider only some of the factors before making a decision. For example, you might choose to discard a poorly organized selection on an unfamiliar and uninteresting topic without examining the piece in great detail. Or, you might plan to use a particularly interesting piece even though it displayed a number of difficult features. Of course, in the latter case, you may design a very supportive SRE to assist students in dealing with the text.

More generally, in concluding we want to note again that as part of the task of matching texts and students, several elements—the factors discussed here, the students who will be reading the selection, your purposes and their purposes in reading the selection, and the scaffolding you will provide to help them deal successfully with the selection—all deserve and require your consideration.

References

Adams, M. L., & Bruce B. (1982). Background knowledge and reading comprehension. In J. A. Langer & T. M. Smith-Burke (Eds.), *Reader meets author: Bridging the gap* (pp. 2–25). Newark, DE: International Reading Association. A very readable introduction to the importance of background knowledge.

Anderson, R.C., & Freebody, P. (1981). Vocabulary knowledge. In J. Guthrie (Ed.), *Comprehension and teaching* (pp. 77–117). Newark, DE: International Reading Association. An intriguing examination of three hypotheses about the relationship between vocabulary knowledge and reading comprehension.

Anderson, R.C. (1984). The role of the readers' schema in comprehension, learning, and memory. In R.C. Anderson, J. Osborn, & R.J. Tierney (Eds.), *Learning to read in American schools* (pp. 243–257). Hillsdale, NJ: Erlbaum. Another readable introduction to the importance of background knowledge.

Anderson, R.C., & Davison, A. (1988). Conceptual and empirical bases of readability formulas. In A. Davison & G.M. Green (Eds.), *Linguistic complexity and text comprehension* (pp.

23–53). Hillsdale, NJ: Erlbaum. Sophisticated argument against the bases of readability formulas.

Anderson, R.C., Shirey, L.L., Wilson, P.T., & Fielding, L.G. (1987). Interestingness of children's reading material. In R. Snow & M. Farr (Eds.), *Aptitude, learning and instruction: Cognitive and affective process analyses*. Hillsdale, NJ: Erlbaum. Describes the substantial effects of reading interest.

Anderson, T.H., & Armbruster, B.B. (1984). Content area textbooks. In R.C. Anderson, J. Osborn, & R.J. Tierney (Eds.), *Learning to read in American schools* (pp. 193–226). Hillsdale, NJ: Erlbaum. Influential article on what is wrong with textbook writing and how it can be improved.

Asher, S. (1980). Topic interest and children's reading comprehension. In R.J. Spiro, B.C. Bruce, & W.F. Brewer. *Theoretical issues in reading comprehension*. Hillsdale, NJ: Erlbaum. Brief review of research suggesting that interest does positively affect reading comprehension.

Beck, I.L., & McKeown, M.G. (1989). Expository text for young readers. The issue of coherence. In L. Resnick (Ed.), *Essays in honor of Robert Glaser* (pp. 47–66), Hillsdale, NJ: Erlbaum. Insightful overview of text characteristics that reduce coherence.

Beck, I.L., McKeown, M.G., & Gromoll, E.W. (1989). Issues that may affect social studies learning: Examples from four commercial programs. *Cognition and Instruction, 6,* 99–158. An extended and sophisticated examination of text factors affecting learning.

Bransford, J. D., & Johnson, M. K. (1972). Contextual prerequisites for understanding: Some investigations of comprehension and recall. *Journal of Verbal Learning and Verbal Behavior, 11,* 717–726. A classic article on the effects of elaboration.

Britton, B.K., & Black, J.B. (Eds.). (1985). *Understanding expository text: A theoretical and practical handbook for analyzing explanatory text*. Hillsdale, NJ: Erlbaum. A comprehensive and fairly technical collection on expository text.

Calfee, R.C., & Chambliss, M. (1988, April). *Structure in social studies textbooks: Where is the design?* Paper presented at the meeting of the American Educational Research Association. New Orleans. Analysis showing that many social studies texts are poorly designed.

Carroll, J.M. (1990). *The Nurnberg funnel: Designing minimalist instruction for practical computer skills*. Cambridge, MA: MIT Press. Advances the intriguing concept that less detail is sometimes preferable for learning.

Chambliss, M., & Calfee, R.C. (in press). *Textbooks for learning: Nurturing children's minds*. Cambridge, MA: Basil Blackwell. An in-depth and insightful look at textbooks and textbook adoption.

Charney, D.H., & Reder, L.M. (1988). Studies in elaboration of instructional texts. In S. Doheny-Farina (Ed.), *Effective documentation: What we have learned from research* (pp. 47–72). Cambridge, MA: MIT Press. A summary of the authors' research on elaboration.

Coleman, E.B. (1971). Developing a technology of written instruction: Some determiners of the complexity of prose. In E.Z. Rothkopf & P.E. Johnson (Eds.), *Verbal learning research and the technology of written instruction*. New York: Teachers College Press. An early look at factors affecting text difficulty.

Cullinan, B.E., & Fitzgerald, S. (1984–1985). Background information bulletin on the use of readability formulae. *Reading Today, 2* (3). The source of the joint IRA/NCTE pronouncement against overreliance on readability formulas.

Drum, P. (1984). Children's understanding of passages. In J. Flood (Ed.), *Promoting reading comprehension* (pp. 61–78). Newark, DE: International Reading Association. A very lucid examination of what children understand from narrative and expository texts.

Duffy, T.M., Higgins, L., Mehlenbacher, B., Cochran, C., Burnett, R., Wallace, D., Hill, C., Haugen, D., McCaffery, M., Sloane, S., & Smith, S. (1989). Models for the design of instructional text. *Reading Research Quarterly, 24,* 434–457. Study showing the superiority of less adorned text.

Freebody, P., & Anderson, R.C. (1983). Effects on text comprehension of differing proportions and locations of difficult vocabulary. *Journal of Reading Behavior, 15,* 19–39. Study indicating that a large proportion of difficult vocabulary must be present to affect comprehension.

Garner, R. (in press). "Seductive details" and learning from text. In K.A. Renninger, S. Hidi, & A. Krapp (Eds.). *The role of interest in learning and development.* Hillsdale, NJ: Erlbaum. Review of research showing the negative effects of seductive details.

Graves, M.F., Prenn, M.C., Earle, J., Thompson, M., Johnson, V., & Slater, W.H. (1991). Improving instructional text: Some lessons learned. *Reading Research Quarterly 26,* 110-120. Reports a study and reviews a series of studies indicating the negative effects of seductive details.

Green, G.M., & Olsen, M.D. (1988). Preferences and comprehension of original and readability-adapted materials. In A. Davison & G.M. Green (Eds.), *Linguistic complexity and text comprehension* (pp. 115–140). Hillsdale, NJ: Erlbaum. Study showing that students prefer original text to supposedly more readable adapted versions.

Grobe, J.A. (1970). Reading rate and study time demands on secondary students. *Journal of Reading, 13,* 286–288, 316. Illustrates the huge task that lengthy readings pose for slow readers.

Leder, J.M. (1986). *Walter Payton.* Mankato, MN: Crestwood House. High interest/easy reading biography of the great Chicago Bears back.

McKeown, M.G., Beck, I.L., Sinatra, G.M., & Loxterman, J.A. (1992). The contribution of prior knowledge and coherent text to comprehension. *Reading Research Quarterly, 27,* 78–93. Study showing that both of these factors have significant effects on comprehension.

Muth, K.D. (Ed.). (1989). *Children's comprehension of narrative and expository text: Research into practice.* Newark, DE: International Reading Association. A teacher-oriented collection of articles on text comprehension.

Pearson, P.D. (1974–1975). The effects of grammatical complexity on children's comprehension, recall, and conception of certain semantic relations. *Reading Research Quarterly, 10,* 155–192. Probably the first study to show that syntactically more complex text can sometimes be comprehended better than syntactically less complex text.

Reder, L.M. (1982). Elaborations: When do they help and when do they hurt? *Text, 2,* 211–224. Study indicating that elaboration does not always facilitate learning.

Reder, L.M, Charney, D.H., & Morgan, K.I. (1986). The role of elaborations in learning a skill from an instructional text. *Memory and Cognition, 14,* 64–78. Study indicating cases in which elaboration does facilitate learning.

Sawyer, M.H. (1991). A review of the research in revising instructional text. *Journal of Reading Behavior, 23,* 307–333. Comprehensive review of the literature on revising text to facilitate learning.

Spiro, R. J., & Taylor, B. M. (1987). On investigating children's transition from narrative to expository discourse: The multidimensional nature of psychological text classification. In R. J. Tierney, P. L. Anders, & J. N. Mitchell (Eds.), *Understanding readers' understanding* (pp. 77–93). Hillsdale, NJ: Erlbaum. Sophisticated essay on factors influencing text comprehension.

Williams, U. (1981). *Style: Ten lessons in clarity and grace.* Glenview, IL: Scott, Foresman. An erudite and enlightening little book on style.

B

Sources of Information on Children's Books

The rapid growth in the number of trade books published over the past several years has vastly increased the chances for teachers to find just the right book for a particular student, as well as books dealing with particular subjects or themes. However, with that increase in opportunity also comes the challenge of identifying appropriate titles from the myriad of possibilities. Thankfully, there are a number of publications available to help locate materials.

The resources for selecting student reading materials range from general bibliographies that provide a simple listing of titles and authors or brief annotations to monthly periodicals that provide in-depth reviews of recently published children's books. Here, we will mention only a selected few of the plethora of resources available. For a more complete listing, we highly recommend Arlene M. Pillar's "Resources to Identify Children's Books," which is found in *Invitation to Read*, edited by Bernice E. Cullinan and published in 1992 by the International Reading Association.

To narrow the possibilities yet provide a useful starting point in locating appropriate material for your students, we present three main categories of resources— general bibliographies, specialized bibliographies, and review sources. These three types of resources have similar components yet slightly different purposes, and they employ a variety of formats. In the remainder of this appendix, we describe each type briefly and provide 8-10 annotated references for each. Our annotations generally include:

- Number of titles listed
- Range of target audience
- Selection process
- Description of features
- An example or a description of annotations
- An example or a description of bibliographic information

General Bibliographies

Some of the resources included in this section are simply listings of books, such as *Children's Books in Print* and *Subject Guide to Children's Books in Print*. Others provide brief annotations of the books cited, and still others provide reviews. Also, some of these bibliographies are organized by subheadings which identify books in a certain subject area, genre, or reading level, while others are not. What distinguishes these general bibliographies from the more specific bibliographies described in the next section is their broader focus and the number of titles they cover. Each of the bibliographies described in this section provides a sizeable listing and offers a starting point for identifying appropriate selections for your students. Because the entries for the general bibliographies vary a great deal, we have included samples to give you an idea how the information is presented.

The following three resources are comprehensive lists of titles.

A to Zoo: Subject Access to Children's Picture Books (3rd ed.), by Carolyn W. Lima and John A. Lima. New York: Bowker, 1989.

> This resource lists approximately 12,000 picture books catalogued under 700 subjects and alphabetized by author. For example, under the subject Moving, the first three titles listed are

> > Adshead, Gladys L. *Brownies—they're moving*
> >
> > Aliki. *We are best friends*
> >
> > Asch, Frank. *Goodbye house*

> Also included is a bibliographic guide and author, title, and illustrator indexes. The bibliographic guide is arranged alphabetically by author; and each entry includes title, publisher, publication date, and subjects. International Standard Book Numbers (ISBNs) are included for entries new to this edition.

> > Abisch, Roz. The Clever Turtle. ill. by Boche Kaplan. Prentice-Hall, 1969.
> >
> > Subj: Animals. Folk and fairy tales. Foreign lands-Africa. Reptiles-turtles, tortoises.

Children's Books in Print. New York: Bowker (updated annually).

> This two-volume resource is a comprehensive listing by author, title, and illustrator of children's books in print. The 1993 publication contains 81,198 titles.

> Volume 1 — Awards, Authors, and Illustrators

> Volume 2 — Titles and Publishers. A typical title entry from this volume looks like this:

> > North American Indian Masks. Frieda Gates. Illus. by Frieda Gates. 64p. (gr. 5 up) 1982. 8.95 (0-8027-6462-2) lib bdg 9.95 (0-8027-6463-0)

Subject Guide to Children's Books. New York: Bowker (updated annually).

> This companion volume to *Children's Books in Print* lists children's books in print according to subject. In the 1993 publication, some 63,293 titles appear under 6,821 subject categories. Titles are arranged alphabetically within various subjects areas. The following is an entry under the subject Newspapers.

Fleming, Thomas. Behind the Headlines. (gr. 5 up). 1989.
14.95 (0-8027-6890-3); PLB 15.85 (0-8027-6891-1) Walker & Co.

The next five resources contain annotated lists of children's materials, and each lists from 1,000 to 12,000 titles. Some annotations simply state the plot in a sentence or two; others provide an evaluation or review; and some even offer suggestions for use in the classroom. A few of these volumes, such as *Children's Catalog* and *The Elementary School Library Collection,* are quite costly but can generally be found in a public library or school media center. Others, such as *Adventuring With Books* and *Collected Perspectives,* are more moderately priced, and you may want to purchase these for your own professional library.

Adventuring With Books, edited by Julie Jensen. Urbana, IL: National Council of Teachers of English, 1993.

Adventuring With Books, edited by Mary Jett-Simpson. Urbana, IL: National Council of Teachers of English, 1989.

Adventuring With Books, edited by Dianne Monson. Urbana, IL: National Council of Teachers of English, 1985.

> *AWB* is published every four years by NCTE and contains annotations of approximately 1,500-1,800 childrens' trade books. These titles, which have been selected from a pool of approximately 8,000 recently published books, have been chosen by reviewers for their literary and artistic quality as well as their appeal for readers pre-K through grade 6. Entries are listed alphabetically by author under a variety of categories and subcategories. For example, under the category Modern Fantasy, some of the subcategories from the 1985 edition include: Animal Fantasy, High Fantasy, and Humorous Fantasy. *AWB* also includes a listing of professional books, a directory of publishers, and author and title indexes.

> Annotations vary from 25-100 words and include curriculum connection statements where appropriate. The following is an entry from the Science section under the subtopic Prehistoric Life in the 1985 edition.

>> Asimov, Isaac. How Did We Find Out about the Beginning of Life?
>> Illus. by David Wool. Walker, 1982. 10-13.
>> Asimov describes experiments in which scientists through the ages attempted to trace the beginnings of life. The book really doesn't end; it just opens into the future. Black-and-white drawings throughout the book illustrate important phenomena and experiments.

Best Books for Children: Preschool Through the Middle Grades. (4th ed.), by John T. Gilespie and Corinne J. Naden. New York: Bowker, 1990.

> This volume, which is revised every three years, contains annotations of 12,000 favorably reviewed books for preschool through grade 6 children. Books are listed under 500 subheadings. The four major review sources for this volume are *Booklist, The Bulletin of the Center for Children's Books, The Horn Book,* and *School Library Journal.*

The following is a typical entry in the Literature section. As shown, the book is categorized as a picture book, an imaginative story, and a fantasy.

Picture Books
Imaginative Stories
Fantasies

566 Adoff, Arnold. Flamboyan (PS-3). Illus. by Karen Barbour. 1988, Harcourt $14.95. (0-15-228404-4). Named for the tree outside her window, red-haired Flamboyan yearns to fly. (Rev: BCB 10/88; BL 10/15/88; SLJ 10/88)

Children's Catalog (16th ed.), edited by Juliet Yaakov. Bronx, NY: H.W. Wilson Co., 1991.

The approximately 6,000 titles in this bibliography are librarian selected for children from preschool through grade 6. Annotations of fiction, nonfiction, short stories, and easy-to-read books are organized by author, title, and subject and classified using the Dewey Decimal system. The following typifies the entries in this volume.

Ekey, Robert

Fire! in Yellowstone; story by Robert Ekey. Gareth Stevens Children's Bks. 1990 32 p il map lib bdg $10.95 (2-4)

574.5

1. Forest fires 2. Yellowstone National Park 3. Forest ecology

ISBN 0-8368-0226-8   LC 89-43156

"A True adventure"

Adapted from an adult book: Yellowstone on fire, published in 1989 by The Billings Gazette

Discusses the fire that ravaged nearly one million acres of Yellowstone National Park during several months in 1988, and explains the two sides to the controversy over letting nature take its course.

A "Well-written and excellently photographed book . . . Good thought-provoking questions stimulate class discussions." Sci Child

Includes glossary and bibliography

Collected Perspectives: Choosing and Using Books for the Elementary Classroom (2nd ed.), edited by Hughes Moir, Melissa Cain, and Leslie Prosak-Beres. Boston, MA: Christopher-Gordon, 1992.

This book contains annotations of nearly 1,000 trade books for students in primary grades through junior high. The entries are alphabetized by author and organized into sections by audience and genre—Picture Story Books, Books for Beginning Readers, Books for Intermediate Grades, Books for Older Readers, Poetry for All Ages, and Nonfiction for All Ages. The book also contains three indexes—author, title, and subject. In addition to listing subjects and themes, the subject index lists activities such as writing poetry, dramatizations, puppetry, and story-telling that might be appropriate to use with certain selections.

The following is an example of an entry.

Bauer, Marion Dane. *On My Honor.* Clarion, 1986. ISBN 0-89919-439-7, $11.95. Ages 9-12.

"On my honor," Joel promised his father, "we won't go anywhere but the park." But when his friend, Tony, challenges him to swim in the treacherous Vermillion River, Joel doesn't want him to think he is scared. Joel dares Tony to swim out to a sandbar, but it's only when Tony disappears that Joel realizes that he can't swim. Back at home, Joel cannot rid himself of the stench of the river. Guilt-ridden and afraid, Joel must find the courage to tell the horrible truth: Tony is dead! With power and sensitivity Bauer tells a gripping, action-filled story. The moral issues are presented realistically through strong and down-to-earth characterizations.

Children are never prepared for the death of a peer. Death often seems removed from their daily lives as they know it, restricted to pets, unknown people in news stories, or older people of different generations. When a peer dies, it can be someone who sat right next to them, someone they played with, and there is a void. On My Honor *deals realistically and honestly with the beginning stages of the grieving process. Other helpful books are Katherine Paterson's* Bridge to Terabithia *(Crowell, 1977), Candy Dawson Boyd's* Breadsticks and Blessing Places *(Macmillan, 1985), Doris Buchanans Smith's* A Taste of Blackberries *(Crowell, 1973), and Anna W. M. Wolf's* Helping Your Children to Understand Death *(Child Study, 1973). These may deepen children's understanding of death.*

The Elementary School Library Collection: A Guide to Books and Other Media (18th ed.), edited by Lois Winkel. Williamsport, PA: Brodart, 1992.

This volume, which is updated every two years, contains librarian-selected materials with annotations for approximately 8,000 fiction, non-fiction, and easy-to-read books suitable for elementary school children. Using a three-point rating system, the *ESLC* also suggests books that are most likely to be of value in the elementary classroom. In addition, the *ESLC* contains appendices and 2,000 listings of audiovisual materials incorporated into the sections describing books on the same subject. The *ESLC* also lists periodicals, reference books, and professional collections for librarians and teachers. Below is a typical entry from the Non-fiction section of the *ESLC*.

> **CE 590.74**   Ph-1 K-2/4 $12.89 FH068
>
> GIBBONS, GAIL. Zoo. Crowell ISBN 0-690-04633-2, 1987. unp col illus. Sound filmstrip available from Live Oak 0-87499-098-X, 60fr, color, 1 sound cassette (8 min), guide. $24.95.
>
> Provides a behind-the-scenes tour of a zoo showing the tasks performed by many different zoo workers. Numerous small, colorful pictures and an economical text describe the work of vendors, animal keepers, and the veterinarian. The care and feeding of the animals, the creation of new exhibits, and the work of zoos in animal conservation are among the many topics covered in this attractive introduction.
>
> SUBJ: Zoos.

This volume also includes author, title, and subject indexes and the following appendices: Media for Pre-School Children; Books for Independent Reading; Author's Series; Publisher's Series; and a Directory of Publishers, Producers, & Distributors.

Specialized Bibliographies

Specialized bibliographies focus on certain areas of interest—for example, award-winning books, science books, or multicultural books. All of these books provide annotations of the titles listed, and some give evaluations and teaching suggestions as well.

The books we have chosen to include represent a cross-section of interests and have been recommended either by children's librarians or educators specializing in children's literature. For the first eight titles, we give brief descriptions; after describing these, we simply list a few more titles to give you an idea of the possibilities. A quick trip to the library will reveal the range of specialized bibliographies available.

Eyeopeners! How to Choose and Use Children's Books about Real People, Places, and Things, by Beverly Kobrin. New York: Penguin, 1988.

> In addition to 10 short chapters (69 pages) which provide background information on selecting and using informational books with children, this book gives annotations for 500 nonfiction books and 150 activity suggestions. Titles are organized alphabetically according to subject—ABC Books, Adoption, Airplanes . . . Marine Life, Math and Counting . . . Wordless Picture Books, Words, Zoos. Annotations, ranging from one sentence to several, are generally evaluative summaries and include the following bibliographic information: title, author, publisher, publication date, illustrator, recommended audience, and number of pages. Two indexes are included: a subject index and an index that includes authors, illustrators, and book titles.

Growing Pains: Helping Children Deal with Everyday Problems Through Reading, by Maureen Cuddigan and Mary Beth Hanson. Chicago, IL: American Library Association, 1988.

> This book provides annotations for approximately 250 books that deal with the pains of growing up. The majority of titles included were published between 1976 and 1986 and are appropriate for youngsters from preschool through fourth grade. Thirteen topics, such as Behavior, Child Abuse and Neglect, Death and Dying, Friendship, are addressed in separate chapters. Each chapter is then broken down into subtopics. For example, for the Chapter "Emotions and Feelings," some of the subtopics are greed, jealousy, joy, love, and serenity. Annotations are 50-word synopses and include the following bibliographic information: title, author, illustrator, publisher, publication date, and recommended audience. Two indexes are included: a subject index and an author-title index.

Kids' Favorite Books, Children's Choices 1989-1991. The Children's Book Council, Inc. and The International Reading Association, Newark: DE, 1992.

This book lists about 300 recently published trade books that 2,000 participating children ages 5-13 have identified as their favorites from among 1,500 titles. Selections are grouped alphabetically by title and organized by year (1989, 1990, 1991) into five reading levels—all ages, beginning independent reading, younger readers, middle grades, and older readers. Annotations provide two or three-sentence reviews of each title. The bibliographic information for each includes: title, author, illustrator, publisher, publication date, and recommended audience. This source would be particularly useful for locating recently published books with proven reader appeal. Two indexes are included: an author index and a title index.

More Exciting, Funny, Scary, Short, Different, and Sad Books Kids Like About Animals, Science, Sports, Families, Songs and Other Things, edited by Frances Laverne Carroll and Mary Meacham. Chicago: American Library Association, 1992.

This bibliography contains approximately 500 annotations of books on topics that librarians know interest children, with an emphasis on titles for children from 2nd to 5th grade. It is divided into sections to help locate books on subjects children often ask for. For example, some of the sections are "I Want to Be Really Scared," "Where Are the Animal Books?", and "I Want a Book Where Disaster Happens." Each section provides 6-10 annotations which run about 50-100 words each and give a summary of the book. Bibliographic information for each includes: title, author, publisher, and publication date. Two indexes are included: an author-title index and a subject index.

Multicultural Literature for Children and Young Adults, by Ginny Moore Kruse. University of Wisconsin, Madison: Cooperative Children's Book Center, 1991.

Annotations of 483 books with multicultural themes or topics published for children and young adults between the years 1980-1990 are included in this bibliography. Books are grouped into sections under a variety of headings. Some of these are History, People, and Places; Seasons and Celebrations; Issues in Today's World; Poetry; Picture Books; and Fiction for Young Readers. Annotations provide a 25-100 word summary of the selection and include the following bibliographic information: author, title, illustrator, publisher, publication date, number of pages, and ISBN. This publication also includes an author/title index and two appendices—an Authors and Illustrators of Color appendix and an appendix listing the Ethnic/Cultural Social Groups represented in the bibliography.

The Museum of Science and Industry Basic List of Children's Science Books, compiled by Bernice Richter and Duane Wenzel. Chicago, IL: American Library Association, 1988. (There are also three other volumes of *The Museum of Science and Industry Basic List of Children's Science Books* available—1973-84; 1986, and 1987. The 1988 edition represents the third annual supplement to the 1973-84 volume.)

This bibliography contains annotations for 600 science books appropriate for children preschool through grade 8. Titles are arranged alphabetically within 18 subject groupings. For example, Animals, Astronomy, Mathematics/Computer Science, Physics, and Chemistry. Annotations are 25–50 word synopses and include a rating from AA (strongly recommended, excellent) to D (not recommended). Books are evaluated on such criteria as accuracy, currency, literary quality, and promotion of scientific skills and attitudes. In addition to an overall rating for each book, a review citation is provided. Bibliographic information includes: title, author, illustrator, place of publication, publisher, distributor, publication date, price, and recommended audience. Also included are a Directory of Publishers, Sourcebooks for Adults, Science Magazines and Review Journals, and title and author indexes.

Portraying Persons with Disabilities—An Annotated Bibliography of Non-fiction for Children and Teenagers, by Joan Brest Friedberg, June B. Mullins, and Adelaide Wier Sukiennik. Providence, NJ: Bowker, 1992.

Portraying Persons with Disabilities—An Annotated Bibliography of Fiction for Children and Teenagers, by Joan Brest Friedberg, June B. Mullins, and Adelaide Wier Sukiennik. Providence, NJ: Bowker, 1992.

Approximately 600 titles appropriate for children from preschool through grade 12 are described in these two volumes, although most of the titles are targeted toward middle- to upper-grade students. The first few chapters in each book discuss patterns and trends and list reference books on disabilities and persons with disabilities. Annotations are provided for books on these topics—Dealing with Physical Problems, Dealing with Sensory Problems, Dealing with Cognitive Behavior Problems, and Dealing with Multiple/Severe Disabilities. Annotations are approximately 250-500 words long and include a description of the book's content and a critical analysis that often includes suggestions on ways to use the book. Bibliographic informations includes: author, title, illustrator, publisher, publication date, number of pages, ISBN, recommended audience, review citation, and disability portrayed.

The Single-Parent Family in Children's Books: An Annotated Bibliography (2nd ed.), by Catherine Townsend Horner. Metuchen, NJ: Scarecrow, 1988.

This book includes annotations for 600 children's books published between 1965-1986 dealing with families fractured by divorce, desertion, separation, or death of a parent. Titles are organized into these six categories—Divorce/Separation/Desertion, Widowhood, Unwed Mothers, Orphans/Wards of the Court with a Single Guardian, Protracted Absense of One Parent, and Indeterminable Cause. Annotations are approximately 100-word plot summaries and include a rating of the book. Bibliographic information includes: author, title, publisher and publication date, number of pages, recommended audience, and rating. Title and author/subject indexes are also included.

Additional titles

Best of the Best for Children, edited by Denise Perry Donavin. New York: Random House, 1992. (American Library Association recommended books, magazines, videos, audio, software, toys, and travel)

Books Kids Will Sit Still For, by Judy Freeman. Hagerstown, MD: Alleyside, 1984. (Recommended read-alouds)

Books in Spanish for Children and Young Adults: An Annotated Guide, by Isabel School. Metuchen, NJ: Scarecrow, 1985.

Children's Literature Awards and Winners (2nd ed.), compiled by Dolores Blythe Jones. Detroit, MI: Gale, 1988.

Distinguished Children's Literature, by Claudette Hegel Comfort. Minneapolis, MN: Dennison, 1990. (Newbery and Caldecott winners)

Fantasy Literature for Children and Young Adults: An Annotated Bibliography (3rd ed.), by Ruth Nadelman Lynn. New York: Bowker, 1989.

Girls are People Too! A Bibliography of Non-traditional Female Roles in Children's Books, by Joan E. Newman. Metuchen, NJ: Libraries Unlimited, 1987.

Sensitive Issues: An Annotated Guide to Children's Literature K-6 by Timothy V. Rasinski and Cindy S. Gillespie. Phoenix, AR: Oryx Press, 1992.

Review Sources

In addition to the resources noted thus far, there are a number of publications devoted exclusively to reviewing newly published children's materials. Here, we list ten of these and give a brief description of each. The first five we list are published several times a year; the second five annually. These publications can be obtained through the public library, school media centers, or through personal subscription.

Periodicals

Book Links, Connecting Books, Libraries, and Classrooms, edited by Barbara Elleman. Chicago, IL: American Library Association.

> Published bimonthly, this 64-page periodical features articles on strategies for using books with children and annotations of approximately 200 books for children from preschool through grade 8. Articles focus on various topics. For example, three features of the May 1993 issue were a spring round-up of big books, books on the American Revolution, and books about endangered animals. Annotations are generally evaluative as well as descriptive and range from 25-100 words. Bibliographic information includes: author, illustrator, title, publication date, number of pages, price, and ISBN.

Bulletin of the Center for Children's Books, edited by Betsy Hearne. Champaign, IL: The Graduate School of Library and Information Science of the University of Illinois at Urbana-Champaign and the University of Illinois Press.

> Published monthly except August, this 30-page publication contains approximately 70 reviews of newly published books for preschool children through young adults. Annotations are approximately 100-150 words long and provide an evaluation as well as a summary of the book. Entries are also given code symbols

to denote whether or not they are recommended or might be of specialized interest. Astericks denote books of special distinction. Entries are alphabetized by author and include the following bibliographic information: title, publisher, publication date, number of pages, ISBN, price, and recommended audience.

The Five Owls, edited by Susan Stan. Minneapolis, MN: The Five Owls, Inc.

Published five times a year, this 24-page publication features a combination of articles and reviews of children's books by leaders in children's literature. The approximately 50 titles reviewed in each edition reflect a variety of selected themes and topics. For example, one issue highlighted books about emotions, books of merit published in the summer and fall, new books for the holidays, and a feature on author/illustrator Kevin Henkes. Annotations of books vary from 50-300 words and provide the following bibliographic information: title, author, illustrator, publisher, publication date, number of pages, ISBN, price, size of book, and recommended audience.

The Horn Book Magazine, edited by Anita Silvey. Boston, MA: The Horn Book, Inc.

Published bimonthly, this 125-page periodical features articles and essays by authors, illustrators, librarians, teachers, and others involved in children's literature, as well as reviews of approximately 150 newly published trade books for children and young adults. Most issues contain 10 features such as articles, essays, and booklists. Reviews vary from 25-300 words and include the following bibliographic information: author, title, number of pages, publisher, publication date, ISBN, price, illustrator, and recommended audience. The magazine also gives announcements of awards and conferences and has an index to books reviewed and advertisers.

The Kobrin Letter, edited and published by Beverly Kobrin, Palo Alto, CA.

The Kobrin Letter is a four-page newsletter "concerning children's books about real people, places and things" published seven times a year. The 20 or so nonfiction books described in the newsletter are organized into two or three topics. For example, in the October 1992 issue, two of the topics were Pilgrims and People They Met and Recycling the 3Rs. Annotations are approximately 50 words long and written from a teacher's perspective, suggesting why and how students might respond to these books. Bibliographic information given with the reviews includes: title, publisher, publication date, price, recommended audience, and number of pages.

Annuals

Children's Choices. *The Reading Teacher*. (annually, in October). Newark, DE: The International Reading Association.

A joint project of the International Reading Association and the Children's Book Council, Children's Choices are fiction and nonfiction titles that students in elementary and middle schools have identified as some of their favorites among recently published trade books. In 1992, a total of 124 books were selected out of a pool of the 650 submitted by publishers. Annotations are categorized by reading level—all ages, beginning independent, younger readers, middle grades, and older readers—and alphabetized by title. The approximately 30-word annotations provide an evaluative synopsis of each selection and include the following bibliographic information: title, author, illustrator, publisher, recommended audience, number of pages, ISBN, and price. This list is available free by sending a self-addressed 9 x 12 envelope stamped with postage for four ounces to the International Reading Association. (PO Box 8139, Newark, DE 19714-8139; Attn: Children's Choices).

New Books for Young Readers, edited by Dianne Monson. (annually each spring). Minneapolis, MN: The College of Education at the University of Minnesota.

This 85-page publication includes reviews of approximately 500 recently published trade books selected for their appropriateness and appeal for readers from age 3 to young adult. Annotations range from one sentence to several and often include comments about the illustrations as well as the text. The list is arranged alphabetically by author and includes the following bibliographic information: author, title, illustrator, publisher, publication date, number of pages, price, ISBN, and recommended audience.

Notable Children's Trade Books in the Field of Social Studies. (annually, in April/May). *Social Education*. Washington, DC: The National Council for the Social Studies.

The April/May issue of *Social Education* includes a section featuring reviews of approximately 150 notable social studies trade books for children from kindergarten through grade 8 published during the previous year. A joint project of the National Council for the Social Studies and the Children's Book Council, books are selected for their humanity, diversity, originality, literary quality, and visual appeal. Books are alphabetized by title within various categories such as Public Policy Issues and North America History, Culture, and Life. Annotations are primarily plot or content summaries and include the following bibliographic information: title, author, illustrator and type of illustrations, publisher, number of pages, ISBN, price, and recommended audience. This list is available free by sending a self-addressed, stamped 6 x 9 envelope to the Children's Book Council. (568 Broadway, New York, NY 10012).

Outstanding Science Trade Books for Children. (annually, in March). *Science and Children*. Washington, DC: The National Science Teachers Association.

The March issue of *Science and Children* features approximately 100 reviews of outstanding science trade books published during the previous year for children from preschool through grade 8. A joint project of the National Science Teachers Association and the Children's Book Council, books are selected for their accuracy, readability, appropriateness, and appeal for the intended audience. The annotated list is divided into various categories—Biography; Environment and Conservation; Physics, Technology, and Engineering; and so on—with selections alphabetized according to title. The approximately 50-word annotations provide an evaluative synopsis of each selection and include the following bibliographic information: title, author, illustrator, publisher, recommended audience, number of pages, ISBN, and price. This list is available free by sending a self-addressed, stamped 6 x 9 envelope to the Children's Book Council. (568 Broadway, New York, NY 10012).

Teacher's Choices. *The Reading Teacher.* (annually, in November). Newark, DE: The International Reading Association.

> Teacher's Choices are fiction and nonfiction trade books that teachers have selected for their high literary quality and applicability across the curriculum, and that students from kindergarten through grade 8 are not likely to find on their own. For 1992, 36 titles were selected out of a pool of approximately 500 books submitted by publishers. Books are categorized by reading level—Primary (Grades K-2), Intermediate (Grades 3-5), and Advanced (Grades 6-8)—and alphabetized by title. Annotations (which range from 100-150 words) include a synopsis of the book and a comment by the reviewer as to how the book was used in the classroom and how students responded to it. Annotations also contain the following bibliographic information: title, author, illustrator, publisher, recommended audience, number of pages, ISBN, and price.

Concluding Comments

Of the resources we have described here, which will be of most use to you will of course depend on the students who will be reading the books and what sort of reading experiences you are planning for them. If you are looking to provide additional nonfiction titles for your classroom, you might begin with *Eyeopeners!* If you are looking for books for a unit on physics for your fifth graders, *The Subject Guide to Children's Books, The Museum of Science and Industry Basic List of Children's Science Books,* and *Outstanding Science Tradebooks for Children* might work well. If you are seeking ongoing inspiration and information on newly published books and how you might use them in the classroom, you might consider subscribing to *Book Links* or *The Five Owls.*

In closing, we would like to mention that the children's librarian at your public library and the media specialist at your school are also invaluable aids for locating material for your students and for recommending bibliographies to help you find just the right book or books for your classroom.

Libraries, bookstores, and publishers' warehouses are filled with wonderful materials that will excite, delight, and inform your students. We hope the resources listed here will help you latch onto the treasures that are waiting to be discovered by you and your students.

Author and Title Index

Grade Level Index

Subject Index

L = Literature
SS = Social Science
ST = Science and Technology

Academic Author Index

Adams, M.J., 25, 41, 209, 213
Allington, R.L., 189, 200
Almasi, J., 198, 202
Alvermann, D.E., 123, 148
Anderson, R.C., 19, 41, 189, 196, 200, 205, 209, 212, 213, 214, 215
Anderson, T.H., 203, 207, 208, 214
Applebee, A.N., 27, 41
Armbruster, B.B., 203, 207, 208, 214
Aronson, E., 193, 200
Asher, S., 212, 214
Atwell, N., 93, 112

Beach, R.W., 27, 41
Beck, I.L., 110, 112, 118, 119, 120, 121, 148, 189, 200, 203, 207, 208, 214, 215
Beretz, M., 54, 82
Bergman, J.L., 198, 202
Betts, E., 5, 17
Black, J.B., 203, 214
Blaney, N., 193, 200
Bransford, J.D., 206, 207, 214
Britton, B.K., 203, 214
Brophy, J., 20, 42
Brown, C.S., 199, 200
Brown, R., 198, 202
Bruce, B., 25, 41, 209, 213
Bruner, J.S., 2, 4
Buikema, J.L., 66, 82

Burkes, A.M., 189, 200
Burnett, R., 214

Calderhead, J., 37, 42
Calfee, R.C., 54, 82, 199, 201, 203, 208, 214
Campione, J., 30, 42
Carnine, D.W., 63, 82
Carr, E., 175, 185
Carroll, J.M., 206, 214
Chambliss, M.J., 54, 82, 203, 208, 214
Charney, D.H., 207, 214, 215
Chen, H.S., 62, 82
Cochran, C., 214
Cohen, P.A., 195, 200
Coleman, E.B., 205, 214
Collins, P., 199, 202
Cooke, C.L., 60, 62, 82, 181, 185
Cullinan, B.E., 39, 42, 199, 200, 203, 214

Davison, A., 204, 213, 214
Dewey, J., 37, 42
Dishner, E.K., 17
Dole, J.A., 62, 82, 197, 201
Doyle, M.A., 132, 148, 198, 201
Drum, P., 208, 214
Duffy, G.G., 36, 42, 197, 202
Duffy, T.M., 212, 214
Duin, A.H., 195, 201
Durkin, D., 197, 200

Academic Subject Index

About the Authors

Michael F. Graves received his Ph.D. from Stanford University and is currently head of the Literacy Education Program at the University of Minnesota. Prior to attending Stanford, he taught English and reading in California public schools. He is coauthor of *Quest,* a reading program for students in grades 4–8, and of several books, including *Essentials of Classroom Teaching: Elementary Reading Methods, Reading and Learning in Content Areas,* and *A Word Is a Word . . . Or Is It?* He has published monographs for the International Reading Association and the National Council of Teachers of English; and his articles have appeared in journals such as *American Educator, Child Development, Elementary School Journal, English Journal, Journal of Educational Psychology, Journal of Reading, Journal of Reading Behavior,* and *Reading Research Quarterly.*

Bonnie B. Graves received her B.A. in English and an elementary teaching certificate from California State University at Long Beach. She taught in California public schools for seven years, has taken advanced courses in reading and instructional design at the University of Minnesota, and has written instructional materials for Scholastic, Glencoe/McGraw-Hill, Globe Book Company, the National Science Foundation, Science Research Associates, and Twin Cities Public Television. In addition, she has coauthored *Easy Reading: Book Series and Periodicals for Less Able Readers* and *Essentials of Classroom Teaching: Elementary Reading Methods.* She has also published several short stories for young readers and has received recognition for her fiction writing, including a grant from the Society of Children's Book Writers and Illustrators for a middle-grade novel.